Modern Phrase Structure Grammar

Blackwell Textbooks in Linguistics

1 Liliane Haegeman — *Introduction to Government and Binding Theory (Second Edition)*

2 Andrew Spencer — *Morphological Theory*

3 Helen Goodluck — *Language Acquisition*

4 Ronald Wardhaugh — *Introduction to Sociolinguistics (Second Edition)*

5 Martin Atkinson — *Children's Syntax*

6 Diane Blakemore — *Understanding Utterances*

7 Michael Kenstowicz — *Phonology in Generative Grammar*

8 Deborah Schiffrin — *Approaches to Discourse*

9 John Clark and Colin Yallop — *An Introduction to Phonetics and Phonology (Second Edition)*

10 Natsuko Tsujimura — *An Introduction to Japanese Linguistics*

11 Robert D. Borsley — *Modern Phrase Structure Grammar*

Modern Phrase Structure Grammar

Robert D. Borsley

Copyright © Robert D. Borsley, 1996

The right of Robert D. Borsley to be identified as author of this work has been asserted in accordance with the Copyright, Designs and Patents Act 1988.

First published 1996
2 4 6 8 10 9 7 5 3 1

Blackwell Publishers Ltd
108 Cowley Road
Oxford OX4 1JF
UK

Blackwell Publishers Inc.
238 Main Street
Cambridge, Massachusetts 02142
USA

British Library Cataloguing in Publication Data

A CIP catalogue record for this book is available from the British Library.

Library of Congress Cataloging-in-Publication Data

Borsley, Robert D.
    Modern phrase structure grammar / Robert D. Borsley.
       p.   cm. — (Blackwell textbooks in linguistics; 11)
    Includes bibliographical references (p.) and index.
    ISBN 0–631–18406–6 (alk. paper). — ISBN 0–631–18407–4 (pbk.:
alk. paper)
    1. Phrase structure grammar.   I. Title. II. Series.
    P158.3.B66 1996
    415—dc20

                                               95–53164
                                               CIP

Typeset in 10 on 13 pt Sabon
by Graphicraft Typesetters Ltd., Hong Kong
Printed in Great Britain by T.J. Press Ltd, Padstow, Cornwall

This book is printed on acid-free paper

To my mother and the memory of my father

Contents

Preface   x

1 Preliminaries   1
   1.1 Introduction   1
   1.2 What is Modern PSG?   1
   1.3 The attractions of Modern PSG   4
   1.4 Some further background   6
   1.5 Summary   8

2 Classical Phrase Structure Grammar   11
   2.1 Introduction   11
   2.2 The nature of Classical PSG   11
   2.3 The strengths and weaknesses of Classical PSG   16
   2.4 Classical and Modern PSG   19
   2.5 Summary   21

3 Syntactic Categories   24
   3.1 Introduction   24
   3.2 Some history   24
   3.3 The power of complex categories   27
   3.4 Categories in GPSG   31
   3.5 Categories in HPSG   35
   3.6 The lexicon   38
   3.7 Summary   40

4 Rules and Principles   44
   4.1 Introduction   44
   4.2 ID and LP rules   44
   4.3 Principles   48
   4.4 Rules and trees   51
   4.5 More on ID and LP rules   53
   4.6 Metagrammars   59
   4.7 Summary   60

5 Semantics   65
   5.1 Introduction   65
   5.2 GPSG semantics   65
   5.3 HPSG semantics   68
   5.4 Quantification   72
   5.5 Summary   77

6 Some Basic Structures   80
   6.1 Introduction   80
   6.2 Head–complement structures   80
   6.3 Subject–predicate structures   91
   6.4 Summary   101

7 Some Further Structures   106
   7.1 Introduction   106
   7.2 Specifier–head structures   106
   7.3 Adjuncts   110
   7.4 Markers   113
   7.5 Coordinate structures   115
   7.6 Summary   122

8 Raising and Control   126
   8.1 Introduction   126
   8.2 Preliminaries   126
   8.3 The GPSG approach   128
   8.4 The HPSG approach   133
   8.5 Some further data   140
   8.6 Summary   144

9 Unbounded Dependencies   146
   9.1 Introduction   146
   9.2 The basic approach   146
   9.3 Island constraints   154
   9.4 Some further constructions   162
   9.5 Summary   170

10 Anaphora   175
   10.1 Introduction   175
   10.2 The GPSG approach   175
   10.3 The HPSG approach   180
   10.4 More on control   187
   10.5 Summary   189

11 Valency Alternations 192
   11.1 Introduction 192
   11.2 Passives 192
   11.3 Other valency alternations 198
   11.4 Other approaches to passives 203
   11.5 Summary 209

12 Some Further Phenomena 212
   12.1 Introduction 212
   12.2 Verb-initial clauses 212
   12.3 Some Germanic phenomena 220
   12.4 Romance clitics 225
   12.5 Free word order 229
   12.6 Summary 234

13 Modern PSG and Other Frameworks 237
   13.1 Introduction 237
   13.2 Principles and Parameters theory 237
   13.3 Categorial Grammar 242
   13.4 Summary 247

References 251

Index 265

Preface

This book provides an introduction to what has been a major current in syntactic theory since 1980. I call this current Modern Phrase Structure Grammar. Its main exemplars are Generalized Phrase Structure Grammar (GPSG) and Head-driven Phrase Structure Grammar (HPSG). I assume no prior knowledge of these frameworks, but I do assume that the reader has some knowledge of the basic concepts and the central phenomena of syntax. Thus, this is an introduction to an important body of ideas about syntax for people who already know something about syntax.

GPSG and HPSG each has a rather different status. The latter is very much alive and evolving; the former is largely a thing of the past, at least within theoretical linguistics. However, it is worth discussing for two reasons. Firstly, the way ideas have developed is of some importance: knowing how they have developed can help one to understand their nature and significance. Secondly, not all GPSG ideas can be consigned to history. Some are still potentially important. Sections of the book that are exclusively concerned with GPSG are identified as such, so readers who want to concentrate on HPSG can ignore them.

I take the view that there is just one version of GPSG that deserves detailed attention, the standard version presented in Gazdar et al. (1985), but that there are three versions of HPSG that should be considered, the version presented in Pollard and Sag (1987), the version presented in the first eight chapters of Pollard and Sag (1994) and the version presented in chapter 9 of Pollard and Sag (1994). The main emphasis is on the last of these.

Each chapter in the book includes notes and exercises. The notes qualify and elaborate on the discussion in the text, raise further issues, and give suggestions for further reading. The exercises reinforce the points made in the text and in some cases raise various questions.

I am grateful to a number of colleagues for valuable comments and advice on various parts of the book, notably Gerald Gazdar (University of Sussex), Danièle Godard (Université Paris 7), Dick Hudson (University College London), Andreas Kathol (University of Groningen), Ewan Klein (University of Edinburgh), Philip Miller (Université de Lille 3), Carl Pollard (Ohio State University), Geoff Pullum

(University of California, Santa Cruz), Ivan Sag (Stanford University), and Richard Sharman (IBM UK). I am especially grateful to Bob Levine (Ohio State University), who provided detailed and perceptive comments on the entire book, from which I have benefited immensely. I alone am responsible for what I have done (or failed to do) with the comments and advice that I have received.

I would like to thank Margaret Aherne for her excellent editorial work.

I am also grateful to the British Academy for a travel grant, which enabled me to attend the First International Workshop on HPSG at Ohio State University, Columbus, Ohio, in July and August 1993. The weather was far too hot but the intellectual climate was excellent.

Robert D. Borsley

1 Preliminaries

1.1 Introduction

The term 'Modern Phrase Structure Grammar' is used in this book to refer to a number of related approaches to the syntax of natural languages which have formed one of the most important currents in syntactic theory since 1980. Most notable are Generalized Phrase Structure Grammar (GPSG), which was developed in the early 1980s by Gerald Gazdar, Ewan Klein, Geoffrey Pullum and Ivan Sag, and Head-driven Phrase Structure Grammar (HPSG), which has been developed since the mid-1980s by Carl Pollard and Ivan Sag. GPSG enjoyed considerable influence in the mid-1980s, and HPSG has had a growing impact in more recent years. Both frameworks have been influential not only in theoretical linguistics but also in computational linguistics. The two frameworks and other versions of Modern PSG contain a rich body of ideas which deserve the attention of anybody interested in syntax. This book explores these ideas.[1]

In this chapter, I will first introduce Modern PSG. Then, I will consider the features which have attracted syntacticians to it. Finally, I will say something about the relation between Modern PSG and Transformational Grammar (TG) including Chomsky's Principles and Parameters (or Government and Binding) framework (P&P).

1.2 What is Modern PSG?

Modern PSG has its origins in two (unpublished) papers written by Gerald Gazdar in 1979: 'Constituent structures' and 'English as a context-free language'. In these papers, he revived the idea, implicit in pre-Chomskyan work on syntax, that sentences have a single level of structure characterized by rules specifying how constituents can be concatenated to form larger constituents.[2]

Gazdar's proposals were in part a natural outcome of certain developments in syntactic theory in the 1970s. A central feature of the work of the 1970s was a concern to restrict the power of transformations. One way to do this was to reduce the distance between deep and surface structure by assuming less abstract deep structures. A number of syntacticians showed that this was possible with a richer conception of the lexicon and a more sophisticated conception of semantics. Among other works, one can cite Brame (1975, 1976), Bresnan (1978), Freidin (1975), McCloskey (1979) and Oehrle (1976). Gazdar's proposals can be seen as a continuation of this work.

Gazdar, however, went beyond any of this work. He was particularly concerned with the so-called unbounded dependencies that characterize *wh*-questions like (1) and relative clauses like the bracketed string in (2).

(1)   Who do they think he talked to?
(2)   the man [who they think he talked to]

In both constructions, there is a dependency between the *wh*-word and the preposition *to*. Before Gazdar's work, it was generally accepted that unbounded dependencies required a transformation moving a constituent from one position to another. Those who rejected this view, e.g. Koster (1978), assumed a non-local interpretive rule associating a constituent in one position with some other position. Gazdar demonstrated that unbounded dependencies could be accommodated within a framework assuming a single level of structure defined by phrase structure (PS) rules, which are a simple means of specifying how constituents can be concatenated to form larger constituents. GPSG owed much of its early impact to this demonstration, and these constructions have continued to be a major concern for Modern PSG.

Gazdar's papers laid the foundations of GPSG. Within GPSG, we can distinguish the early version presented in Gazdar (1981a, 1981b, 1982) and Gazdar, Pullum and Sag (1982), and the mature version presented in Gazdar et al. (1985). The mature version differed from the early version in not assuming PS rules, and in having a well-worked out theory of syntactic categories. GPSG was one of the main influences on the development of the HPSG framework. This has its origins in a number of papers written by Carl Pollard in 1985 (Pollard 1985a, 1985b, 1988). The earliest version of the framework differed both from GPSG and from later versions of HPSG in assuming a procedural formulation of rules and principles, in which they specify how expressions can be constructed from smaller expressions. Pollard and Sag (1987) adopt a declarative formulation of rules and principles, in which they specify what sorts of complex expressions are well-formed. Pollard and Sag (1994) adopt a new view of the relation between syntax and semantics. Finally, chapter 9 of Pollard and Sag (1994) adopts a new view of dependent elements, building on the proposals of Borsley (1987, 1989a, forthcoming).

GPSG and HPSG share two main characteristics. Firstly, both assume that sentences have a single level of syntactic structure. This distinguishes them from most other frameworks and especially from TG. Secondly, both assume very local syntactic rules. Again, this distinguishes them from most other frameworks. In standard versions of GPSG and HPSG, rules just specify how constituents can be concatenated to form larger constituents. As we have noted, PS rules provide a simple way of doing this. However, it is possible to maintain this assumption without assuming PS rules, and, as we will see, standard versions of GPSG and HPSG do not assume PS rules.

In addition to the standard versions of GPSG and HPSG, there have been certain non-standard versions, such as the version of GPSG presented in Ojeda (1987, 1988) and the version of HPSG presented in Reape (forthcoming, 1994), and there are intermediate frameworks presented in Levine (1989a), Miller (1992) and Fodor (1992a). There are also other versions of Modern PSG, most notably the Japanese Phrase Structure Grammar (JPSG) framework presented in Gunji (1987). Thus, there is a rich body of work here.

As noted above, GPSG and HPSG have also had a major impact within computational linguistics. In fact, they have probably been the most influential theories of syntax within computational linguistics. They have certainly had a much greater influence than P&P. Works such as Alshawi (1992), Pereira and Shieber (1987), Gazdar and Mellish (1989) and Grover et al. (1988) illustrate the relevance of the theories in a computational context.

As we have indicated, the idea that natural languages are limited to rules specifying how constituents can be concatenated to form larger constituents was implicit in pre-Chomskyan linguistics. Chomsky and others formalized pre-Chomskyan ideas about syntax and applied the term PSG to the result, which they argued to be an inadequate conception of grammar. I will call this formalization Classical PSG. Although this book is about Modern PSG, it will be necessary to say something about Classical PSG. I will look at Classical PSG in some detail in chapter 2, where, among other things, I will distinguish between the context-free (CF) form and a more powerful context-sensitive (CS) form. As we will see, the former has had considerable influence.

An obvious question about Modern PSG is: how far is it like and unlike Classical PSG? GPSG was seen by its developers and others as a continuation of Classical PSG. Thus, Gazdar (1982: 132) remarks of GPSG that: 'This type of generative grammar . . . is to all intents and purposes, simply a variant of CF phrase structure grammar.' In similar vein, Sampson (1984) asserts that 'Theorists such as Gazdar are telling us, effectively, that grammar involves only the fairly simple kind of structure that was taken for granted long before the "Chomskyan revolution".' It would be surprising, however, if there were no significant differences between Modern and Classical PSG. There are important similarities between Modern and Classical PSG, but there are also important differences, which mean that Modern PSG does not have the weaknesses that

Classical PSG has. We will discuss the similarities in chapter 2, and focus on the differences in chapters 3, 4 and 5.

1.3   The attractions of Modern PSG

I want now to take a look at the attractions of Modern PSG, the features that have led syntacticians to adopt one or other version of the approach.

One feature that has undoubtedly attracted some syntacticians to Modern PSG is its relative simplicity. For most theories of syntax, sentences have a number of levels of structure, but for Modern PSG, as we have said, they have just one. Other things being equal, a conception of grammar which assigns a single level of structure to sentences must be preferable to one that assigns a number of levels. Proponents of approaches assuming more than one level of structure would argue that other things are not equal, but it is not clear that there are any very strong arguments for more than one level. It is notable in this context that at least one proponent of P&P has argued for a single-level version of the framework. (See Koster 1986.)

Another feature of the various versions of Modern PSG that has attracted some syntacticians is that they are well-understood frameworks, permitting precise and explicit analyses. Gazdar (1982: 132) stresses this feature of GPSG, arguing that one reason for adopting the GPSG approach is that its grammars are relatively well-understood systems because they have much in common with grammars instantiating the context-free version of Classical PSG, which have been extensively studied since the 1950s. As we will see, the most important difference between Modern PSG and Classical PSG is that Modern PSG assumes complex syntactic categories whereas Classical PSG assumes simple atomic categories. However, the properties of complex categories have been studied fairly extensively. (See, for example, Gazdar et al. (1988), Kasper and Rounds (1990), Carpenter (1992) and Moshier and Pollard (1994).) Thus, the fact that Modern PSG grammars involve complex categories does not mean that their properties are obscure. In this area, Modern PSG compares very favourably with P&P, which is characterized by considerable vagueness. Not surprisingly, Barton, Berwick and Ristad (1987) remark in their discussion of the formal properties of various theories that 'we lack a complete, faithful formalization of GB [i.e. P&P] theory'.

A further feature of the various versions of Modern PSG that has been an attraction for some syntacticians is that they are quite restrictive frameworks in the sense that they offer a limited range of potential solutions to any descriptive problem. There is a fairly clear contrast here with P&P. Given its multiple levels of representation and its vagueness about crucial matters, P&P inevitably allows a broader range of solutions to any descriptive problem.

GPSG is restrictive in another way. GPSG grammars can only generate so-called context-free languages, sets of strings of symbols which can be generated by a grammar instantiating the context-free version of Classical PSG. When GPSG was being developed, there were no good arguments against the claim that natural languages are context-free languages: this was demonstrated by Pullum and Gazdar (1982). It has since become clear, however, that natural languages are not necessarily context-free languages. Thus, this is no longer an advantage of GPSG. We should note, however, that this fact does not show that GPSG is fundamentally misguided, only that it needs to be extended in some way. We will say more about this matter in the next chapter.

Both GPSG and HPSG have been seen as receiving some support from what is known about human language processing. An important claim in the early GPSG literature is that GPSG grammars, unlike transformational grammars, provide a basis for an explanation of the fact that human parsing is 'easy and quick' (Gazdar 1982). This argument raises two obvious questions: is human parsing in fact 'easy and quick'? If so, does GPSG provide a basis for an explanation?

Chomsky and Lasnik (1993) reject the assumption that human parsing is easy and quick. They write that:

> It has sometimes been argued that linguistic theory must meet the empirical condition that it account for the ease and rapidity of parsing. But parsing does not, in fact, have these properties. Parsing may be slow and difficult, or even impossible, and may be 'in error' in the sense that the percept assigned (if any) fails to match the SD [structural description] associated with the signal . . .

The obvious response to this is that it may be true that parsing is sometimes 'slow and difficult, or even impossible' but this is quite compatible with the claim that parsing is normally easy and quick. This is essentially the view of Fodor (1991: 108–9), who writes that:

> the human parsing system does most of things it has to do both quickly and accurately. The places where it breaks down are striking and interesting; but most of them involve temporarily ambiguous constructions where the grammar does not provide the relevant information at the point at which the parser is faced with a choice. No parser could be blamed for sometimes making the wrong decision in such circumstances. In unambiguous constructions, errors seem to be quite rare and may be attributable to simple processing overload (as in the case of multiply centre-embedded constructions). . . . if the human parser is indeed a highly efficient, well-oiled system, that is in itself an important empirical finding, one that couldn't have been anticipated, and one that should constrain future theory building. The most plausible variety of grammar (other things, such as descriptive coverage, being equal) would be the one that is optimal as a database for an efficient parser.

Thus, human parsing is normally easy and quick and an adequate conception of grammar should be compatible with this.[3]

Does GPSG in fact provide the basis for an explanation of parsing efficiency? Things are far from simple here. Barton, Berwick and Ristad (1987) highlight computational problems associated with certain features of GPSG.[4] However, it is clear that GPSG grammars and HPSG grammars are more open to computational implementation than P&P grammars. This is why they have been influential in computational linguistics. It is interesting to note in this context that a number of the papers in Berwick, Abney and Tenny's (1991) book on principle-based parsing reformulate P&P grammars as something more like Modern PSG grammars to make them suitable for implementation. In particular, they follow Modern PSG in assuming just a single level of structure.[5]

It has also been suggested that HPSG receives some support from what is known about human language processing. As we will discuss in chapter 4, HPSG is a unification-based framework. This means that all rules and principles are on a par and none takes precedence over any other. Pollard and Sag (1994) argue that this permits an explanation for some important features of human language processing. They highlight four features. Firstly, it is highly incremental in the sense that 'speakers are able to assign partial interpretations to partial utterances'. Secondly, it is highly integrative in the sense that 'information about the world, the context, and the topic at hand is skillfully woven together with linguistic information whenever utterances are successfully decoded'. Thirdly, 'there is no one order in which information is consulted which can be fixed for all language use situations'. Finally, it consists of various kinds of activity: 'comprehension, production, translation, playing language games, and the like'. They argue that these features are unproblematic for unification-based grammars but pose serious problems for other sorts of grammars.

Thus, a number of general considerations favour the Modern PSG theories. However, for syntacticians the most important argument in favour of these theories is that they can provide illuminating analyses of diverse syntactic phenomena. This will be the main focus of later chapters.

1.4   Some further background

In this final section, I want to say something about the relation between Modern PSG and TG, including P&P.

From the standpoint of Modern PSG, Classical TG was in a sense a mistake, but it was not just a mistake. Classical TG uncovered a rich body of data and generalizations, which any theory, including the various forms of Modern PSG, must accommodate. Island constraints, conditions on anaphora, the distinction between control and raising verbs are all the product of Classical TG. Classical TG also explored some important theoretical ideas, most notably the idea of complex categories, which, as we have said, is central to Modern PSG. Thus, Classical TG is an important influence on Modern PSG.

Probably most proponents of Modern PSG would share this assessment of Classical TG, but one finds rather different attitudes to P&P in the literature of Modern PSG. References in the GPSG literature are quite dismissive. For example, Gazdar et al. (1985: 6) remark that ' "generative grammar" . . . includes little of the research done under the rubric of the "Government–Binding" [i.e. P&P] framework, since there are few signs of any commitment to the explicit specification of grammars or theoretical principles in this genre of linguistics.' In contrast, in the HPSG literature, P&P is identified as one of a number of theories that have had an influence on the development of the framework. Pollard and Sag (1987: v) comment that HPSG 'freely avails itself of ideas from categorial grammar, discourse representation theory, generalized phrase structure grammar, government–binding theory, lexical functional grammar and situation semantics'. The influence of P&P on HPSG can be seen especially in HPSG approaches to unbounded dependencies (discussed in chapter 9) and anaphora (discussed in chapter 10). Not surprisingly, then, HPSG is much more like P&P than GPSG is.

Proponents of Modern PSG and of P&P sometimes suggest that they are fundamentally different enterprises. It is not clear, however, that there is any real basis for this view. There are some important differences of emphasis, but it seems best to regard them as broadly similar enterprises.

Some proponents of Modern PSG have taken a rather different view of what syntactic theory is about from that which underlies P&P. For P&P, syntactic theory is concerned with what Chomsky (1986a) calls I-language, 'some element of the mind of the person who knows the language, acquired by the learner, and used by the speaker-hearer'. In contrast, for Gazdar et al. (1985), syntactic theory is concerned with languages in the sense of 'collections whose membership is definitely and precisely specifiable'. This is essentially what Chomsky (1986a) calls E-language, language seen as 'a collection of actions, or utterances, or linguistic forms' and 'understood independently of the properties of the mind/ brain'. Chomsky argues at some length that E-language is not an appropriate focus for syntactic theory. Here, then, there might seem to be an important difference between Modern PSG and P&P. However, there is no reason why Modern PSG should not be seen as an approach to I-language, and in fact this seems to be how Pollard and Sag (1994) see HPSG. They write that '. . . we have accepted the conventional wisdom that linguistic theory must account for linguistic knowledge . . . Indeed, we take it to be the central goal of linguistic theory to characterize what it is that every linguistically mature human being knows by virtue of being a linguistic creature, viz. universal grammar' (1994: 14).

Another matter that has figured prominently in discussions of the relation between Modern PSG and P&P is the importance of formalization. There is undoubtedly greater concern with the precision implied by the term 'generative' in Modern PSG than in P&P. On the face of it, however, there is no reason why P&P should not place as much emphasis as Modern PSG on formalization. It should also be noted that not all Modern PSG work has been fully formalized. For example, the earliest work in GPSG made crucial use of complex categories but there was no real theory of categories. It is doubtful whether there is any fundamental difference here.[6]

A final matter that we should consider here is the relation between Modern PSG and computational linguistics. There have been links between the two since the earliest work in Modern PSG. It is important, however, not to exaggerate the significance of these links. Work in Modern PSG has had essentially the same aim as other work in syntactic theory – to provide illuminating analyses of syntactic phenomena – and the possibility of computational implementations has never been the main concern. In fact, computational linguists have found it necessary to modify GPSG and HPSG in various ways to implement them, and one finds titles like 'A simple reconstruction of GPSG' (Shieber 1986). As noted earlier, it was also demonstrated by Barton, Berwick and Ristad (1987) that some aspects of GPSG are quite problematic from a computational point of view. Thus, although there are significant links between Modern PSG and computational work, their importance should not be exaggerated.

1.5   Summary

In this chapter, we have provided a preliminary characterization of Modern PSG and distinguished its main forms. We have also looked at the features which have attracted syntacticians to Modern PSG. Finally, we have considered the relation between PSG and TG, including P&P. We will say more about all these matters in the following chapters.

Notes

1 Textbook introductions to GPSG can be found in Bennett (1995) and Horrocks (1987). Borsley (1991) provides a textbook introduction to some of the basic ideas of both GPSG and HPSG together with some of the basic ideas of P&P. Useful discussion of GPSG can also be found in Hukari and Levine's (1986) review article of Gazdar et al. (1985).

2   For some discussion of the background to the emergence of Modern PSG, see
    Newmeyer (1986: ch. 7.2.1).
3   For more recent discussion of the problems of parsing, see Tomita (1991).
4   For some useful discussion of the problems of implementing the standard version of
    GPSG see Bennett (1995: ch. 14) and the references cited there.
5   For a critical assessment of the papers in Berwick, Abney and Tenny (1991) see
    Pullum (1993).
6   Stabler (1993) provides a formalization of the 'Barriers' (Chomsky 1986b) version of
    P&P in first order logic, which could be the basis for an implementation of the theory.

Exercises

1   Show how the PS rules in (1) will allow both the grammatical and the
ungrammatical examples in (2). Explain how this highlights the problem
posed by unbounded dependencies. Brackets in the rules indicate an optional
constituent. The rules assume that auxiliary-initial clauses have a ternary-
branching structure.

(1)   a.   S ⟶ NP S
      b.   S ⟶ V NP VP
      c.   VP ⟶ V PP
      d.   PP ⟶ P (NP)
      e.   S ⟶ (NP) VP
      f.   VP ⟶ V S

(2)   a.   Who did Kim talk to?
      b.   Who do you think saw Sandy?
      c.   Did Kim talk to Sandy?
      d.   Do you think Kim saw Sandy?
      e.   *Do you think saw Sandy?
      f.   *Did Kim talk to?
      g.   *Who do you think Kim saw Sandy?
      h.   *Who did Kim talk to Sandy?

2   It has sometimes been assumed in transformational grammar that
idioms form a constituent in underlying structure and that if they do not form
a constituent in the superficial structure of a sentence, this is a result of a
movement process. The idiom *make headway* in the following examples provides evidence against this assumption.

(1)   We discussed [NP the headway [S that we had made]]
(2)   We made [NP all the headway [S that we expected]]

Explain how.

3   The following sentences are potentially misleading, that is, they may lead the human parsing system astray. Explain why, using relevant grammatical terminology.

(1)   The performer sent the flowers was very pleased.
(2)   Is that liquid spreading across the floor blood?
(3)   I saw John and Mary saw him too.
(4)   When I woke up Mary had left.
(5)   I told the boy that the girl seduced the story.
(6)   Without her contributions to the fund would be quite inadequate.

4   Pollard and Sag (1994: Introduction) point out that the number of the noun *sheep* is determined before the intended interpretation of *pen* in (1) but that the reverse is true in (2).

(1)   The sheep that was sleeping in the pen stood up.
(2)   The sheep in the pen had been sleeping and were about to wake up.

Explain why this is and what sort of information is involved.

2 Classical Phrase Structure Grammar

2.1 Introduction

As we noted in the last chapter, an important question about Modern PSG is: how far is it like and unlike Classical PSG? Are proponents of Modern PSG suggesting that the ideas of Chomsky's predecessors constitute a satisfactory approach to the syntax of human languages, as some have suggested? I have already suggested that this is not the case. Rather, there are major differences between Classical and Modern PSG. In this chapter I will introduce Classical PSG, highlight its strengths and weaknesses, and identify the main features that it shares with Modern PSG. In the following chapters, we will look at the main differences between Modern PSG and Classical PSG.

2.2 The nature of Classical PSG

As we observed in chapter 1, Classical PSG is a conception of grammar assumed to be implicit in pre-Chomskyan work on syntax. Pre-Chomskyan American linguistics did not really have any explicit conception of syntax. It was dominated by methodological questions. It was concerned with how one should arrive at a grammatical description, and there was little interest in the formal properties of the descriptions that were produced. These were first investigated in a number of early papers of Chomsky's, in which he suggested that what he called Phrase Structure Grammar was an adequate formalization of the descriptive practices of the American linguists of the time, and argued that it was an untenable conception of grammar.

Chomsky did not try to show in any detail that Classical PSG represents an adequate formalization of pre-Chomskyan assumptions about syntax. In Chomsky (1957), he describes Classical PSG as an approach 'customarily' taken to syntactic analysis. In Chomsky (1962), he presents it as a modification of the

'Morpheme to Utterance' procedures of Harris (1951). In Chomsky (1964: fn. 4) he calls Classical PSG the 'taxonomic model' and suggests that it is 'a generalization of Harris' morpheme-to-utterance statements'. The most detailed attempt to show that Classical PSG was indeed an adequate formalization of pre-Chomskyan assumptions is Postal (1964). Postal argues that 'the so-called theory of phrase structure . . . correctly represents the underlying conception of grammatical description prevalent in modern linguistics generally, especially modern American linguistics' (1964: v) and that 'modern American syntactic ideas are correctly represented, formalized, or explicated by this theory' (1964: vi).[1]

Given that Classical PSG was generally regarded as an adequate formalization of pre-Chomskyan work on syntax, it is not surprising that showing that Classical PSG is untenable was a major concern of early work in TG such as Chomsky (1957) and Postal (1964). The weaknesses of PSG were also a prominent theme of textbook introductions to TG in the 1960s and 1970s, such as Akmajian and Heny (1975), Bach (1973), Baker (1978) and Huddleston (1976).

How satisfactory was Classical PSG as a formalization of pre-Chomskyan views of syntax? We will see that there are some grounds for thinking that it was not that satisfactory. It is possible, then, that Classical PSG is a conception of grammar that nobody has ever been committed to. It is certainly one that has never been explicitly advocated. In spite of this, it is important for two reasons. Firstly, as we have noted, it was assumed in the 1960s and 1970s to be implicit in pre-Chomskyan work on syntax, and standard arguments for TG took the form of arguments for the superiority of TG over Classical PSG. Secondly, it has been studied and exploited in computer science, especially the context-free form. For these two reasons, it is important to compare Modern PSG with Classical PSG even if nobody was ever in fact committed to it.

As we noted in the last chapter, there are two distinct forms of Classical PSG, a context-free form and a more powerful context-sensitive form. For both, grammars are sets of phrase structure (PS) rules containing simple, atomic categories. For the context-free version, these rules are applicable in all contexts; for the context-sensitive version they may be restricted to specific contexts. Following standard practice, I will refer to grammars instantiating the context-free version as context-free grammars (CFGs) and to grammars instantiating the context-sensitive version as context-sensitive grammars (CSGs).

In standard presentations of Classical PSG, for example Chomsky (1957) or Postal (1964), PS rules are string rewriting rules of the form $XAY \longrightarrow XZY$ (or $A \longrightarrow Z/X\_\_Y$), where A is a single non-terminal symbol and X, Y and Z are strings of terminal and/or non-terminal symbols, and at least Z is non-null. Such rules are context-free if X and Y are null and context-sensitive if they are non-null. They allow a symbol to be rewritten as a string of symbols and generate so-called derivations, sequences of strings of symbols. Provided the derivations meet certain conditions, a single tree can be constructed from any derivation. We can illustrate with the following CF-PS rules from Chomsky (1957: 26–7):

(1) (i)   S ⟶ NP VP
     (ii)   NP ⟶ Art N
     (iii) VP ⟶ V NP
     (iv) Art ⟶ the
     (v)   N ⟶ man, ball, etc.
     (vi) V ⟶ hit, took, etc.

Notice that (v) and (vi) allow N and V to be rewritten in more than one way. In other words, they allow alternatives. These rules allow derivations like the following:

(2) S
     NP VP   (i)
     Art N VP   (ii)
     Art N V NP   (iii)
     the N V NP   (iv)
     the man V NP   (v)
     the man hit NP   (vi)
     the man hit Art N   (ii)
     the man hit the N   (iv)
     the man hit the ball   (v)

Each line in this derivation is derived from the immediately preceding line by the rule whose number is given in brackets. For example, the second line is derived from the first by the rule (i). From this derivation, we can obtain the following tree, in which each category has as its daughters the string of symbols that replaces it in the derivation:

(3)

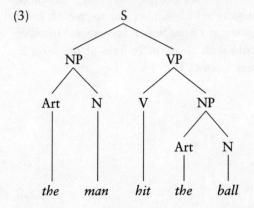

In general, a single tree corresponds to a number of derivations. We would have the same tree here if N was replaced before Art, V before N, etc.

It has been argued that both context-free and context-sensitive versions of Classical PSG were implicit in pre-Chomskyan work. Chomsky (1964: fn. 4) writes that 'most modern work in syntax is actually more adequately formalized in terms of rewriting systems with null context (i.e. *context free grammar* – in particular, this seems to be true of Pike's tagmemics, as of most work in IC analysis)'. Postal (1964) argues that Pike (1954–60), Lamb (1962), Hockett (1961) and Harris (1962) implicitly assumed context-free rules while Bloch (1946), Wells (1947), Harris (1951) and Hockett (1954) implicitly assumed context-sensitive rules. The earliest work in TG assumed both context-free and context-sensitive PS rules but after Chomsky (1965) only context-free rules were assumed.

In an important paper, McCawley (1968) pointed out that it is not necessary to interpret PS rules as rewrite rules. Instead, they can be interpreted as node admissibility conditions, statements that specific local trees consisting of a category and its daughters are well-formed. Thus, the rule in (4) can be understood as saying not that (5a) and (5b) are legitimate consecutive lines in a derivation, but that the local tree in (6) is well-formed.

(4) A $\longrightarrow$ B C

(5) a. ...A...
     b. ...BC...

(6)   A
        / \
       B   C

McCawley pointed out that interpreting PS rules as node admissibility conditions has a number of advantages. If PS rules are rewrite rules, they cannot be allowed to have a right-hand side category which is identical to the left-hand side category since, if they do, derivations can arise which correspond to more than one tree. For example, a derivation with consecutive lines of the form in (7) will correspond to the two different trees in (8).

(7) a. ...AB...
     b. ...ACB...

(8) ...A   B...   ...A   B...
        /\   /\
       A C   C B

If PS rules are node admissibility conditions, there is no problem about having a right-hand side category which is identical to the left-hand side category. There is considerable motivation for local trees in which a daughter category is identical to the mother category. Thus, this is an important reason for viewing PS rules as node admissibility conditions and not as rewrite rules.[2]

If PS rules are rewrite rules, it is also necessary to exclude rules with the null string as their right-hand side; rules, that is, of the form in (9).

(9) X $\longrightarrow$ e

Again, such rules allow derivations which correspond to more than one tree. For example, a derivation with consecutive lines of the form in (10) will correspond to the two different trees in (11).

(10) a. ... AB ...
      b. ... C ...

(11) ... A   B ...   ... A   B ...
          | | | |
          e   C   C   e

Rules with the null string as their right-hand side are unproblematic if PS rules are node admissibility conditions. Since it is quite widely assumed that empty categories are a feature of natural languages, this is another advantage for the node admissibility conception.

Given these two advantages, one might wonder why PS rules were originally viewed as rewrite rules. McCawley (1982: 92) suggests that this was probably the result of 'a historical accident that early transformational grammarians knew some automata theory but no graph theory'.

Somewhat surprisingly, McCawley's paper had little influence within the textbooks of the 1970s, which generally continued to present PS rules as rewrite rules. This is true, for example, of Baker (1978: 36), Akmajian and Heny (1975: ch. 3.3) and Huddleston (1976: 36). However, the earliest work in GPSG (Gazdar 1981a, 1982) assumes PS rules interpreted as node admissibility conditions.

In addition to the restrictions we have mentioned, two other constraints are assumed in standard descriptions of Classical PSG. Firstly, it is assumed that no rule may allow a node to have an unlimited number of daughters. This is somewhat surprising because TG analyses have often incorporated PS rules which do just this. For example, such rules play an important role in the analyses of Jackendoff (1977), where they are invoked in connection with adjuncts and coordinate structures. Secondly, it is assumed that the daughters of a node must form a continuous string, in other words that there can be no trees of the following form:

(12)

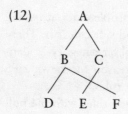

This restriction is assumed in most work in TG and in standard versions of Modern PSG. However, it was rejected in Harman's (1963) defence of PSG and some work in Modern PSG has also rejected it, as we will see in chapter 12.

As we have noted, an important question about Classical PSG is: how satisfactory is it as a formalization of the syntactic ideas of pre-Chomskyan linguistics? Manaster-Ramer and Kac (1990) argue that it is not very satisfactory from this point of view. They contend that what they call the IC (immediate constituent) model implicitly assumed various devices excluded from Classical PSG. In particular, they claim that it allowed null elements, unlimited numbers of daughters, and discontinuous constituents, all of which, as we have just seen, are excluded from Classical PSG. They also argue that IC analysis implicitly assumed complex categories, and separate immediate dominance and linear precedence statements, which as we will see in the next two chapters are central features of Modern PSG. They conclude that: 'the issue of the adequacy of the IC model and that of PSG are quite independent. Chomsky's arguments may dispose of PSG as a plausible candidate for a theory of human language syntax, but, insofar as they ignore various components of Bloomfield's, Bloch's and Harris's models, they have little to say about the adequacy of the latter' (1990: 348). It seems, then, that it is doubtful whether Classical PSG is a satisfactory formalization of pre-Chomskyan views of syntax. However, as noted earlier, Classical PSG is important even if no one was ever committed to it because of its role in arguments for TG and its importance in computer science. It is perhaps worth adding that the fact that none of Chomsky's predecessors presented a critique of the claim that PSG was a formalization of their conceptions shows how little attention they paid to the formal properties of their descriptions.

2.3 The strengths and weaknesses of Classical PSG

We now consider the strengths and weaknesses of Classical PSG as a conception of natural language syntax. The most obvious strength is that it is a simple conception. It is also a well-understood conception. Both the context-free and the context-sensitive version have been extensively studied within the branch of computer science known as formal language theory. In particular, their weak generative capacity, what sorts of sets of strings of symbols can be generated, and their parsing properties, have been major topics of investigation.

As noted in chapter 1, the context-free version of Classical PSG is a restrictive framework in the sense that it can only generate certain stringsets. For example, a CFG cannot generate the language $a^n b^n c^n$, the language all of whose strings consist of a certain number of a's followed by the same number of b's and the same number of c's. However, this language can be generated by a CSG. Similarly, as Gazdar and Mellish (1989) point out, a CFG cannot generate the language xx, x in $\{a, b, c\}^*$, a language consisting of strings made out of the symbols a, b, and c, where each string consists of two halves, the second being identical to the first. Again, however, a CSG can generate this language. As noted earlier, languages that can be generated by a CFG are standardly referred to as context-free languages (CFLs). Languages that can be generated by a CSG are standardly referred to as context-sensitive languages (CSLs). The former are a subset of the latter.[3]

Whether or not natural languages are CFLs has been discussed sporadically since the earliest work in generative grammar. There were a number of attempts during the 1960s and 1970s to show that natural languages are not CFLs. However, Pullum and Gazdar (1982) demonstrated that all the attempts were flawed in one way or another. Thus, when GPSG was emerging it was reasonable to suppose that natural languages were CFLs. GPSG grammars can only generate CFLs. This was seen as an important argument in favour of such grammars in the early GPSG literature. Thus, Gazdar (1982: 132) remarks that 'if we allow ourselves to employ apparatus restricted to CF generative capacity, then we are making a very strong universal claim about the properties of natural languages, one which is presently unfalsified'. More recently, however, it has become clear in the work of Shieber (1985) and Huybregts (1985) that natural languages are not necessarily CFLs.[4] They focus on Swiss German, which has subordinate clauses like the following:

(13)   mer d'chind   em Hans   es huus   lönd hälfed
        we the children-ACC Hans-DAT the house-ACC let   helped
        aastriiche
        paint
        'we let the children help Hans paint the house'

Here, *d'chind* is the object of *lönd*, *em Hans* is the object of *hälfed*, and *es huus* is the object of *aastriiche*. The dependencies cross over each other. Such 'cross-serial dependencies' are beyond the capacity of CFGs. Thus, the fact that GPSG grammars can only generate CFLs is not an advantage but a weakness. HPSG grammars are not restricted to generating CFLs; hence, the fact that natural languages are not necessarily CFLs is not a problem for HPSG.[5]

Another feature of CFGs is that they permit relatively efficient parsing. In the worst case, a CFG allows a sentence to be parsed in an amount of time proportional to the cube of the number of words it contains. This fact was presented in Gazdar (1982) as a reason for preferring GPSG-type grammars to transformational grammars. His argument has essentially the following form:

(14)   Natural languages are efficiently parsable.
        CFLs are efficiently parsable.
        Therefore, it is plausible to suppose that natural languages are CFLs and
        a theory whose grammars can only generate CFLs is preferable, other
        things being equal, to one that is less restricted.

Since it is now clear that natural languages are not necessarily CFLs, this argument has been overtaken by events. However, before this became clear, it was subject to certain criticisms, notably in Berwick and Weinberg (1982); they point out that some CSLs are efficiently parsable, so that the fact that some theory allows grammars that generate CSLs does not necessarily provide an argument against it. They also stress that parsing efficiency is affected by the size of the grammar: the bigger the grammar, the more time the parsing algorithm will spend running through the rules to find one that is applicable. As we will see in the next chapter, CFGs need very large numbers of rules to achieve significant coverage, so this is an important matter. A further weakness of Gazdar's argument, highlighted, for example, in Barton, Berwick and Ristad (1987), is that the fact that some type of grammar can only generate CFLs does not entail that it has the same parsing properties as CFGs, any more than it entails that it has the same ability to capture generalizations. (See also Rounds 1991.) GPSG and HPSG grammars differ from CFGs in their ability to capture generalizations and may well differ from CFGs in their parsing properties.

It is fairly clear, then, that the parsing efficiency of CFGs cannot be used as an argument for GPSG. Nevertheless, Gazdar was clearly right to draw attention to the relevance of parsing considerations in evaluating theories of syntax, and his argument has led to some important research.[6]

We turn now to the weaknesses of Classical PSG. An obvious weakness of the context-free version is that it is too restricted, given that natural languages are not necessarily CFLs. Most discussion of Classical PSG in the linguistic literature has focused on the context-free version but the objections that have been advanced have not generally been concerned with weak generative capacity. Thus, Postal (1964: 73–5) advances eight objections to Classical PSG and none involve weak generative capacity. Chomsky's arguments against Classical PSG are similar. As Manaster-Ramer and Kac (1990: 335) note, they are such that 'weak generative capacity cannot be the issue'. The main focus of the objections is strong generative capacity, the ability to generate the right structures, and descriptive adequacy, the ability to capture linguistically significant generalizations.

In connection with strong generative capacity, we find objections that simply assume with no real argument that more than one level of structure is necessary. This is the second of Postal's objections and also figures in Bach (1973: 73). We also find objections which assume dubious restrictions on Classical PSG. Thus, Postal claims that Classical PSG will assign the wrong structure to coordinate structures. He is assuming here that no rule may allow a node to have an unlimited number of daughters, and hence that Classical PSG cannot generally assign a flat structure to coordinate structures.

Turning to descriptive adequacy, we find Akmajian and Heny (1975: 83) arguing that a Classical PSG approach to *yes–no* questions misses a generalization, and Baker (1978: 65) arguing that it is 'unrevealing'. These objections are sound ones. It is interesting to note, however, that there was no discussion in these texts of the possibility of accommodating the data with PS rules containing complex categories, in spite of the fact that they all assume complex categories. As we will see in the next chapter, complex categories allow Modern PSG to capture most of the generalizations that elude Classical PSG.

2.4   Classical and Modern PSG

We now consider the relation between Classical and Modern PSG. We will say something about both the similarities and the differences: we will deal with the latter more fully in the next three chapters.

The most obvious similarity between Classical and almost all versions of Modern PSG is the following:

(15)   Classical and Modern PSG are monostratal frameworks, in which the syntactic structure of a sentence is a single tree.

This distinguishes Classical and almost all versions of Modern PSG from all versions of TG, including P&P, and from certain other frameworks, such as Relational Grammar. (In chapter 12 we will consider a version of Modern HPSG which arguably assumes two levels of structure.) A second similarity is the following:

(16)   For context-free versions of Classical PSG and standard versions of Modern PSG, grammatical statements are strictly local, never referring to anything larger than a local tree. Hence, a tree is well-formed if and only if every local tree is well-formed.

Here, we are only concerned with the context-free version of Classical PSG and standard versions of Modern PSG. As we have seen, for the context-sensitive version of Classical PSG, rules may refer not just to a local tree but to its context. There is also at least one non-standard version of GPSG, that of Ojeda (1988) discussed in chapter 12, that has this property. Nevertheless, this is an important property shared by the most influential form of Classical PSG and almost all versions of Modern PSG, and one that distinguishes them from P&P. As we will see, however, complex categories allow some kinds of context sensitivity without explicit reference to context in rules.

It is these two similarities that justify regarding Classical and Modern PSG as forms of PSG. They are important similarities but they are compatible with the existence of major differences. There are three important differences between Modern and Classical PSG. They are as follows: (1) Modern PSG, unlike Classical PSG, assumes complex categories; (2) standard versions of Modern PSG, unlike Classical PSG, do not assume PS rules; (3) Modern PSG analyses, unlike Classical PSG analyses, are allied to semantic analyses. We will consider these matters in some detail in the following chapters.

It is natural to ask here how different Modern and Classical PSG are. They are not fundamentally different if one's main concern is the nature of syntactic representations and the scope of syntactic rules. As we have seen, standard versions of Modern PSG are similar to the context-free version of Classical PSG in this area. They also are not necessarily fundamentally different if one's main concern is with weak generative capacity. As we have noted, GPSG grammars have the same weak generative capacity as CFGs. From this perspective, the fundamental distinction is between the context-free version of Classical PSG and GPSG on the one hand and the context-sensitive version of Classical PSG and HPSG on the other. However, Classical and Modern PSG are very different if one is concerned, as syntacticians are, with capturing generalizations. As we will see in the next two chapters, complex categories and the replacement of PS rules by various different types of conditions on local trees allows the various versions of Modern PSG to capture generalizations that are beyond the reach of Classical PSG.

It is interesting in this context to recall Chomsky's (1966) discussion of Harman's (1963) version of PSG. Harman's framework makes use of complex categories and is essentially an early version of Modern PSG. Calling Harman's framework 'extended' PSG and Classical PSG 'restricted' PSG, Chomsky suggests that 'extended phrase structure grammar has no more connection with restricted phrase structure grammar than antelopes have with ants' (1966: 41). This is a very strange remark. When Chomsky (1965) introduced complex categories into TG, there was no suggestion that he was proposing a new type of grammar with no more connection with earlier TG than, say, caterpillars have with cats. In any event, it is clear that Modern and Classical PSG have much more in common than ants and antelopes. However, they do differ greatly in their descriptive potential, as we will see in the next two chapters.

2.5 Summary

In this chapter, we have looked at the central features of Classical PSG and distinguished between the context-free and the context-sensitive version. We have also outlined the strengths and weaknesses of Classical PSG. Finally, we have looked at the relation between Classical and Modern PSG. We have noted two important similarities, but we have also noted three major differences. We will look in detail at these differences in the next three chapters.

Notes

1 For some further discussion of pre-Chomskyan American linguistics and Chomsky's criticisms of it, see Newmeyer (1986: ch. 1).
2 McCawley (1968) pointed out that PS rules could also be interpreted as tree formation rules, rules mapping trees onto trees by adding daughters to hitherto terminal nodes.
3 For discussion of the properties of CFL's and CF-PSGs, see Aho and Ullman (1972).
4 Further evidence that natural languages are not necessarily CFLs is presented in Culy (1985) and Miller (1991).
5 The fact that natural languages are not necessarily CFLs does not entail that they require the full power of CSGs. It has been argued that natural languages are only 'mildly context-sensitive'. See, for example, Partee, Wall and ter Meulen (1990: ch. 7), Joshi, Vijay-Shanker and Weir (1991) and Gazdar (1988). For surveys of mathematical work on natural languages, see Partee, Wall and ter Meulen (1990: Part E), Perrault (1984) and Gazdar and Pullum (1985).
6 For some discussion of the generative power of HPSG grammars, see Carpenter (1991).

Exercises

1 The CS-PS rules in (1), combined with a suitable lexicon, will allow the grammatical examples in (2) while excluding the ungrammatical examples in (3). Explain how these results are achieved.

(1)
   a. NP $\longrightarrow$ Det $\begin{Bmatrix} \text{Nsing} \\ \text{Nplur} \end{Bmatrix}$

$$\text{b.} \quad \text{VP} \longrightarrow \begin{Bmatrix} \text{Vsing NP/Nsing} \underline{\quad} \\ \text{Vplur NP/Nplur} \underline{\quad} \end{Bmatrix}$$

(2) a. The boy likes cricket.
     b. The boys like cricket.

(3) a. *The boy like cricket.
     b. *The boys likes cricket.

The additional rules in (4) are not sufficient to accommodate the examples in (5). Explain why this is.

(4) VP $\longrightarrow$ Adv VP
     V $\longrightarrow$ V *and* V

(5) a. The boy really likes cricket.
     b. The boy likes and plays cricket.

2 Show how the bracketed strings in the following provide evidence for local trees in which a daughter category is identical to a mother category.

(1) a. a [handsome man]
     b. a [dark, handsome man]
     c. a [tall, dark, handsome man]

(2) a. Kim [did it on Wednesday]
     b. Kim [did it on Wednesday in the pub]
     c. Kim [did it on Wednesday in the pub for a bet]

(3) a. [Kim] did it.
     b. [Kim and Sandy] did it.

(4) a. Kim [ran]
     b. Kim [ran and walked]

3 As noted in the text, Jackendoff (1977) assumes that coordinate structures require a rule allowing a node to have an unlimited number of daughters. Data like the following appear to provide motivation for this assumption:

(1) Kim and Sandy
(2) Kim (and) Sandy and Lee
(3) Kim (and) Sandy (and) Lee and Fido

One might propose, however, that what look like coordinate structures with more than two conjuncts are in fact coordinate structures with two conjuncts, one or both of which is a coordinate structure. Discuss the implications of the following data for this idea.

(4)   both Kim and Lee and Sandy
(5)   *both Kim, Lee and Sandy
(6)   Kim and both Lee and Sandy
(7)   *Kim, both Lee and Sandy

4   The following grammar, based on one in Gazdar and Mellish (1989: 136), will generate the context-sensitive language $a^n b^n c^n$. Its crucial feature is that a category can consist of a basic category and a list (possibly empty) of categories. Show how it can generate the strings *abc, aabbcc,* and *aaabbbccc.*

(1)   S[ ] $\longrightarrow$ a A[z]
(2)   A[...] $\longrightarrow$ a A[a...]
(3)   A[...] $\longrightarrow$ B[...]
(4)   B[a...] $\longrightarrow$ b B[...] c
(5)   B[z] $\longrightarrow$ b c

5   Summarize an argument for a transformational treatment of some phenomenon presented in an introduction to transformational grammar. Identify what kind of argument it is, whether it relates to weak generative capacity, strong generative capacity, or descriptive adequacy, and consider whether it has any obvious defects.

3 Syntactic Categories

3.1 Introduction

We can turn now to the features that distinguish Modern PSG from Classical PSG as described in the last chapter. In this chapter, we shall look at the most important, the fact that syntactic categories are complex entities made up of smaller elements generally known as features or attributes in Modern PSG. Modern PSG is not unique in assuming complex syntactic categories: in fact, most current approaches to syntax make this assumption. The potential of complex categories was highlighted by various kinds of work before the emergence of Modern PSG, but it was essentially ignored within mainstream syntactic theory, and it only became fully apparent with the appearance of GPSG, and subsequently HPSG.

In this chapter, we will begin by looking at the history of these matters. Then we will consider the descriptive power of complex categories. Next we will look in detail at the GPSG and HPSG conception of categories. Finally we will consider the implications of complex categories for the lexicon.

3.2 Some history

The idea that syntactic categories are complex entities composed of smaller elements is implicit in traditional discussion of grammar, where labels like 'masculine singular noun' and 'feminine plural noun' are employed. However, complex categories are not a feature of Classical PSG and they were not assumed in early TG. Gazdar and Mellish (1989: 141) trace the idea that syntactic categories are complex back to Yngve (1958). As we noted in the last chapter, it was a central feature of Harman (1963), and it gained general acceptance after it was adopted in Chomsky (1965). Chomsky was influenced by phonology, in which the idea that phonological segments are made up of smaller elements was firmly established. It had also been proposed in semantics, for example in Katz and Fodor (1963), that meanings are made up of smaller semantic features. Chomsky in fact proposed not that all syntactic categories are complex, but only that lexical categories such as noun and verb are. He proposed that features should only be used to provide a more refined classification of lexical items than is possible with labels like 'N' and 'V'. In particular, he used features to subclassify verbs, to distinguish, for example, between verbs like *pause*, which take no complements, and verbs like *kick*, which take an NP complement, marking the former as [+___0] and the latter as [+___NP]. He argued that 'There is apparently no motivation for allowing complex symbols to appear above the level of lexical categories' (1965: 188).

The idea that it is only lexical categories that are complex was abandoned by Chomsky in Chomsky (1970). In the course of a discussion of the theoretical implications of derived nominal phrases like *John's criticism of the book*, he argues that the distinction between features and categories is an artificial one, and that categories are 'sets of features' (1970: 49).

Complex categories were assumed in most syntactic theorizing of the 1970s, but there was little interest in the potential of such categories within mainstream syntactic theory. Two aspects of the work of the 1970s are worth noting. The first is that it was generally assumed that features are binary, with just two possible values: '+' and '−'. This assumption appears to live on within P&P. A central concept within this theory is Case, and it seems to be generally assumed that this is represented formally by a set of binary features ±nominative, ±objective, etc. rather than by a single feature with nominative, objective and other case names as its values.

The second is that information about what is often known as the 'bar level' of an expression, whether it is lexical, full phrasal or something in between, was generally regarded as something distinct from other types of information. Only the latter was seen as encoded by features. This position was made explicit by Bresnan (1976), who proposed that a syntactic category is an ordered pair <i,M>, where i is the bar level of the category, 0 for lexical, 1 for intermediate phrasal, and 2 for full phrasal, and M is the feature matrix of the category.

Outside mainstream theoretical linguistics, the potential of complex categories was demonstrated during the 1970s in work of a number of kinds. They were a central characteristic of the approach known as Systemic Grammar and the related framework Daughter Dependency Grammar. (See Hudson 1971, 1976.) They were also exploited in natural language processing, where 'augmented' context-free grammars, essentially context-free grammars with complex categories, dominated the scene (see, for example, Sager 1981).

The value of complex categories was also highlighted by work in Montague grammar. (See, for example, Partee 1976.) This work exploited a conception of syntactic categories that derives from Categorial Grammar, an approach to grammar which was originally developed between the wars by the Polish logician Ajdukiewicz. In one version of Categorial Grammar all categories apart from a small number of basic categories are of the form α/β or α\β, where α and β are categories. An α/β is an expression which combines with a following β to form an α, and an α\β is an expression which combines with a preceding β to form an α. Within this approach, an English VP might be analysed as an S\NP, an expression which combines with a preceding NP to form an S, and an English transitive verb might be analysed as an (S\NP)/NP, an expression that combines with a following NP to form an expression which combines with a preceding NP to form an S. With such categories, grammars need very few rules. (We shall say more about Categorial Grammar in chapter 13.)

A further demonstration of the value of complex categories was provided at the end of the 1970s by work in Artificial Intelligence on Definite Clause Grammars (DCGs). These are essentially sets of PS rules involving complex categories in a format that derives from the computer language PROLOG. Their potential was demonstrated in Pereira and Warren (1980), who showed *inter alia* that they could provide a simple account of English subject–verb agreement, something which was argued in Grinder and Elgin (1973) to be beyond the scope of phrase structure grammars.

While the potential of complex categories had been highlighted before 1980, it only became clear within mainstream theoretical linguistics with Gazdar's (1981a) demonstration that complex categories permit an interesting monostratal approach to so-called unbounded dependencies. Interestingly, however, this paper does not present a theory of syntactic categories. It is only in Gazdar and Pullum (1982) that such a theory is outlined.

Since Gazdar and Pullum's paper the nature of syntactic categories has been a major concern of Modern PSG. This distinguishes Modern PSG quite sharply from P&P, in which the nature of syntactic categories has received very little attention. As noted above, it seems to be generally assumed within P&P that all features are binary. It looks, then, as if syntactic categories must be sets of binary feature specifications. It is not uncommon, however, to find discussion within the framework which appears to assume that categories are simple, atomic entities. For example, one finds Ouhalla (1991) arguing that English aspectual auxiliaries cannot be verbs because they differ from typical verbs in their behaviour. This would only follow if categories were simple entities. One also finds discussion which appears to assume, as in *Aspects* (Chomsky 1965), that categories are atomic elements possibly supplemented by certain feature specifications. For example, one finds Chomsky (1986b: 47) suggesting that an empty complementizer is 'featureless'. Clearly, this could not really be the case if categories are sets of feature specifications.

3.3   The power of complex categories

Why is the use of complex categories such an important difference between Modern and Classical PSG? The answer is that complex categories have immense descriptive potential. Hence, a grammar that employs such categories can be quite different from a grammar that contains the same sorts of rules but employs simple, atomic categories.

Complex categories allow all sorts of generalizations to be captured which cannot be captured with simple, atomic categories. It seems reasonable to say that a generalization is captured when it is formulated as a single simple statement. With simple, atomic categories, a single simple statement is only possible where expressions behave in exactly the same way so that they can be assigned to the same category. It is an important fact about language that expressions which are different in some way can be similar in other ways. In other words, there are generalizations about expressions which are not identical in their behaviour. With complex categories such generalizations can be formulated as a single simple statement. The expressions can be assigned to categories that are different in some way but similar in many ways. With simple categories the expressions would be assigned to different categories, and many different statements would be necessary (or a disjunctive statement). Hence, the generalization would be missed.

One situation which highlights the difference between simple and complex categories is where members of a number of different categories appear in the same position. Consider the following examples:

(1)   Mary sings the song.
(2)   Mary sings a song.
(3)   Mary sings the songs.
(4)   Mary sings songs.

Each of these examples involves a verb with a noun phrase object. One might suppose that the noun phrases could be assigned to the same category. However, the following show that it is necessary in English to distinguish singular and plural noun phrases:

(5)   The song annoys/*annoy her.
(6)   The songs annoy/*annoys her.

The following show that it is also necessary to distinguish definite and indefinite NPs.

(7)   All of the/*some songs were popular.
(8)   There was a/*the song on the radio.

It is clear, then, that we need four different categories for the NPs in (1)–(4). If we have simple, atomic categories, we might assume the following categories:

(9)   NP1 = definite singular noun phrase
      NP2 = indefinite singular noun phrase
      NP3 = definite plural noun phrase
      NP4 = indefinite plural noun phrase

Given these categories, we will have four different local trees for the verb phrases in (1)–(4), and we will require either the four separate rules in (10) or the single disjunctive rule in (11).

(10) VP $\longrightarrow$ V NP1
      VP $\longrightarrow$ V NP2
      VP $\longrightarrow$ V NP3
      VP $\longrightarrow$ V NP4

(11)
$$VP \longrightarrow V \begin{Bmatrix} NP1 \\ NP2 \\ NP3 \\ NP4 \end{Bmatrix}$$

The situation is quite different with complex categories. Given complex categories, the four types of noun phrase will have broadly similar categories. For example, we might have the following:

(12)
$$\begin{bmatrix} nominal\ + \\ phrasal\ + \\ definite\ + \\ number\ sing \end{bmatrix} \quad \begin{bmatrix} nominal\ + \\ phrasal\ + \\ definite\ - \\ number\ sing \end{bmatrix}$$

$$\begin{bmatrix} nominal\ + \\ phrasal\ + \\ definite\ + \\ number\ plur \end{bmatrix} \quad \begin{bmatrix} nominal\ + \\ phrasal\ + \\ definite\ - \\ number\ plur \end{bmatrix}$$

Given such categories, we will have four similar verb phrases in (1)–(4), which we can provide for with a single rule of the following form:

(13)   VP $\longrightarrow$ V $\begin{bmatrix} \text{nominal} + \\ \text{phrasal} + \end{bmatrix}$

'VP' and 'V' are abbreviations for certain feature complexes. One point to note is that it is not just in object position that we have these four types of NPs. They also appear in prepositional object position and in subject position in non-finite clauses. Thus, this is an important matter.

A second situation which highlights the difference between simple and complex categories is where a language shows agreement, that is, where one constituent varies as another varies. Examples (5) and (6) provide an illustration. The following Welsh data provide a more complex illustration.

(14)   arnaf   i
       on-1SG I

       arnat   ti
       on-2SG you(SG)

       arno   ef
       on-3SGM he

       arni   hi
       on-3SGF she

       arnom   ni
       on-1PL we

       arnoch chwi
       on-2PL you(PL)

       arnynt hwy
       on-3PL they

Here, we have a preposition with seven different forms used with different objects. Thus, we have PPs consisting of seven different pairs of categories, and within Classical PSG we would need seven separate statements here. In contrast, within Modern PSG, we can require categories in the same local tree to have the same value for certain features, and a single statement is possible. We might propose a rule of the following form:

(15)   PP $\longrightarrow$ P   NP
       $\begin{bmatrix} \text{number } \alpha \\ \text{person } \beta \\ \text{gender } \gamma \end{bmatrix}$ $\begin{bmatrix} \text{number } \alpha \\ \text{person } \beta \\ \text{gender } \gamma \end{bmatrix}$

'PP', 'P' and 'NP' are abbreviations. The variables α, β and γ will ensure that the features person, number and gender have the same value in the two categories.[1]

It is clear, then, that complex categories allow Modern PSG to capture a variety of generalizations that are quite beyond the reach of Classical PSG. Thus, they allow Modern PSG to avoid most of the objections that can be levelled against Classical PSG.

In earlier discussion, we implicitly assumed that a category in a tree can be more complex than the corresponding category in the licensing rule. If we did not assume this, every distinct local tree type would require a distinct rule, and we would derive no benefit from complex categories. A category in a tree must have all the feature specifications of the corresponding category in a rule but it may have additional feature specifications. We can express this in terms of the notion 'subsumes', which we can define as follows:

(16)   A category X subsumes another category Y if and only if Y contains all the feature specifications in X together possibly with certain additional feature specifications.

We can now characterize the relation between tree categories and rule categories as follows:

(17)   A category in a tree matches a category in a rule if and only if the latter subsumes the former.

We can illustrate these ideas with the following categories:

(18)   a. $\begin{bmatrix} \text{nominal} + \\ \text{phrasal} + \end{bmatrix}$ b. $\begin{bmatrix} \text{nominal} + \\ \text{phrasal} + \\ \text{number sing} \end{bmatrix}$

     c. $\begin{bmatrix} \text{nominal} + \\ \text{phrasal} + \\ \text{number plur} \end{bmatrix}$ d. $\begin{bmatrix} \text{nominal} + \\ \text{phrasal} - \end{bmatrix}$

(18a) subsumes both (18b) and (18c) but not (18d) because it has a different value for the feature phrasal. This means that (18b) and (18c) match (18a) but (18d) does not.

It is worth noting that these ideas are implicit in P&P work. The α in Move α is essentially a completely unspecified category. What exactly is moved is some specific category, but whatever it is, it is subsumed by α.

Sometimes a category contains two instances of some variable. In this situation, it can only subsume another category if the two instances are replaced by the same constant. Thus, (19a) subsumes (19b) but not (19c).

(19)   a. $\begin{bmatrix} F^1 \ \alpha \\ F^2 \ \alpha \\ \ldots \end{bmatrix}$ b. $\begin{bmatrix} F^1 \ V^1 \\ F^2 \ V^1 \\ \ldots \end{bmatrix}$ c. $\begin{bmatrix} F^1 \ V^1 \\ F^2 \ V^2 \\ \ldots \end{bmatrix}$

This means that (19b) but not (19c) matches (19a).

As we have seen, a grammar with complex categories can have a single rule where a grammar with simple categories has a number of rules. There is more to be said here. For each of the verb phrases in (1)–(4), there are four other verb phrases identical except that they involve a different form of the verb. Thus, corresponding to (1), we have the following:

(20) a. The girls sing the song.
      b. Mary may sing the song.
      c. Mary is singing the song.
      d. Mary has sung the song.

In each case we have a different VP headed by a different form of the verb and appearing in a different context. (*Sing* in (20a) looks like *sing* in (20b) but it differs in that it only allows a plural subject. We do not have ***The girl sing the song* whereas we do have *The girl may sing the song*.) We will have four similar examples corresponding to (2), (3) and (4). What this means is that within Classical PSG we would have not four different rules but 20 in this area. In GPSG, a single rule provides for the VPs in all 20 examples. This is not a PS rule but an immediate dominance rule, but this does not affect the basic point. (We will introduce the concept of an immediate dominance rule in the next chapter.) The GPSG rule is one of 48 rules for head–complement structures listed in the appendix to Gazdar et al. (1985). Each corresponds to a number of PS rules with simple categories. As we will see in chapter 6, HPSG has a single rule for all head–complement structures. This rule corresponds to a considerable number of GPSG rules since it is clear that more than just the 48 rules in the appendix are necessary. Thus, the HPSG rule corresponds to a massive number of PS rules with simple categories. It is clear that a GPSG grammar captures generalizations that a grammar containing PS rules with simple categories misses, and that an HPSG grammar captures generalizations that a GPSG grammar misses. Thus, we can see the number of rules in a grammar as a measure of sorts of how far it captures generalizations.[2]

3.4 Categories in GPSG

Having looked at the power of complex categories, we now look at the GPSG conception of categories, more precisely the theory of syntactic categories presented in Gazdar et al. (1985).[3]

On Gazdar et al.'s theory, categories are sets of feature specifications, a feature specification being a feature name and a feature value. Feature values are either atoms or syntactic categories. Where the feature value is an atom there may be more than two possible values. Hence, atomic-valued features are not necessarily binary. Category-valued features are obviously not binary. Categories are standardly represented as attribute-value matrices (AVMs), box-like arrays with feature names on the left and feature values on the left. The following is a simple example:

(21)
$$\begin{bmatrix} N\,+ \\ V\,- \\ BAR\ 2 \\ PER\ 3 \\ PLU\,- \end{bmatrix}$$

This is the GPSG category for a third person singular NP. Alternatively, a category can be represented by a directed acyclic graph. Thus, instead of (21), we might have the following:

(22)

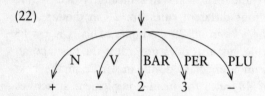

It is worth looking briefly at the value of multi-valued features. We can illustrate this with a consideration of the various forms that regular verbs have in English. The following, in which the crucial items are italicized, illustrate:

(23)　a.　He *works* hard.
　　　b.　He may *work* hard.
　　　c.　He is *working* hard.
　　　d.　He has *worked* hard.

Gazdar, Pullum and Sag (1982) provide for these forms with a number of binary features. This necessitates a stipulation that if a category has the value '+' for any of these features it must have the value '−' for all the others. Gazdar et al. (1985) avoid the need for such a stipulation by providing for the various forms with a feature VFORM with the values FIN (finite), BSE (base), PRP (present participle), and PSP (past participle). Given this feature, the verb forms above will have the following feature specifications:

(24)　a.　[VFORM FIN]
　　　b.　[VFORM BSE]
　　　c.　[VFORM PRP]
　　　d.　[VFORM PSP]

There is one other multi-valued feature that should be noted here. This is the BAR feature, which encodes the bar level of expressions. It has three possible values, 0 (lexical), 1 (intermediate phrasal) and 2 (full phrasal). We noted earlier that information about bar level was generally regarded as something distinct from other types of information in the work of the 1970s. It may be that this was because it involves at least a three-way contrast, and hence is not naturally reducible to binary features.

Proponents of GPSG have also made use of unary features, features with just one possible value. These are used in Sag et al. (1985) to provide an account of person in coordinate NPs. Their approach, however, is criticized in Warner (1988).

As we have said, GPSG allows features that take syntactic categories as their values. One such feature is the SLASH feature, which is central to the GPSG analysis of unbounded dependencies. The feature encodes the information that a constituent contains an unbounded dependency gap. Thus, the bracketed string in (25) will include [SLASH NP] within its categorial makeup.

(25) Who [did Kim talk to]

We will see how exactly this feature is used in chapter 9. GPSG also employs a category-valued feature AGR to encode information about what kind of subject an expression requires. Thus, the bracketed VP in (26) will include [AGR NP[3SG]] in its categorial makeup.

(26) Kim [likes Sandy]

We will consider this feature further in chapter 6 and chapter 8. It is worth noting here that category-valued features are implicit in Categorial Grammar. As is noted in Uszkoreit (1986), a typical Categorial Grammar category can be formalized in terms of three features, two taking a category as their value. For example, S\NP can be formalized as follows:

(27) $\begin{bmatrix} \text{Val S} \\ \text{dir left} \\ \text{arg NP} \end{bmatrix}$

This makes it explicit that an S\NP combines with an NP to its left to form an S.

Two devices that play an important role in the GPSG theory of categories are feature co-occurrence restrictions (FCRs) and feature specification defaults (FSDs). The former either require certain feature specifications to co-occur or prevent them from co-occurring. The latter identify the normal or unmarked values of certain features or combinations of features.

We look first at FCRs. Typical examples are the following:

(28)   [INV +] ⊃ [AUX +, VFORM FIN]
(29)   VFORM ⊃ [V +, N −]

(28) ensures that only finite auxiliaries can be [INV +] and hence head a verb-initial clause in English. (29) ensures that only verbs have a value for VFORM.

We turn now to FSDs. Here, we have for example the following:

(30)   [INV −]
(31)   [NFORM] ⊃ [NFORM NORM]

(30) ensures that verbs are normally [INV −] in English and hence accounts for the marked character of verb-initial sentences. (31) ensures that normal NPs are [NFORM NORM], i.e. not expletives.

Both FCRs and FSDs may be either universal or language-specific. However, Fodor (1992a, 1992b) argues against language-specific FCRs from the standpoint of learnability. She argues that language-specific FCRs are unlearnable if it is true, as is generally accepted, that children have no access to negative data, that is, information that certain things are not possible. She goes on to argue that universal FSDs play an important role in syntactic theory. The marked exceptions to the generalizations they embody can be learned from positive data. Hence, there are no learnability problems.[4]

For both GPSG and HPSG, features fall into a number of different types which behave rather differently. For example, some features are (typically) shared by a head and its mother while others are not. This raises the question: how should this be made explicit? Gazdar and Pullum (1982) identify features as belonging to the same type by grouping them together as the value of another feature.[5] As we will see, this is the approach that is taken in HPSG. Gazdar et al. (1985) abandon this approach and propose instead that grammars simply stipulate that certain features belong to the same type. This approach allows a number of possibilities which are not allowed in the first approach. Firstly, it allows features to be assigned to two separate classes where neither is a subset of the other. According to Gerald Gazdar (personal communication), this was Gazdar et al.'s main reason for adopting the approach. As we will see in chapter 9, they analyse SLASH as both a HEAD feature and a FOOT feature. Secondly, it allows the classification of a feature to vary from context to context; this possibility is exploited in Hukari and Levine (1987). Finally, it allows the classification of a feature to depend on its value; this possibility is utilized in Warner (1988).

3.5 Categories in HPSG

We turn now to the HPSG conception of syntactic categories. As we will see, it is rather more complex than the GPSG conception.

HPSG allows features to have a variety of complex values. Many features have a feature structure, i.e. a number of other features, as their value. For example, so-called HEAD features are identified as such by being grouped together as the value of a feature HEAD. This is like the approach of Gazdar and Pullum (1982) referred to above. However, the HPSG approach is more complex than Gazdar and Pullum's because every feature value is labelled with a sort symbol, which indicates the kind of value that it is. For example, the feature HEAD has as its value a feature structure of sort *head*. Sorts have subsorts. Thus, *head* has the subsorts *substantive* (*subst*) and *functional* (*func*); *subst* in turn has the subsorts *noun*, *verb*, *adjective* (*adj*), *preposition* (*prep*), *relativizer* (*rltvzer*), and *func* has the subsorts *marker* (*mark*) and *determiner* (*det*). In short, we have a sort hierarchy, part of which takes the following form:

(32)

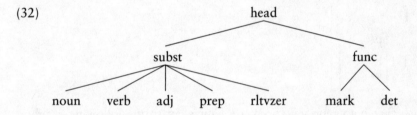

Different features are appropriate for different sorts. For example, *noun* has the feature CASE, while *verb* has the features VFORM, AUX and INV(ERTED). All *subst* sorts have the feature PRED. Atomic values are simply sorts for which no features are specified. For HPSG, a central part of a grammar is a specification of a sort hierarchy and of what features are appropriate for what sorts. This specification does the work that is done within GPSG by FCRs. Hence, there is no need for any separate FCRs.

As in GPSG, categories are standardly represented as attribute-value matrices (AVMs). The following is a very partial category for a finite verb.

(33)
$$\begin{bmatrix} \text{HEAD} & \begin{bmatrix} \text{VFORM fin} \\ \text{AUX } - \\ \text{INV } - \end{bmatrix}_{verb} \end{bmatrix}$$

Notice that the sort label *verb* appears as a subscript on the brackets that represent the feature structure that it labels. I will often omit sort labels in later discussion. It is also often convenient to omit many attributes from a feature structure. I will often omit higher level attributes in subsequent discussion. I will also follow Pollard and Sag in using 'X | Y' to identify the attribute Y that is within the value of X.

An important feature of the HPSG conception of categories is that it allows two or more features to have the same feature structure as their value. This situation is commonly referred to as structure-sharing (or re-entrancy). Structure-sharing is represented in AVMs with boxed numerals called *tags*. Consider, for example, the following:

(34)
$$\begin{bmatrix} F^1 \ [1] \begin{bmatrix} F^3 \ \dots \\ F^4 \ \dots \\ F^5 \ \dots \end{bmatrix} \\ F^2 \ [1] \end{bmatrix}$$

Here, the shared value appears just once and the sharing is indicated by the tag '[1]'. Notice that the following is an equivalent representation:

(35)
$$\begin{bmatrix} F^1 \ [1] \\ \\ F^2 \ [1] \begin{bmatrix} F^3 \ \dots \\ F^4 \ \dots \\ F^5 \ \dots \end{bmatrix} \end{bmatrix}$$

Notice also that both representations are equivalent to the following graph:

(36)

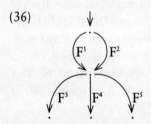

Another important feature of the HPSG conception of categories is that it allows negative and disjunctive feature values in rules and lexical entries. That is, it allows the value of some feature to be ¬ X, where X is a possible value, or X ∨ Y, where both X and Y are possible values. A number of situations in which such feature specifications appear to be necessary are discussed in Kartunnen (1984), and they are an important element of HPSG.

Perhaps the most important feature of HPSG categories is the use of list-valued and set-valued features. As we will see in chapter 6, list-valued features are central to the HPSG account of the combinatorial properties of lexical items. In one version of the framework, expressions have a feature SUBCAT whose value is a list of so-called *synsem* objects, combinations of syntactic and semantic information. The list identifies what kind of subject and complements the expression requires. Thus a verb like *think*, which takes an NP subject and an S complement, has the following specification:

(37)   [SUBCAT <NP,S>]

I use categories here to represent *synsem* objects. For HPSG, the SLASH feature is a set-valued feature. It takes as its value a set of local feature structures. Thus, we have feature specifications such as the following:

(38)   [SLASH {NP}]

I use a category here to stand for a local feature structure.

We noted earlier that HPSG has no FCRs. FSDs have also generally been rejected in HPSG. Calder (1994) advances some general criticisms, and Green and Morgan (1996) argue against the FSD in (30). Sag et al. (1992) demonstrate that defaults are unnecessary in one particularly interesting case, Icelandic 'quirky case'.

A further point that we should note here is that HPSG requires categories in trees to be fully specified. More precisely, it requires them to be totally well-typed and sort-resolved. The former means that every appropriate feature is actually present. The latter means that feature values are maximally specific sorts, for example *nom* or *acc* as the value of CASE and not *case*. Categories in rules and lexical entries, which are essentially descriptions of linguistic expressions, are not subject to this requirement.

An important feature of HPSG which we can introduce here is that all properties of expressions are represented in terms of feature structures, not only their syntactic category but also their semantic interpretation, their phonological properties and their internal structure where they are complex. In the version of HPSG presented in Pollard and Sag (1987), the phonological properties of an expression are identified by a PHON feature, the syntactic properties by a SYN feature, the semantic interpretation by a SEM feature, and what daughters a complex expression consists of is identified by a DTRS feature. We can illustrate with the simple NP *the dog*. Ignoring the SEM feature and using standard orthography as the value of PHON, we can represent this as follows:

$$(39) \quad \begin{bmatrix} \text{PHON} & \textit{the dog} \\ \text{SYN} & \text{NP} \\ \text{DTRS} & \left\langle \begin{bmatrix} \text{PHON} & \textit{the} \\ \text{SYN} & \text{Det} \end{bmatrix}, \begin{bmatrix} \text{PHON} & \textit{dog} \\ \text{SYN} & \text{N} \end{bmatrix} \right\rangle \end{bmatrix}$$

Notice that there is no real distinction between categories and trees on this approach. In later discussion, I shall generally use fairly standard trees. It should be borne in mind, however, that this is an informal representation.[6]

There are two further points that we should note here. Firstly, as we shall see in the next chapter, rules are also expressed as feature structures in HPSG. A rule is simply a schematic complex expression. Secondly, as we shall see in chapter 5, syntactic and semantic information are combined in Pollard and Sag's (1994) version of HPSG in a way that means that, strictly speaking, it does not have syntactic categories in the traditional sense.

3.6   The lexicon

As the foregoing discussion has made clear, syntactic categories are complex things in Modern PSG. This is true in GPSG, but is especially true in HPSG. It is true of lexical categories as much as of phrasal categories. One might suppose that this means that the lexicon of a GPSG or an HPSG grammar will be very large and cumbersome. It would mean this if it were necessary to give the categories of all lexical entries in full, but this is not necessary.

The main device that makes it unnecessary to give all lexical entries in full is an inheritance hierarchy, a device originally employed in Artificial Intelligence knowledge representation systems. The basic idea is a simple one. We can illustrate with the verb form *gives*. This is one of a number of third person singular, present tense ditransitive verbs. This means that it shares part of its feature makeup with all third person singular present tense verbs and part of its feature makeup with all ditransitive verbs. The shared information can be stored in two generic lexical entries for third person singular present tense and ditransitive, from which individual verbs can draw part of their feature makeup. Given such generic entries, the lexical entries for *gives* and similar verbs need only include phonological and semantic information and the information that they draw on these generic entries. Within HPSG, these generic entries are lexical sorts, subsorts of the sort *word*, and they are part of the sort hierarchy discussed in the last section.

Just as ordinary lexical entries can be simplified by drawing on generic entries, so generic entries can be simplified by drawing on other generic entries. Ditransitive verbs share part of their feature makeup with all other verbs. This shared information can be stored in a generic entry for verb, on which various verb-types can draw. Similarly, the third person singular present tense verbs share part of their feature makeup with other present tense verbs. The shared information can be stored in a generic entry for present tense. Thus, we have the following situation:

(40)

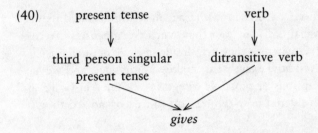

third person singular
present tense

gives

With such an inheritance hierarchy, information that is shared by a class of words is only listed once. Thus, the complexity of lexical entries does not mean a large and cumbersome lexicon.

In the case we have just considered, the full lexical category is simply the result of combining information from a number of sources. This is known as simple inheritance. It has often been proposed that specific entries should be allowed to include information which conflicts with some more general entry on which they draw, and which takes precedence over the more general entry. This is known as default inheritance. We can illustrate the basic idea with English modal auxiliaries. As the following show, they normally take a bare infinitive complement:

(41)   John may/must/will/can/could go home.

However, two modals *ought* and *is* take a *to*-infinitive complement.

(42)   John ought/is to go home.

One way to handle the data would be to formulate a generic entry for modal auxiliaries, which includes the information that they take a bare infinitive complement, and then to include in the entries for *ought* and *is* the information that they take a *to*-infinitive complement. This will override the information in the generic entry.[7]

A second device which permits a major simplification of the lexicon is lexical rules, which derive lexical entries from lexical entries. These have been assumed in a variety of frameworks (see, for example, Jackendoff 1975 and Bresnan 1982a), and they are important features of both GPSG and HPSG. For example, both assume a lexical rule deriving passive participles from the related active verbs by adding the appropriate morphology and modifying the feature makeup. We will be concerned with lexical rules in chapter 9 and especially in chapter 11.

3.7   Summary

In this chapter, we have been concerned with the most important difference
between Modern and Classical PSG, the fact that syntactic categories are complex entities for Modern PSG whereas they are simple, atomic entities for Classical PSG. We have considered how exactly this makes a difference, and we have
looked at the detailed conceptions of syntactic categories assumed in GPSG and
HPSG. Finally, we have considered how the lexicon can be organized to avoid
redundancy.

Notes

1 The discussion of the Welsh preposition in (14) ignores the fact that it also has a form
   which appears with a non-pronominal object, either singular or plural. The following
   illustrates:

   (i) ar y   dyn/ dynion
        on the man men

   This means that the analysis given in (15) is too simple.
2 Some early computational grammars, which were essentially instantiations of Classical PSG, involved very large numbers of rules. For example, Grishman (1986: 33)
   reports that the Harvard predictive analyser of Kuno and Oettinger (1962) included
   2,100 rules and did not have an account of subject–verb agreement.
3 GPSG assumptions about syntactic categories are set out in Gazdar et al. (1985:
   ch. 2) and formalized in Gazdar et al. (1988). HPSG ideas are set out in Pollard and
   Sag (1987: ch. 3) and Pollard and Sag (1994: ch. 1). The formal foundations are
   explored in Kasper and Rounds (1990), Carpenter (1992) and Moshier and Pollard
   (1994).
4 For further discussion of defaults and learnability from an HPSG point of view, see
   Wacholder (1995).
5 The idea that a feature can have a group of features as its value has been explored
   quite extensively in phonology, where 'feature geometry' is a major concern. See
   Clements (1985) and, for textbook discussion, Kenstowicz (1994: ch. 9).
6 HPSG approaches to phonology are developed in Bird (1991), Bird and Klein (1993)
   and Scobbie (1991, 1993). HPSG approaches to morphology are developed in
   Riehemann (1992), Kathol (forthcoming) and Krieger and Nerbonne (1993).
7 For further discussion of the role of inheritance in the lexicon, see Flickinger (1987),
   Flickinger, Pollard and Wasow (1985) and Flickinger and Nerbonne (1992). For a
   detailed lexical analysis of English auxiliaries utilizing default inheritance, see Warner
   (1993a, 1993b). For some general discussion of default inheritance, see Gazdar (1987)
   and Daelemans, De Smedt and Gazdar (1992).

Exercises

1   The following sentences illustrate the relation between English declaratives and *yes–no* interrogatives. Formulate a generalization about this relationship and show how PS rules containing simple, atomic categories will fail to capture it.

(1)   a.   He will go/*gone/*going to London.
      b.   He has gone/*go/*going to London.
      c.   He is going/*go/*gone to London.

(2)   a.   Will he go/*gone/*going to London?
      b.   Has he gone/*go/*going to London?
      c.   Is he going/*go/*gone to London?

2   Replace the informal classifications of expressions in the following statements with precise GPSG categories using the features, N, V, BAR and others:

(1)   *Done* is the past participle of an auxiliary verb.
(2)   *Them* is an accusative third person plural pronoun.
(3)   *As old as the hills* is an equative adjective phrase.
(4)   *The women* is a feminine plural noun phrase.
(5)   *Stories about Kim* is a neuter, singular N′.

3   Drawing on the discussion in 3.3, provide PS rules for S and VP which will handle the agreement exhibited in the following Polish examples:

(1)   a.   Ja lubię   piwo.
         I   like-1SG beer
         'I like beer.'

      b.   Ty   lubisz   piwo.
         you(SG) like-2SG beer
         'You(SG) like beer.'

      c.   On/ona/ono lubi   piwo.
         he she it   like-3SG beer
         'He/she/it likes beer.'

      d.   My lubimy   piwo.
         we like-1PL beer
         'We like beer.'

      e.   Wy   lubicie piwo.
         you(PL) like-2PL beer
         'You(PL) like beer.'

    f.   Oni lubią   piwo.
         they like-3PL beer
         'They like beer.'

4 Which categories in the following are subsumed by which other categories?

(1) $\begin{bmatrix} \text{BAR 2} \\ \text{N +} \\ \text{V –} \end{bmatrix}$

(2) $\begin{bmatrix} \text{BAR 2} \\ \text{N +} \\ \text{V –} \\ \text{CASE ACC} \end{bmatrix}$

(3) $\begin{bmatrix} \text{BAR 2} \\ \text{N –} \\ \text{V +} \\ \text{VFORM FIN} \\ \text{PAST +} \end{bmatrix}$

(4) $\begin{bmatrix} \text{BAR 0} \\ \text{N +} \\ \text{V –} \\ \text{CASE ACC} \end{bmatrix}$

(5) [BAR 2]

(6) $\begin{bmatrix} \text{BAR 2} \\ \text{N –} \\ \text{V +} \\ \text{PERS 3} \\ \text{NUM SG} \end{bmatrix}$

(7) $\begin{bmatrix} \text{BAR 2} \\ \text{N –} \\ \text{V +} \\ \text{VFORM FIN} \end{bmatrix}$

(8) $\begin{bmatrix} \text{BAR 0} \\ \text{N –} \\ \text{V +} \end{bmatrix}$

5 The words *need*, *near*, *sheep*, and *enough* in the following sentences are atypical members of the class of modals, adjectives, nouns and degree words

(words like *more*, *so* and *too*), respectively, and hence strong candidates for an analysis involving default inheritance. Explain how they are atypical.

(1) I need not elaborate.
(2) The theatre is near (to) the river.
(3) The sheep were in the field.
(4) Kim is old enough to be selected.

4 Rules and Principles

4.1 Introduction

In this chapter, we will consider the second important difference between Modern PSG and Classical PSG: the fact that standard versions of Modern PSG assume not PS rules but a number of different rules and principles, which jointly determine whether or not a local tree is well-formed. In this, Modern PSG is a modular framework rather like P&P.

We will look first at the motivation for separate immediate dominance and linear precedence rules. Then we will consider the motivation for various general principles. Next we will consider the relation between rules and trees. We will go on to look in more detail at immediate dominance and linear precedence rules in GPSG and HPSG. Finally we will consider the notion of a metagrammar, which played an important role in early GPSG.[1,2]

4.2 ID and LP rules

The deficiencies of PS rules were recognized in Modern PSG at much the same time as they were in P&P. In Modern PSG, they were first pointed out in Gazdar and Pullum (1981), while in P&P they were first highlighted in Stowell (1981). In both cases, it was argued that PS rules should be replaced by separate immediate dominance and linear precedence statements. In Modern PSG, these are known as immediate dominance (ID) and linear precedence (LP) rules.

There are two main objections to PS rules. The first is that they miss generalizations about the order of sister constituents. Somewhat surprisingly, this was ignored in Classical TG criticisms of PS rules. We can illustrate this objection with a set of PS rules that might be proposed for English:

(1) a. V′ $\longrightarrow$ V NP
     b. V′ $\longrightarrow$ V PP

c. V′ ⟶ V S
d. V′ ⟶ V NP PP
e. V′ ⟶ V NP S
f. V′ ⟶ V́ PP S

(2) a. N′ ⟶ N PP
b. N′ ⟶ N S

(3) a. A′ ⟶ A PP
b. A′ ⟶ A S
c. A′ ⟶ A PP S

(4) a. P′ ⟶ P NP
b. P′ ⟶ P PP
c. P′ ⟶ P S

These rules would provide for the italicized strings in the following examples:

(5) a. Kim *watched Sandy.*
b. Kim *looked at Sandy.*
c. Kim *knows Sandy did it.*
d. Kim *put the book on the shelf.*
e. Kim *persuaded Lee that Sandy did it.*
f. Kim *said to Lee that Sandy did it.*

(6) a. a *picture of Sandy.*
b. the *belief that the earth is flat.*

(7) a. Kim is *aware of the problem.*
b. Kim is *aware that there is a problem.*
c. It is *obvious to everyone that Kim is here.*

(8) a. Kim is *in the bath.*
b. Kim appeared *from behind the wall.*
c. Kim arrived *before Sandy arrived.*

The rules miss a number of generalizations about the order of sisters. The most important is the following:

(9) A lexical category precedes any phrasal category that is its sister.

All the rules exemplify this generalization. Another important generalization is the following:

(10)   An NP precedes any other phrasal category that is its sister.

This is exemplified by rules (1d) and (1e). A further generalization is the following:

(11)   An S follows all its sisters.

This is exemplified by (1e) and (1f), and (3c). Here, then, we have a rather serious objection to PS rules.

The second objection to PS rules is that they obscure similarities between different languages. Consider, for example, a language in which V', N', A' and P' allow exactly the same constituents as in English but in which the order of constituents is reversed. If we assume PS rules, we will have the following rules:

(12)   a.   V' $\longrightarrow$ NP V
       b.   V' $\longrightarrow$ PP V
       c.   V' $\longrightarrow$ S V
       d.   V' $\longrightarrow$ PP NP V
       e.   V' $\longrightarrow$ S NP V
       f.   V' $\longrightarrow$ S PP V

(13)   a.   N' $\longrightarrow$ PP N
       b.   N' $\longrightarrow$ S N

(14)   a.   A' $\longrightarrow$ PP A
       b.   A' $\longrightarrow$ S A
       c.   A' $\longrightarrow$ S PP A

(15)   a.   P' $\longrightarrow$ NP P
       b.   P' $\longrightarrow$ PP P
       c.   P' $\longrightarrow$ S P

Given such rules, the two languages look very different. In particular, we completely miss the fact that they allow exactly the same immediate constituents. Here, then, we have another objection to PS rules.

Both these objections to PS rules can be solved by replacing them with separate ID and LP rules. In both GPSG and HPSG, ID rules are commonly distinguished from PS rules by the separation of the right-hand side categories by commas. In other words, ID rules are represented as follows:

(16) $C^0 \longrightarrow C^1, C^2, \ldots C^n$

We can interpret such a rule as (17):

(17)   A C^0 can immediately dominate a C^1 and a C^2 and ... and a C^n.

LP rules are commonly represented as follows:

(18) $C^1 < C^2$

At least in GPSG, we can interpret such a rule as follows:

(19)   A C^1 must precede (may not follow) C^2

We might capture the generalizations in (9)–(11) with the following rules:

(20)   a. $X^0 < YP$
      b. $NP < XP$ $(X \neq N)$
      c. $XP < S$

We will see in section 4.4 that it may be necessary to interpret LP rules rather differently in HPSG.

If PS rules are replaced by separate ID and LP rules, whether or not a local tree is well-formed becomes a more complex matter than it is if one assumes just PS rules. If the grammar is a set of PS rules, we have the following statement about local trees:

(21)   A local tree is well-formed if and only if it matches a PS rule.

If the grammar consists of separate ID and LP rules, we have the following, more complex statement:

(22)   A local tree is well-formed if and only if it matches an ID rule and conforms to all relevant LP rules.

We can illustrate this with the following trees:

(23)   a.   V′   b.   V′

             V   NP   NP   V

Both these trees match the following ID rule, which will replace the PS rule in (1a):

(24)   V′ $\longrightarrow$ V, NP

However, only (23a) conforms to the LP rule in (20a).[3]

   A further point that we should note here is that it is only if the order of sister categories is the same whatever their mother is that PS rules can be replaced by ID and LP rules. If two sister categories could appear in one order with one type of mother and in the opposite order with another, it would be impossible to replace PS rules by separate ID and LP rules. Thus, any framework that assumes separate ID and LP rules is committed to the following assumption:

(25)   Sister categories have the same order whatever their mother is.

In the GPSG literature, a grammar which has this property is said to show Exhaustive Constant Partial Ordering (ECPO). Gazdar et al. (1985: 49) suggest that this is a statistically unexpected property and therefore that it is of considerable interest if it is a linguistic universal.[4]

4.3   Principles

A grammar consisting of a set of ID rules and a set of LP rules will capture many generalizations that a grammar consisting solely of PS rules cannot capture. There are generalizations, however, that a grammar consisting solely of ID rules and LP rules cannot capture. Such generalizations require certain general principles imposing additional conditions on local trees and ruling out some of the possibilities allowed by ID rules.

We begin by looking at the bracketed expressions in the following examples:

(26)   Kim saw [the man]
(27)   [Which man] did Kim see?

Both expressions are NPs but they are not identical NPs. The second is interrogative, and it is interrogative because it contains an interrogative determiner. This suggests that both the NP and the determiner should be marked [WH +] or something similar. Thus, we will have something like the following local trees here:

(28)   a.

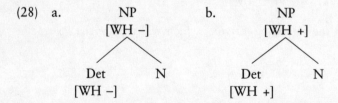

We need to allow these local trees, while excluding the following:

(29) a.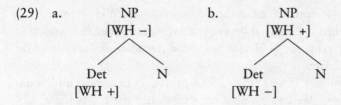

One way to do this would be to assume the following ID rule:

(30) NP[WH α] $\longrightarrow$ Det[WH α], N

The variable here will ensure that NP and Det have the same value for WH, either both '+' or both '−'.

Consider now the bracketed expressions in the following examples:

(31) Kim relied [on Sandy]
(32) [On whom] did Sandy rely?

Both expressions are PPs but they are not identical. The second is interrogative because it contains an interrogative pronoun as its complement. Here, then, it seems that both the PP and the complement should be marked [WH +]. Hence, we will have something like the following local trees:

(33) a.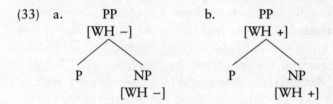

We need to allow these trees while excluding the following:

(34) a. PP   b. PP
         [WH −]   [WH +]

      P   NP   P   NP
          [WH +]   [WH −]

We might do this by assuming the following ID rule:

(35) PP[WH α] $\longrightarrow$ P, NP[WH α]

This will ensure that PP and NP have the same value for WH. Notice now, however, that we have proposed two different rules which stipulate that a mother category has the same value for WH as a non-head daughter. It looks as if we are missing a generalization.

We can avoid this problem if we allow various principles to impose additional constraints on local trees. We can propose something like the following condition on the WH feature:

(36)   a.   If a category is [WH +], its mother must be too.
       b.   If a category is [WH +], one of its daughters must be too.

Given this principle, we can have the following ID rules with no mention of the WH feature:

(37)   NP ⟶ Det, N
(38)   PP ⟶ P, NP

These rules will interact with the principle in (36) to allow the trees in (28) and (33) but not the trees in (29) and (34). In fact (36a) is rather too strong. It entails that every node dominating a [WH +] node will be [WH +]. In chapter 9 we will consider how this undesirable consequence can be avoided, when we consider the FOOT Feature Principle of GPSG and the related Nonlocal Feature Principle of HPSG.

Another general principle is required to capture the relation between heads and mothers. A variety of different structures licensed by different rules have a head which is largely identical in feature makeup to the mother. This is true both for a structure consisting of a head and its complement(s) and for a structure consisting of a specifier and a head. Among the former we have V′ with a V daughter, P′ with a P daughter, etc. Among the latter, we have NP with an N′ daughter and AP with an A′ daughter. One could stipulate this identity in the various rules that license headed structures. This, however, would miss a generalization. Therefore, we need a general principle to require the identity. GPSG has a principle called the Head Feature Convention (HFC), and HPSG has a principle called the Head Feature Principle (HFP). We can formulate the two principles as follows:

(39)   HEAD FEATURE CONVENTION
       The HEAD feature specifications of a head are identical to those of its mother unless some rule or principle requires otherwise.

(40)   HEAD FEATURE PRINCIPLE
       The HEAD value of a headed phrase is identical to the HEAD value of the head daughter.

There are a number of differences to note here. Recall that for GPSG the set of HEAD features is identified as such by stipulation whereas for HPSG they are the value of the feature HEAD. This means that the HFC must require a number of different features to have the same value in head and mother whereas the HFP just has to require a single feature, HEAD, to have the same value in head and mother. A second difference is that whereas the HFP is an absolute principle, the HFC is a default principle.[5] It can be overridden by rules and other principles. We will introduce a more complex version of the HFC when we consider coordinate structures in chapter 7.

With the introduction of principles like those we have just discussed, whether or not a local tree is well-formed becomes rather more complex. Instead of (22), we need something like the following:

(41)   A local tree is well-formed if and only if it matches an ID rule and conforms to all relevant LP rules and general principles.

In fact, however, the situation is somewhat more complex than this in GPSG, and this formulation also somewhat misrepresents the HPSG situation. We will consider this in the next section.

4.4   Rules and trees

In this section, we look more closely at the relation between rules and trees in Modern PSG, highlighting the similarities and the differences between GPSG and HPSG and also introducing the important notion of unification.[6]

In GPSG, the relation between rules and trees is more complex than (41) suggests because of the role played by feature co-occurrence restrictions (FCRs) and feature specification defaults (FSDs). It involves a sequence of definitions. Simplifying somewhat, we can formulate them as follows:

(42)   a.   A projection of an ID rule is a local tree that accords with the ID rule and respects all the FCRs in the grammar.
       b.   A candidate projection is a projection that respects the LP rules of the grammar and satisfies the feature instantiation principles.
       c.   An admissable projection is a candidate projection that satisfies all FSDs.

Notice that these definitions make it clear that rules and principles take precedence over FSDs.

Turning to HPSG, the relation between rules and trees is one aspect of the definition of a language, which crucially involves the notion of unification. The unification of two feature structures A and B, written A $\wedge$ B, is the feature structure which contains all the information in both A and B and nothing more. To take an abstract example, the unification of the feature structures in (43) is (44).

(43) $\quad \begin{bmatrix} F^1 \begin{bmatrix} F^2 \ P \\ F^3 \ Q \end{bmatrix} \end{bmatrix}$

$\quad [F^1 \ [F^4 \ R]]$

(44) $\quad \begin{bmatrix} F^1 \begin{bmatrix} F^2 \ P \\ F^3 \ Q \\ F^4 \ R \end{bmatrix} \end{bmatrix}$

If two feature structures contain incompatible information, they have no unification, or, in other words, they do not unify.

Assuming the notion of unification, Pollard and Sag (1987: 44) note that if $P_1, \ldots P_n$ is the set of universal principles and $P_{n+1}, \ldots P_{n+m}$ the set of English-specific principles, and if $L_1, \ldots L_p$ are the lexical signs of English and $R_1, \ldots R_q$ the grammar rules of English, then English can be defined as follows:

(45)   English = $P_1 \wedge \ldots \wedge P_{n+m} \wedge (L_1 \vee \ldots \vee L_p \vee R_1 \vee \ldots \vee R_q)$

We can paraphrase this as follows:

(46)   An object is an English sign just in case (i) it satisfies all the universal and English-specific principles and (ii) either it is subsumed by one of the English lexical signs or it is subsumed by one of the English grammar rules.

They assume that the LP rules of a language constitute a language-specific Constituent Ordering Principle, one of the language-specific principles. Pollard and Sag (1994: 38) suggest that grammar rules should be formulated as a disjunctive Immediate Dominance Principle. One could also formulate the lexical signs as a disjunctive Lexical Principle. With this revision, we could reformulate the definition and the paraphrase as follows:

(47)   English = $P_1 \wedge \ldots \wedge P_{n+m}$

(48)   An object is an English sign just in case it satisfies all the universal and English-specific principles.

One thing that the two definitions make' clear is that all the principles are on a par and none takes precedence over any others. This means that the principles can be used in any order. It is this that makes a unification-based framework attractive from a processing point of view.

Unlike HPSG, GPSG is not a purely unification-based framework. This is so for two reasons. Firstly, it assumes FSDs and by definition other rules and constraints take precedence over them. Secondly, the HFC is a default principle unlike its HPSG counterpart, the HFP. This means that other rules and principles take precedence over it. We should note here that arguments have been advanced for the default nature of the HFC, notably in Pullum (1991), who argues that a default HFC allows an attractive account of nominal gerunds such as the bracketed string in the following:

(49) We heard about [his leaving early]

He proposes that the construction involves an NP with a VP as its head. Such an analysis is only available if the HFC is a default principle, which doesn't require head and mother to have identical categorial features under all circumstances.[7]

4.5   More on ID and LP rules

In section 4.2, we looked at the motivation for separate ID and LP rules. In this section, we will look more closely at ID and LP rules in both GPSG and HPSG. We begin with ID rules.

We saw in section 4.3 that both GPSG and HPSG assume a principle requiring heads to be identical in many respects to their mother. These principles raise an obvious question: how are heads identified? In both frameworks, head is a primitive notion and heads are explicitly identified as such although in rather different ways.

In GPSG, heads are only identified as such in ID rules. GPSG employs an informal notation in which heads are identified with an H. We have rules like the following:

(50) $V' \longrightarrow H°, NP$

Here, 'H°' stands for an X° which is a head. Formally, a headed ID rule is an ordered pair whose first member is an ID rule and whose second member is a multiset of categories, the head daughters. (A multiset is like a set except that the same item may appear more than once.) An ID rule is an ordered pair whose first member is a category, the mother, and whose second member is a multiset of categories, the daughters. Thus, the formal counterpart of (50) is the following:

(51)   <<V', {X°, NP}$_m$>, {X°}$_m$>

The second part of the rule identifies the X° as a head. As we have said, heads are only identified as such in rules in GPSG. This means that one has to consider the licensing rule to determine whether some daughter in a tree is a head.

We now consider HPSG. In HPSG, heads are identified as such both in rules and in trees. In fact, a number of different types of daughters are distinguished both in rules and in trees. In the version of HPSG presented in Pollard and Sag (1987) and the first eight chapters of Pollard and Sag (1994), both complement and adjunct daughters are distinguished. In the version of HPSG presented in chapter 9 of Pollard and Sag (1994), subject and specifier daughters, which are regarded as complements in the earlier framework, are distinguished. Formally, different daughters are distinguished by taking the value of the DTRS attribute to be a feature structure consisting of such attributes as HEAD-DTR and COMP-DTRS. This means that we will have the following feature structure for the sentence *Kim likes Sandy* if we assume that subjects are complements:

(52) $\begin{bmatrix} \text{PHON} & \textit{Kim likes Sandy} \\ \text{SYN} & \text{S} \\ \text{DTRS} & \begin{bmatrix} \text{HEAD-DTR} & \text{<[PHON } \textit{likes Sandy}\text{]>} \\ \text{COMP-DTRS} & \text{<[PHON } \textit{Kim}\text{]>} \end{bmatrix} \end{bmatrix}$

This is, of course, simplified in various ways. It ignores the semantic properties of the sentence, and it ignores everything except the phonological properties of the two daughters. As I noted in the last chapter, I will generally use fairly standard trees to represent sentence structures. Where it is necessary to distinguish different types of daughters, this can be done by labelling the branches 'H', 'C', etc. Thus, (52) can be represented informally as follows:

(53)

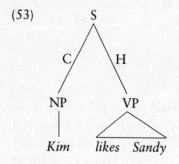

We noted in the last chapter that not only structures but also rules are represented as feature structures in HPSG. However, I will use the notation introduced in section 4.2 for HPSG ID rules and indicate the status of daughters by writing HEAD, etc. immediately beneath them.

We turn now to LP rules. They have had rather less attention than ID rules. Nevertheless there is some interesting discussion of such rules in the literature.

We suggested earlier that LP rules identify certain orders as necessary, at least in GPSG. The situation is less clear in HPSG. Pollard and Sag (1987) implicitly assume that LP rules identify necessary orders. Hukari and Levine (1991b) argue, however, that the HPSG conception of rules entails that LP rules must identify possible orders. For HPSG, rules are schematic complex phrases, and a specific complex phrase conforms with a rule if and only if the rule subsumes it, as we saw in the last section. It seems to follow that all rules, including LP rules, must identify certain situations as possible.

One might wonder whether it makes any difference whether LP rules identify necessary or possible orders. In fact, it does seem to matter. It matters especially in connection with the phenomenon of free word order. If LP rules identify necessary orders, languages with very free word order will require very few rules. On the other hand, if LP rules identify possible orders, languages with very free word order will require a large number of rules. Thus, if LP rules specify necessary orders, languages with free word order should be quite common, whereas if they specify possible word orders, such languages should be uncommon. What the facts really are in this area is not clear to me.

Whether LP rules identify necessary or possible orders also matters in connection with acquisition. Fodor (1992a) points out that it is not clear how negative rules could be learned if children do not have access to negative data. Rules that state that certain situations are necessary are essentially negative rules since they preclude other logically possible situations. Thus, from the standpoint of acquisition, LP rules identifying possible orders are clearly preferable to LP rules identifying necessary orders. Here, then, we have an important argument in favour of LP rules identifying possible orders.

One thing that is clear about HPSG LP rules is that they order not signs but only their PHONOLOGY attributes. More precisely, they specify how the PHONOLOGY attribute of a sign is created by concatenating the PHONOLOGY attributes of its daughters. One consequence of this is that if phonologically empty categories exist they will not be ordered with respect to their sisters.[8]

Although there is some vagueness about LP rules in the HPSG literature, some interesting proposals have been advanced. Particularly interesting is the proposal developed in Sag (1987) and Pollard and Sag (1987: ch. 7) that LP rules may make reference to an ordering of dependants in terms of obliqueness.

As a first approximation, Pollard and Sag propose the following LP rule:

(54)   COMPLEMENT << COMPLEMENT

'<<' designates a special kind of restricted linear precedence constraint which is only in force where the left-hand element is less oblique than the right-hand element. Thus, this rule says that a complement must precede any more oblique complement sister. (Recall that Pollard and Sag assume that LP rules identify necessary orders.) The rule will ensure that an NP complement will precede other types of complement, such as PP, S', given the natural assumption that they are more oblique. It will also ensure the right order of complements in double object sentences such as the following, given the reasonable assumption that the goal NP is less oblique than the theme NP.

(55)   Kim gave Sandy a book.

This is an interesting approach to an ordering fact which is handled in a rather *ad hoc* way in GPSG (see Gazdar et al. 1985: 214). Pollard and Sag proceed to refine this rule. Firstly, they reformulate it as follows:

(56)   COMPLEMENT << COMPLEMENT[LEX−]

This says that a complement must precede any more oblique phrasal complement sister. If we assume that particles are lexical complements, this will allow them to precede or follow objects, giving both of the following:

(57)   I looked up the answer.
(58)   I looked the answer up.

They then reformulate the rule as follows:

(59)   COMPLEMENT[MAJ ¬V] << [LEX−]

This says that a non-verbal complement must precede any more oblique phrasal sister (whether a complement or an adjunct). It will account for the following data if we assume that the infinitival complement of *appear* is less oblique than *to*-complement.

(60)   Kim appeared to be unhappy to Sandy.
(61)   Kim appeared to Sandy to be unhappy.

In (60), the two complements are ordered in terms of obliqueness. In (61), we have the opposite order but this is allowed given that the less oblique complement is verbal. Notice that we can also account for the following data:

(62)   Kim appeared unhappy to Sandy.
(63)   *Kim appeared to Sandy unhappy.

Here, we have an AP complement instead of the infinitival complement, and it has to precede the *to*-complement. Pollard and Sag assume that adjuncts can be sisters of complements but that when they do they are more oblique. Thus, (59) requires a non-verbal complement to precede an adjunct sister, but it allows a verbal complement to follow an adjunct sister. Thus, both examples in (64) and (65) are allowed.

(64) a. I want to participate very much.
    b. I want very much to participate.

(65) a. They argued that Lou should resign convincingly.
    b. They argued convincingly that Lou should resign.

We will say more about adjuncts in chapter 7.[9]

We noted earlier that any theory which assumes separate ID and LP rules is committed to the claim that grammars display Exhaustive Constant Partial Ordering – the claim, that is, that sister categories have the same order whatever their mother is. The following German data might seem problematic for this assumption.

(66) Der Doktor   gibt die Pille   dem Patientem.
    the doctor-NOM gives the pills-ACC the patient-DAT
    'The doctor gives the patient pills.'

(67) dass der Doktor   die Pille   dem Patientem gibt
    that the doctor-NOM the pills-ACC the patient-DAT gives
    'that the doctor gives the patient pills'

The verb precedes its complements in the main clause in (66) but follows them in the subordinate clause in (67). If the verb is a sister of its complements in both cases, we appear to have a case where the ordering of sisters is affected by the nature of their mother. It is in fact quite easy to accommodate these data within a framework assuming separate ID and LP rules. If we assume that main clauses are marked [INV +] and subordinate clauses [INV –] and that verbs are the heads of clauses, the verb in (66) will be [INV +] while the verb in (67) will be [INV –]. (See Uszkoreit (1984) and Pollard (forthcoming) for such analyses.) In other words, the verbs will be members of slightly different categories and it will be quite easy to ensure that the verb precedes its complements in one case and follows in the other. This discussion shows that the claim that grammars display Exhaustive Constant Partial Ordering is not quite as strong as it might appear. Nevertheless it is a claim of some interest. We will return to German word order in chapter 12.[10]

It is natural to ask here if there are any other ordering universals. A number of such universals have been proposed in P&P, for example in Travis (1989). Fodor and Crain (1990), working within GPSG, question whether some proposed ordering universals are necessary. They point out that more general rules are simpler in the sense that they involve fewer feature specifications. Hence, they will be favoured if we make the reasonable assumption that simple rules are preferred to more complex rules. This will mean that certain word order situations will be very unlikely to occur even if they are not strictly impossible. Thus, it may not be necessary to stipulate that certain non-attested word order situations are impossible if simple rules are favoured.

There is one further matter that we should mention here. We noted in section 4.2 that separate ID and LP statements are assumed not only in Modern PSG but also in P&P. There is, however, one important difference between Modern PSG and P&P in this area. For standard versions of Modern PSG, LP rules only affect sister categories. For P&P, however, LP statements can affect non-sisters. A relevant example is the following:

(68)   They considered him to be a threat.

Here, *considered* and *him* are required to be adjacent even though they are not sisters on P&P assumptions. This example highlights a further difference between P&P and standard versions of Modern PSG. P&P assumes that certain items are required to be adjacent, that is, that one element is required to immediately precede another. Some syntacticians have proposed, however, that immediate precedence rules should be incorporated within GPSG. Notable here are Zwicky and Nevis (1986) and Ojeda (1988). Ojeda invokes such a rule to account for the following data from Jacobson (1987a):

(69)   a.   The secretary sent out a schedule.
       b.   The secretary sent a schedule out.

(70)   a.   The stockholders were sent out a schedule.
       b.   *The stockholders were sent a schedule out.

These examples show that whereas a particle can precede or follow an NP complement in an active sentence, it can only precede an NP complement in a passive sentence. Ojeda proposes that this is because of a rule requiring a passive verb to immediately precede a particle which is its sister. Using '<<' to denote immediate precedence, he formulates this as follows:

(71)   V[PAS] << PRT

We will consider other uses that Ojeda makes of an immediate precedence rule in chapters 7 and 12.

4.6 Metagrammars

We have seen that ID rules and LP rules interact in both GPSG and HPSG to determine the set of well-formed local trees. This was not their role, however, when they were first introduced in Gazdar and Pullum (1981). Their role there was to define a set of PS rules which in turn determined the set of well-formed local trees. In other words, they were part not of a grammar but of a meta-grammar which generated a grammar.

The idea that a grammar is generated by a metagrammar was in fact present in Gazdar (1981a, 1982) and it was developed further in Gazdar and Pullum (1982). Gazdar (1981a, 1982) proposed that some PS rules are not listed but are derived from other PS rules by so-called metarules.[11] Gazdar and Pullum (1982) introduce a different conception of metarule. Instead of deriving PS rules from PS rules, they derive partially specified ID rules from other partially specified ID rules. The full set of ID rules which results from the operation of metarules is fleshed out in accordance with various principles. The fully specified ID rules then interact with LP rules to define a set of PS rules. Here, then, we have a metagrammar of some complexity. It can be represented as follows:

(72)

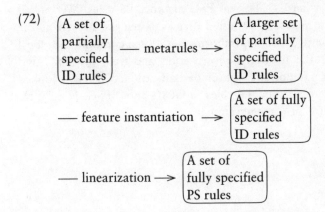

As we have noted, the standard version of GPSG presented in Gazdar et al. (1985) does not assume a complex metagrammar. Partially specified ID rules interact with LP rules, general principles, FCRs and FSDs to determine the set of well-formed local trees. However, the standard version of GPSG does retain a metagrammar because it assumes metarules deriving partially specified ID rules from partially specified ID rules.

Rather surprisingly, Gazdar et al. (1985) give no reasons for moving away from a complex metagrammar. Others, however, have argued against the notion of a metagrammar, notably Stowell (1982) and Shieber (1984). The objection is essentially that it is not clear what sort of psychological reality a metagrammar could have. If a grammar is a model of the speaker's linguistic knowledge it is hard to see what a metagrammar could be. On the other hand, if the metagrammar is a model of the speaker's linguistic knowledge, the grammar can only be a set of representations that can be computed during parsing, and it is odd to call such representations a grammar. Thus, there is no obvious place for a grammar–metagrammar distinction if our aim is to account for grammatical knowledge. It is worth noting, however, that there is a place for such a distinction in natural language processing. It is quite reasonable for a natural language processing system to store its grammatical knowledge in one form (a form that is convenient for the grammar writer) and to use it in another (a form that allows efficient parsing). This just means that the grammatical knowledge must be 'compiled', i.e. converted from one form into another, before it can be used.

4.7 Summary

In this chapter, we have looked at a second important difference between Modern and Classical PSG, the fact that Modern PSG assumes a number of interacting conditions on local trees whereas Classical PSG assumes PS rules. We looked first at the motivation for separate ID and LP rules. Then we looked at the motivation for certain general principles imposing additional conditions on local trees. Next we looked at the relation between rules and trees in GPSG and HPSG and introduced the important notion of unification. Then we looked more closely at the nature of ID and LP rules in GPSG and HPSG. Finally, we looked briefly at the notion of a metagrammar.

Notes

1 GPSG ideas about rules are set out in Gazdar et al. (1985: ch. 3). GPSG ideas about principles are set out in Gazdar et al. (1985: ch. 5). The latter discusses not only the Head Feature Convention and the Foot Feature Principle, but also the Control Agreement Principle, which we consider in chapters 6 and 8.
2 HPSG ideas about rules are presented in Pollard and Sag (1987: chs 6 and 7; 1994: ch. 1.5) and HPSG ideas about principles in Pollard and Sag (1994: ch. 1.4).
3 Shieber (1984) formulates an algorithm for parsing with separate ID and LP rules. Problems are discussed in Barton, Berwick and Ristad (1987: ch. 7).

4 Kilbury (1986) argues within GPSG for the replacement of ID rules by two separate devices: branches and category co-occurrence restrictions (CCRs). A branch is a statement that a category can have some other category as a daughter. It says nothing about any other daughters. For example, the following says that an S can have an NP as a daughter:

(i)   <S, NP>

CCRs impose constraints on the co-occurrence of categories in a single local tree. Among the CCRs that Kilbury proposes are the following:

(ii)   S | [NP ∧ VP] |
(iii) | [AUX ⊃ VP] |

(ii) says that an S must have an NP and a VP among its daughters. (iii) says that if AUX appears as a daughter in a local tree, VP must also.

5 Although the HFP is standardly formulated as an absolute principle, Borsley (1993) argues for a default version of the principle.

6 Unification and various unification-based theories are discussed in Shieber (1987).

7 An important current in theoretical linguistics, which contrasts quite sharply with unification-based approaches, is the Optimality Theory of Prince and Smolensky (forthcoming), which has been applied extensively in phonology and is applied to syntax in Grimshaw (1993). For Optimality Theory, a grammar consists of an ordered set of constraints and it is acceptable to violate one of them if that is the only way to satisfy a more highly ranked one. For some critical discussion of its application to phonology, see Scobbie (1993).

8 The fact that empty categories are not ordered in HPSG means that the ungrammaticality of (i) cannot be attributed to an empty category blocking the contraction of *want + to* to *wanna*, as it has been in P&P.

(i)   *Who do you wanna talk to?

Sag and Fodor (1994) argue that this approach is untenable anyway.

9 Pollard and Sag (1987) also consider so-called heavy-NP-shift, the postposing of a complex or 'heavy' NP, illustrated by the following:

(i)   Kim put on the table the book he bought in Vienna.

They propose that this is the result of an LP rule which places a focused constituent after a non-nominal sister. They formulate it as follows:

(ii)   [MAJ ¬N] < [FOCUS +]

One problem with this rule is that it is in conflict with the rule in (54). They leave this problem unresolved.

10 A language which, like German, shows word order differences between different types of clauses is Breton. Among other things, it shows participle–auxiliary order in affirmative main clauses but auxiliary–participle order in negative main clauses, as the following illustrate:

(i)   Lennet en   deus Yann al levr.
      read   3SGM have Yann the book
      'Yann has read the book.'

(ii) N'   en   deus ket lennet Yann al levr.
      NEG 3SGM have NEG read   Yann the book
      'Yann has not read the book.'

For a GPSG analysis which is compatible with the claim that grammars display
Exhaustive Constant Partial Ordering, see Borsley (1990a).

11 Metarules were first proposed in van Wijngaarden's (1969) work on the computer
    language ALGOL68.

Exercises

1 Replace the following PS rules by an equivalent set of ID and LP rules.

(1) S ⟶ NP VP
(2) VP ⟶ NP V
(3) VP ⟶ V PP
(4) VP ⟶ V S
(5) PP ⟶ NP P
(6) PP ⟶ P PP
(7) PP ⟶ P S

Explain how exactly the two sets of rules are equivalent.

2 If grammar (1) is just rule (1), grammar (2) rules (1) and (2), grammar
(3) rules (1), (2) and (3), and so on, which of the grammars can be replaced
by separate ID and LP rules?

(1) X ⟶ Y Z
(2) X ⟶ Z Y
(3) Y ⟶ Y Z
(4) Y ⟶ X Z
(5) Y ⟶ Z Y
(6) Z ⟶ Z X

3 Consider a grammar consisting of the condition on the WH feature
presented in 4.3, the Head Feature Convention also presented in 4.3, the ID
rule in (1) and the LP rule in (2).

(1) N' ⟶ H°, PP
(2) X° < YP

Assuming this grammar, decide which of the following local trees are well-formed, which are not, and why.

(3)

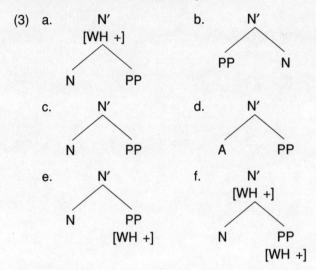

4   Provide formal and informal HPSG analyses parallel to those in (47) and (48) for the following phrases. Assume that any non-head daughter is a complement (C) daughter.

(1)   to London
(2)   afraid of spiders
(3)   give a book to Bill
(4)   Kim's book
(5)   pictures of the cathedral

5   One difference between GPSG and HPSG is that the former assumes that conjuncts are heads of coordinate structures while the latter does not. Explain how the data in (1) and (2) might be seen as evidence that conjuncts are heads while the data in (3)–(5) might be seen as evidence against this idea (or at least a simple version of it).

(1)   a.   I bought a book.
      b.   I bought a book and a newspaper.
      c.   *I bought go home.
      d.   *I bought go home and have a sleep.

(2)   a.   I may go home.
      b.   I may go home and have a sleep.
      c.   *I may a book.
      d.   *I may a book and a newspaper.

(3) a. He did it slowly and with great care.
     b. He is a linguist and proud of it.

(4) a. Kim likes/*like cricket.
     b. Kim and Sandy like/*likes cricket.

(5) a. I am/*are late.
     b. You and I are/*am late.

5   Semantics

5.1   Introduction

We now turn to the final feature which distinguishes Modern PSG from Classical PSG, the fact that its syntactic analyses are associated with explicit semantic analyses. There were some observations about the relation between syntax and semantics in pre-Chomskyan linguistics, but there was no general interest in the relation, in part perhaps because of behaviourist assumptions which tended to make meaning a 'no-go' area. Not surprisingly, then, Classical PSG is just a conception of syntax with no allied conception of semantics. In contrast, both GPSG and HPSG have been concerned not just to specify what the grammatical expressions of a language are, but also with what their meanings are. The present book is mainly concerned with syntax, but it is necessary to say something about the view of semantics taken within the two main versions of Modern PSG, particularly as syntactic and semantic analyses are intimately associated in certain areas in a way that makes it impossible to discuss the syntax without discussing the semantics.

In this chapter, I will look first at the GPSG conception of semantics.[1] Then I will consider the HPSG conception.[2] Finally, I will look at the important topic of quantification.

5.2   GPSG semantics

GPSG draws on the model-theoretic semantics of Richard Montague (Montague, 1974). For Montague, semantics is concerned with the relation between expressions and what they denote. A semantic theory for a language should provide a recursive definition of denotation in a model (an abstract representation of the world) for the expressions of the language. To do this, it must specify denotations for simple expressions and specify how the denotations of complex expressions are determined by their constituents.

In a very simple version of model-theoretic semantics, one might assume that NPs denote individuals, sentences truth values, 1 (true) and 2 (false), and VPs functions from individuals to truth values. In a very simple world, consisting of just three individuals, two of whom are tall and one of whom isn't, the denotation of the VP *is tall* might be the following function:

(1) | Kim ——————→ 1
      | Lee ————————→
      | Sandy ——————→ 0

To determine the denotation of the sentence *Kim is tall*, one simply applies the function which is the denotation of *is tall* to the individual who is the denotation of the NP *Kim*. The result is 1.

More fully developed versions of model-theoretic semantics involve more complex denotations than this simple version. All types of expressions have as their denotations complex set-theoretic constructions out of entities, truth values and possible worlds. For example, in the GPSG version, sentences have functions from possible worlds to truth values as their denotations. The denotations of NPs and VPs are much more complex.

It is standard practice in Montague semantics to provide a recursive definition of denotation by translating the expressions of the language into representations in intensional logic (IL), a rich logical system which has a recursive definition of denotation. However, the intensional logic representations are seen as just a matter of convenience and not as an essential part of the analysis. GPSG follows the standard Montague practice here.

A central feature of IL is that its categories or 'types' reflect in a very direct way the denotation of the expressions with which they are associated. Thus, if we know the type of an expression in IL we know what kind of things it will denote. IL has three basic types, e, t, and s. The denotation of e is the set of entities, and the denotation of t is the set of truth values. For any type a, the denotation of <s,a> is a function from possible worlds to whatever a denotes. For any types a and b, the denotation of <a,b> is a function from whatever a denotes to whatever b denotes.

Having introduced the basic concept of semantic types, we can list some of the type assignments that are assumed in Gazdar et al. (1985).

(2)   NP – <s<<e,t>,t>>
      S   – <s,t>
      VP – <<s<<e,t>,t>>,<s,t>>
      N′ – <e,t>
      Det – <<e,t>,<s<<e,t>,t>>>

As these type assignments make clear, many syntactic categories have very complex denotations. We will comment on just one of the type assignments, that for NP. Here, the idea, stemming from Montague, is that NPs denote sets of properties. Thus, *Kim* denotes the set of properties that Kim has and *every man* denotes the set of properties that every man has. Gazdar et al. often abbreviate semantic types by replacing some of the semantic types that they consist of by the associated syntactic category. Thus, they abbreviate the semantic type for VP as <NP,S> and the semantic type for Det as <NP,N>.

In early GPSG, each syntactic rule is associated with a semantic rule specifying how the interpretation of the constituent it licenses is determined on the basis of the interpretation of its immediate constituents. Thus, we might have the following syntactic–semantic rule pair:

(3)   VP $\longrightarrow$ V NP, V′(NP′)

Here, X′ stands for the interpretation of X. The rule pair states that a VP can consist of a V followed by an NP and that the interpretation of the VP is determined by applying the interpretation of the V as a function to the interpretation of the NP. Klein and Sag (1985) argue that it is not necessary to associate a syntactic rule with a semantic rule because the interpretation of the constituent it licenses is predictable. In the above case, it is not necessary because the semantic types of the V and the NP mean that there is only one way that they can combine semantically to give the interpretation of the VP.

It is normal for there to be just one way in which daughters can combine semantically to give the interpretation of their mother. However, where two daughters have the same semantic type there will be more than one way in which they can combine semantically. This situation arises in the following examples:

(4)   Kim gave Sandy Fido.
(5)   Kim gave Fido to Sandy.

In (4), we have a verb with two NP complements, both of which have the semantic type <s<<e,t>,t>>. In (5), we have an NP and a PP complement, but Gazdar et al. propose that such PPs also have the semantic type <s<<e,t>,t>>. They stipulate that in this situation the verb combines semantically first with the second complement and then with the first. Gazdar et al. propose other stipulations to handle the interpretation of 'semantically potent' features such as [PAST +] and the interpretation of sentences involving unbounded dependencies. However, most types of local tree are brought within the scope of a relatively simple Semantic Interpretation Schema.[3]

For GPSG, the semantic analysis of sentences is not only important in its own right but also has implications for syntax. One of the general principles assumed in GPSG is the Control Agreement Principle, which refers to the semantic interpretation of local trees. This principle accounts *inter alia* for the following contrasts:

(6) a. He likes her.
    b. *They likes her.

(7) a. We expected him to be early.
    b. *We expected there to be early.

We will discuss it in chapters 6 and 8.

5.3 HPSG semantics

The importance of semantics is stressed in HPSG by the use of the term 'sign', which suggests a combination of form and meaning, to refer to linguistic expressions of all kinds. Whereas GPSG draws on model-theoretic semantics, HPSG draws on situation semantics, an approach to semantics originally presented in Barwise and Perry (1983).

For situation semantics, 'Reality consists of situations – individuals having properties and standing in relations at various spatiotemporal locations' (Barwise and Perry 1983: 7). Meaning is analysed as a relation between situation types, and linguistic meaning relates utterance situation types to described situation types. A central concept is a *state-of-affairs* (*soa*) (called a circumstance in Pollard and Sag 1987). A *soa* is a possible way that the world might be, in other words a potential fact. A basic *soa* consists of a relation and the individuals participating in it, and a specification of its polarity, whether it obtains or not. Properties are analysed as unary (one-place) relations. For situation semantics, a relation is seen as something real and not just an ordered n-tuple as in mathematics. The different ways of participating in relations are called roles. Thus, an n-ary relation has n roles. Generally, each relation is assumed to have its own inventory of roles. Thus, the role associated with the subject of *walk* is WALKER and the role associated with the subject of *run* is RUNNER, and they are not both AGENT, as they would be in some other approaches. However, as we will see in chapter 8, Pollard and Sag (1994) assume that the relations that occur in control sentences like the following involve a small number of generalized roles:

(8) a. Kim hoped to impress Sandy.
    b. Kim persuaded Sandy to go home.

Just as important as a *soa* is a *parameterized-state-of-affairs* (*psoa*). A *psoa* is like a *soa* but certain argument roles are not anchored to determinate objects. It determines in part the type of situation described by an utterance of the relevant type of sentence. For HPSG, a *psoa* is the value of the sentence's CONTENT feature.

We now look at how exactly HPSG combines situation semantic analyses with its syntactic analyses. There are in fact two different positions in the literature. In Pollard and Sag (1987), the distinction between syntactic and semantic properties of an expression is very basic, and as a result signs have the following form:

(9)
$$\begin{bmatrix} \text{PHON} \\ \text{SYN} \\ \text{SEM} \\ \text{DAUGHTERS} \end{bmatrix}$$

In Pollard and Sag (1994), the basic distinction is between LOCAL syntactic and semantic properties, which are commonly shared by a sign and its head daughter, on the one hand, and NON-LOCAL syntactic and semantic properties, which are commonly shared between a sign and a non-head daughter, on the other. Signs have the following form:

(10)
$$\begin{bmatrix} \text{PHON} \\ \text{SYNSEM} \begin{bmatrix} \text{LOCAL} \begin{bmatrix} \text{CATEGORY} \\ \text{CONTENT} \\ \text{CONTEXT} \end{bmatrix} \\ \text{NON-LOCAL} \end{bmatrix} \\ \text{DAUGHTERS} \end{bmatrix}$$

Although there is a feature CATEGORY here, it only embodies some of the syntactic properties of the sign. In a sense, then, this version of HPSG does not have syntactic categories of a traditional kind. CONTEXT here is a feature whose value is an object of sort *context* which has the attributes CONTEXTUAL-INDICES and BACKGROUND. The former has as its value a group of features including SPEAKER, ADDRESSEE and UTTERANCE-LOCATION, which give linguistically relevant information about the circumstances of utterance. The latter has as its value a set of *psoas* which embody appropriateness conditions associated with the utterance of a particular type of sign. For example, relative *who* will include in its BACKGROUND value the information that its referent is human.[4]

We now look briefly at the HPSG semantic analysis of nominals. Here, the value of CONTENT is a feature structure of sort *nominal-object* (*nom-obj*). Nominal objects have the subsorts *nonpronoun* (*npro*) and *pronoun* (*pro*), the latter divided into the subsorts *personal-pronoun* (*ppro*) and *anaphor* (*ana*). They have the attributes INDEX and RESTRICTION. The value of INDEX is a structure of sort *index* with three subsorts *referential*, *it* and *there*. Indices have the agreement features PERSON, NUMBER and GENDER. These features are not attributes of syntactic categories. For HPSG, the pronoun antecedent relation involves token-identity of indices. Hence, a pronoun and its antecedent must agree in person, number and gender. Unlike PERSON, NUMBER and GENDER, CASE is not an attribute of indices. Thus, there is no requirement that pronouns and their antecedents have the same case. The value of the RESTRICTION attribute is a set of *psoas*. We can illustrate these ideas with the CONTENT value of the common noun *book*.

$$
(11) \quad \begin{bmatrix} \text{INDEX} & [1] \begin{bmatrix} \text{PRE } 3rd \\ \text{NUM } sing \\ \text{GEND } neut \end{bmatrix}_{index} \\ \\ \text{RESTRICTION} & \left\{ \begin{bmatrix} \text{RELATION } book \\ \text{INSTANCE } [1] \end{bmatrix}_{psoa} \right\} \end{bmatrix}
$$

Notice that the index appears as the value of the INSTANCE role within the *psoa* in the value of RESTRICTION.

We now turn briefly to verbs. Ignoring phonology and simplifying somewhat, we might have the following sign for the verb *walks*.

$$
(12) \quad \begin{bmatrix} \text{HEAD } verb[fin] \\ \text{SUBCAT } <\text{NP}[\text{nom}]_{[1][3rd,sing]}> \\ \text{CONTENT} \begin{bmatrix} \text{RELN } walk \\ \text{WALKER } [1] \end{bmatrix} \end{bmatrix}
$$

This assumes the SUBCAT feature introduced in chapter 3. In this case, it just indicates what sort of subject the verb requires. Notice that the index of subject and its person and number features appear as subscripts. The sign makes it clear that the index of the subject NP is the value of the WALKER role within the CONTENT value, in other words that the subject identifies the walker. For the verb *sees*, we might have the following schematic sign:

(13)
$$\begin{bmatrix} \text{HEAD } verb[fin] \\ \text{SUBCAT } <\text{NP[nom]}_{[1][3rd,sing]}, \text{NP[acc]}_{[2]}> \\ \text{CONTENT} \begin{bmatrix} \text{RELN } see \\ \text{SEER } [1] \\ \text{SEEN } [2] \end{bmatrix} \end{bmatrix}$$

Here, the SUBCAT feature indicates both what sort of subject the verb requires and what type of complement it takes. The sign makes it clear that the index of the subject is the value of the SEER role and the index of the complement the value of the SEEN role. Finally, we might have the following schematic sign for *gives*:

(14)
$$\begin{bmatrix} \text{HEAD } verb[fin] \\ \text{SUBCAT } <\text{NP[nom]}_{[1][3rd,sing]}, \text{NP[acc]}_{[2]}, \text{NP[acc]}_{[3]}> \\ \text{CONTENT} \begin{bmatrix} \text{RELN } give \\ \text{GIVER } [1] \\ \text{GIVEN } [2] \\ \text{GIFT } [3] \end{bmatrix} \end{bmatrix}$$

Again, the SUBCAT feature indicates both what sort of subject the verb requires and what type of complements it takes. The sign makes it clear that the index of the subject is the value of the GIVER role, the index of the first complement the value of the GIVEN role, and the index of the second complement the value of the GIFT role.

An obvious question here is: what is the relation between a verb's SUBCAT feature and its CONTENT feature? Pollard and Sag (1987: ch. 5.3) argue at some length that syntactic selection cannot be reduced to semantic selection. It is clear, however, that not everything is possible in this area. For example, one would not expect to come across a basic verb just like *see* except that the SEEN role is associated with the subject and the SEER role with the complement. For some interesting discussion of the restrictions and how they might be accommodated, see Wechsler (1991, forthcoming).

For HPSG the semantic properties of a sign are derived from those of its daughter signs by a number of general principles. The most important is the CONTENT Principle. This refers to the notion semantic head. The semantic head of a sign is the syntactic head except in the case of adjunct–head combinations when it is the adjunct. Ignoring the question of quantification, we can formulate the principle as follows:

(15) CONTENT PRINCIPLE (preliminary version)
    The CONTENT value of a headed phrase is token-identical to that of the
    semantic head.

As we will see, quantification necessitates a rather more complex principle.

5.4 Quantification

An important aspect of meaning which we have ignored so far is quantification.
Among other things, a satisfactory treatment of quantification must account for
the fact that ambiguities commonly arise when there are two quantifiers in a
sentence. For example, whereas (16) is unambiguous, (17) has two interpretations, given in (18) and (19).

(16) Kim knows 'Beowulf'.
(17) Every student knows a poem.
(18) Every student knows some poem or other.
(19) There is a certain poem that every student knows.

On the first interpretation, *every* is more prominent or has scope over *a*. On the
second interpretation, it's the other way round. GPSG has no account of such
facts, but Pollard and Sag (1994) develop a fairly detailed HPSG analysis.[5]
 Standard predicate logic accounts for ambiguities like that in (17) by separat-
ing quantifiers out from the sentences in which they appear, which contain
variables bound by the quantifiers. The order of quantifiers corresponds to their
scope: each quantifier has scope over any quantifiers that follow it. Within a
version of standard predicate logic that allows quantifiers to be restricted, we
might represent the two interpretations of (17) as follows:

(20) $\forall x$ x a student $\exists y$ y a poem knows(x,y)
(21) $\exists y$ y a poem $\forall x$ a x student knows(x,y)

We can paraphrase these representations within 'logician's English' as follows:

(22) For all students x, there exists a poem y such that x knows y.
(23) There exists a poem y such that for all students x, x knows y.

It is not difficult to incorporate such representations into HPSG. Pollard and Sag
propose that a quantifier is an object with the attributes DET (determiner) and
RESTIND (restricted index). The latter takes as its value an *npro*. Within this

conception, the interpretation of *every student* and *a poem* can be represented as follows:

(24)
$$
\begin{bmatrix}
\text{DET } \textit{forall} \\
\text{RESTIND}
\begin{bmatrix}
\text{INDEX } [1] \\
\text{RESTR } \left\{ \begin{bmatrix} \text{RELN } \textit{student} \\ \text{INSTANCE } [1] \end{bmatrix} \right\}
\end{bmatrix}
\end{bmatrix}
$$

(25)
$$
\begin{bmatrix}
\text{DET } \textit{exists} \\
\text{RESTIND}
\begin{bmatrix}
\text{INDEX } [2] \\
\text{RESTR } \left\{ \begin{bmatrix} \text{RELN } \textit{poem} \\ \text{INSTANCE } [2] \end{bmatrix} \right\}
\end{bmatrix}
\end{bmatrix}
$$

Pollard and Sag also redefine a *psoa* to allow it to include quantifiers. They propose that it has the attributes QUANTS and NUCLEUS. The former takes as its value a list of quantifiers (in order of scope) and the latter takes as its value a *quantifier-free psoa* (*qfpsoa*). If we use [3] as an abbreviation for (24) and [4] as an abbreviation for (25), we can represent the two interpretations of (17) as follows:

(26)
$$
\begin{bmatrix}
\text{QUANTS } <[3], [4]> \\
\text{NUCLEUS}
\begin{bmatrix}
\text{RELN } \textit{know} \\
\text{KNOWER } [1] \\
\text{KNOWN } [2]
\end{bmatrix}
\end{bmatrix}
$$

(27)
$$
\begin{bmatrix}
\text{QUANTS } <[4], [3]> \\
\text{NUCLEUS}
\begin{bmatrix}
\text{RELN } \textit{know} \\
\text{KNOWER } [1] \\
\text{KNOWN } [2]
\end{bmatrix}
\end{bmatrix}
$$

Here, then, we have two CONTENT values for (17). What we need now is some way of associating these CONTENT values with (17).

To associate sentences with CONTENT values like (26) and (27), Pollard and Sag adopt a storage mechanism of the kind proposed within Montague semantics by Cooper (1975, 1983). This allows a quantified NP to be integrated into the interpretation of the sentence that contains it at a higher point in the structure.

Pollard and Sag propose firstly that signs have a QSTORE attribute, whose value is a set of quantifiers. They propose that all quantifiers 'start out in storage'. Thus, the phrase *every book* has the CONTENT and the QSTORE in (28).

(28)

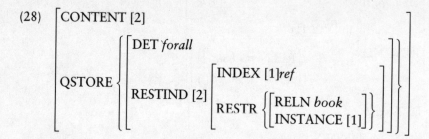

They introduce one more attribute, RETRIEVED, whose value, like that of QUANTS, is a list of quantifiers, the quantifiers retrieved from storage at some node.

To use the various attributes, a number of things are necessary. Firstly, it is necessary to restrict the CONTENT Principle so that it only requires the NUCLEUS of semantic head and mother to be identical where the semantic head is of sort *psoa*.

(29)   CONTENT PRINCIPLE (final version)
       In a headed phrase,
       (Case 1) if the semantic head's CONTENT value is of sort *psoa*, then its NUCLEUS is token-identical to the NUCLEUS of the mother
       (Case 2) otherwise, the CONTENT value of the semantic head is token-identical to the CONTENT value of the mother.

Secondly, it is necessary to ensure the correct relation between RETRIEVED and QSTORE. This is done by the Quantifier Inheritance Principle, which is formulated as follows:

(30)   QUANTIFIER INHERITANCE PRINCIPLE
       In a headed phrase, the RETRIEVED value is a list whose set of elements forms a subset of the union of the QSTOREs of the daughters, and is non-empty only if the CONTENT of the semantic head is of sort *psoa*; and the QSTORE value is the relative complement of the RETRIEVED value.

This ensures (a) that the RETRIEVED value of a headed phrase cannot include quantifiers that are not in the QSTOREs of its daughters – quantifiers cannot appear from nowhere – and (b) that any quantifiers in the QSTORES of its daughters and not in its RETRIEVED value are in its QSTORE – quantifiers cannot just disappear. Finally, it is necessary to ensure the correct relation between QUANTS and RETRIEVED. This is done by the SCOPE Principle, which is as follows:

(31) SCOPE PRINCIPLE
      In a headed phrase whose semantic head is of sort *psoa*, the QUANTS value is the concatenation of the RETRIEVED value with the QUANTS value of the semantic head.

Pollard and Sag go on to bring these principles together in a single Semantics Principle, but we will leave them as three separate principles.

We can illustrate the operation of these principles with the following tree:

(32)

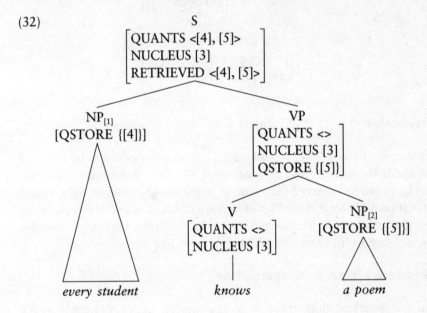

Here, both the subject and the object give rise to a quantifier in storage. The RETRIEVED value of the S is a list whose set of elements is identical to the union of the QSTOREs of its daughters. Hence, by the Quantifier Inheritance Principle, its QSTORE is empty. The QUANTS value of the semantic head, the VP, is the empty list. Hence, by the Scope Principle, the QUANTS value of S is identical to the RETRIEVED value. Notice that we could retrieve quantifier [5] from storage at the VP level. The result would be a tree like (32) but with [5] in the QUANTS value of the VP and just [4] in the RETRIEVED value of S. The QUANTS value of the S would derive partly from the QUANTS value of the VP and partly from its own RETRIEVED value.

(32) provides a representation for (17) when it has the interpretation in (18). If the quantifiers were retrieved from storage in the opposite order, we would

have the following, a representation for (17) when it has the interpretation in (19):

(33)

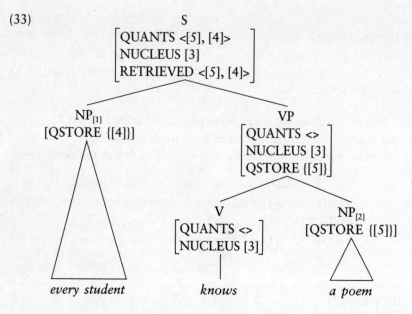

One further point to note here is that nothing requires quantifiers to be retrieved from storage at the first S above the associated NP. Thus, a quantifier in a subordinate clause can be retrieved from storage at the root S, giving it wide scope.[6]

While it is possible for a quantifier to be 'raised' into a higher clause, it is not possible for a quantifier to be 'lowered' into a lower clause. One might suppose that this is necessary in connection with examples like the following:

(34)   A unicorn appears to be approaching.

Here, on one interpretation, there is no assumption that a unicorn actually exists.[7] One might take this as evidence that the scope of *a unicorn* can be the complement of *appears*. Pollard and Sag's analysis does not allow this. This looks like a weakness of the analysis. However, they suggest (1994: fn. 3) that there may be an alternative approach to the data.

Pollard and Sag propose one further condition on quantification in connection with examples like the following:

(35)   One of her$_i$ students approached [each teacher]$_i$.
(36)   [Each man]$_i$ talked to a friend of his$_i$.

Both examples contain a universal quantifier and an existential quantifier with the former acting as antecedent to a pronoun in the latter. In both cases, the universal must have wide scope. Pollard and Sag suggest that such examples show that a condition is necessary to prevent a quantifier from having a scope that is not wide enough to bind all 'occurrences' of the index that 'belong' to it. They propose the following informal condition:

(37)   QUANTIFIER BINDING CONDITION
       Given a quantifier contained within a CONTENT value, every occurrence within that CONTENT value of the quantifier's index must be captured by that quantifier.

They propose that a quantifier captures an occurrence of an index just in case the occurrence is either (1) in the RESTRICTION of the quantifier, (2) in another quantifier to the right of the quantifier in question in the same QUANTS list, or (3) in the NUCLEUS of the *psoa* containing the QUANTS list.

One final point that we should note here is that Pollard and Sag's analysis is quite limited in its scope. In particular, it does not take account of many factors that appear to affect the determination of quantifier scope. Nevertheless, it seems to offer a promising basis for the development of a fuller treatment of quantification.[8]

5.5   Summary

In this chapter, we have outlined the basic approach to semantics that is taken in GPSG and HPSG. Semantics is important in both frameworks. They draw on different conceptions of semantics, model-theoretic semantics in GPSG and situation semantics in HPSG. Hence, they have rather different semantic analyses. Both propose general principles that predict the interpretation of a phrase on the basis of the interpretations of its constituents. However, only HPSG has an account of quantification. As we will see, the semantic analyses of GPSG and HPSG are of considerable importance in connection with raising and control sentences (chapter 8), anaphora (chapter 10), and valency alternations (chapter 11).

Notes

1   The semantic ideas of GPSG are set out in Gazdar et al. (1985: chs 9, 10). For a general introduction to Montague semantics, see Dowty, Wall and Peters (1981) or Cann (1993).

2 The semantic ideas of HPSG are set out in Pollard and Sag (1987: ch. 4) and Pollard and Sag (1994: ch. 8).

3 Gazdar et al. (1985: ch. 10.7) also discuss how idioms should be accommodated within model-theoretic semantics.

4 Vallduvi and Engdahl (1995) propose that *context* has a further attribute INFO-STRUCT, which encodes the information structure properties of expressions.

5 The relation between syntactic dependants and semantic arguments is explored further within HPSG in Davis (forthcoming).

6 An account of quantification must also accommodate *wh*-phrases both in clause-initial position and in situ. *What* and *whom* in the following illustrate:

(i) What did you say to whom?

See Kathol (1995b: ch. 6) for some discussion.

7 Pollard has proposed in unpublished work that the non-existential interpretation of an example like (34) can be accommodated if QSTORE is an attribute not of signs but of LOCAL feature structures.

8 Pollard and Sag (1994: ch. 8.5) note that there are plausible alternatives to a number of their semantic proposals. In particular, they note that a number of plausible alternatives are developed in Cooper (1990, ch. 7).

Exercises

1 In HPSG, many prenominal adjectives can be analysed semantically as placing additional restrictions on the index of the noun, but not all can. Decide which adjectives in the following examples have this character and which do not.

(1) red car
(2) English linguist
(3) alleged spy
(4) black swan
(5) false beard
(6) potential problem

2 Provide schematic HPSG signs like those in (12)–(14) with HEAD, SUBCAT and CONTENT attributes for the items in bold in the following examples. Assume that PPs that are required to contain a specific preposition have an index as their interpretation and select appropriate role names.

(1) Kim **relies** on Sandy.
(2) Kim **sold** his car to Sandy for £500.
(3) Kim **loaded** the cart with hay.
(4) Kim **talked** to Lee about Sandy.

3   The sentence in (1) is ambiguous with the interpretations in (2) and (3).

(1)   Kim thinks that he saw something.
(2)   Kim thinks he saw something or other.
(3)   There is some specific thing that Kim thinks he saw.

On the first interpretation, the scope of *something* is the subordinate clause, while on the second, it is the main clause. Show how the HPSG approach to quantification can represent these two interpretations.

4   Discuss the implications of the following examples for theories of scope, paying particular attention to the words in bold.

(1)   **Some** unicorns **may** be approaching.
(2)   There **may** be **some** unicorns approaching.
(3)   **Everyone** likes **somebody**.
(4)   **Someone** from **every** village thinks it is worth visiting.
(5)   **Not all** the papers were rejected.
(6)   **All** that glitters is **not** gold.
(7)   **Not many** arrows hit the target.
(8)   **Many** arrows did **not** hit the target.

6   Some Basic Structures

6.1   Introduction

Having considered at some length the main features that distinguish Modern
PSG from Classical PSG, we can now begin to look more closely at how Modern
PSG accommodates the central phenomena of syntax. An important assumption
in much work in syntactic theory is that there are a small number of basic types
of structure. This has been a central theme of so-called X-bar theory since its
origins in Chomsky (1970). It did not play an important role in GPSG but it is
of considerable importance in HPSG, one of whose guiding assumptions is that
there should be a single ID rule for each basic type of structure. In this chapter,
I will look at two such structures: head–complement structures, and subject–
predicate structures. In the next chapter, I will consider four more.

6.2   Head–complement structures

Head–complement structures are arguably the most important type of structure in natural languages. This is one reason to look at them first. A second
reason for beginning with such structures is they are an area in which there is
a major difference between GPSG and HPSG. Whereas GPSG has a large number
of category-specific rules for head–complement structures, HPSG has a single
category-neutral rule and rather more complex categories.

The GPSG and HPSG approaches to head–complement structures can be seen
as two different ways of responding to an observation that was made by a
number of syntacticians in the late 1970s. This is that there is a serious redundancy in an approach to head–complement structures which employs category-
specific rules for such structures and associates lexical heads with so-called
subcategorization frames, specifications of the complements that they take. There
are two possible responses to this observation: either one eliminates the specifications of the complements that lexical items take or one eliminates category-
specific rules. GPSG takes the first option. HPSG, like P&P, takes the second.

Central to the GPSG approach is a feature SUBCAT, which takes as its value an arbitrary integer. Within GPSG, we might have ID rules like the following for a range of VPs:

(1) a. VP ⟶ H°[SUBCAT 1]
     b. VP ⟶ H°[SUBCAT 2], NP
     c. VP ⟶ H°[SUBCAT 3], S′
     d. VP ⟶ H°[SUBCAT 4], NP, S′

As noted in chapter 4, H° stands for a lexical head. The Head Feature Convention will ensure that the head is a verb in structures licensed by these rules. To ensure that the correct structures are generated, simple intransitive verbs like *sleep* must be assigned to the category V[SUBCAT, 1], simple transitive verbs like *hit* to the category V[SUBCAT, 2], verbs which take an S′ complement such as *think* to the category V[SUBCAT, 3], and verbs which take an NP and an S′ complement such as *tell* to the category V[SUBCAT, 4]. The rule in (1b) will license the following tree:

(2)

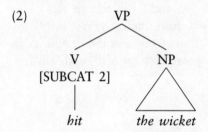

No rule, however, will license a similar tree with a V[SUBCAT 1]. Hence, we will not generate e.g. *slept the wicket*.

One further point to note here is that for GPSG the selection of complements with specific cases is just like the selection of complements with any other property. For example, if a language has some verbs that take an accusative NP complement and others that take a dative NP complement, this can be captured by including ID rules like the following in its grammar:

(3) a. VP ⟶ H°[SUBCAT 7], NP[CASE ACC]
     b. VP ⟶ H°[SUBCAT 8], NP[CASE DAT]

Thus, there seems to be no need for any special case-marking conventions.

The HPSG approach to head–complement structures exploits the Categorial Grammar insight that grammars can be simplified considerably if categories incorporate information about the categories with which they combine. It makes crucial use of a list-valued feature. The nature of this feature is different in different versions of the framework. What I will call the SUBCAT framework, the approach developed in Pollard and Sag (1987) and the first eight chapters of Pollard and Sag (1994), assumes a feature SUBCAT which indicates both what complements a head takes and what kind of subject it requires.[1] In Pollard and Sag (1987) its value is a list of signs, whereas in Pollard and Sag (1994) its value is a list of *synsem* objects. We will consider the difference between these two positions later.[2] In Borsley (1987, forthcoming), it is argued that what complements a head takes and what kind of subject it requires should be encoded in two separate features. In these papers, the two features are called SUBCAT and SUBJ. Pollard and Sag (1994) accept the argument of these papers in their chapter 9, but they call the first feature COMPS, and they retain the original SUBCAT feature for other purposes, which we will consider in chapter 10. (In some recent work, it is renamed ARG-S (argument structure).) I will refer to this framework as the SUBJ–COMPS framework. I will consider some of the arguments that can be advanced for it in the next section.

In Pollard and Sag (1987), SUBCAT lists have the order most oblique to least oblique. In Pollard and Sag (1994), however, both SUBCAT lists and COMPS lists have the order least oblique to most oblique, and I will assume this order throughout this book. Given this order, we will have the categories in (4) for *sleep*, *hit*, *think* and *tell* within the SUBCAT framework and the categories in (5) within the SUBJ–COMPS framework. (We ignore both the SUBJ and SUBCAT features.)

(4)   a.   V[SUBCAT <NP>]
      b.   V[SUBCAT <NP,NP>]
      c.   V[SUBCAT <NP,S'>]
      d.   V[SUBCAT <NP,NP,S'>]

(5)   a.   V[COMPS <>]
      b.   V[COMPS <NP>]
      c.   V[COMPS <S'>]
      d.   V[COMPS <NP,S'>]

'<>' here stands for the empty list. 'NP' and 'S' are abbreviations. We will consider what they stand for later. Given categories like these, there is no need for category-specific rules. All we need is a single category-neutral rule and two general principles.

We look first at the situation within the SUBCAT framework. Here, we need the following rule, which we can refer to as the Head–Complement Rule:

(6) HEAD–COMPLEMENT RULE (SUBCAT framework)
   [SUBCAT <[ ]>] ⟶ [SUBCAT L], [ ]*
                      HEAD   COMPS

'[ ]' stands for an arbitrary list member, and 'L' stands for an arbitrary list. We can paraphrase the rule as follows:

(7) A sign with the feature specification SUBCAT <[ ]> can contain a head daughter with the feature specification SUBCAT L and any number of complement daughters.

Nothing in this rule ensures that we have the right kind of head and the correct number and kind of complements. The former is ensured by the Head Feature Principle, which we considered in chapter 4. The latter is ensured by the Subcategorization Principle. This is rather like the Projection Principle of P&P. We can formulate it as follows:

(8) SUBCATEGORIZATION PRINCIPLE
   In a headed phrase, the SUBCAT value of the head is the concatenation of the phrase's SUBCAT list with the list of SYNSEM values of the complement daughters.

The category in (4b) will interact with the rule and the two principles to allow the tree in (9).

(9)

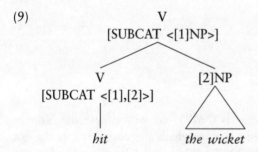

A similar structure with a verb that is V[SUBCAT <NP>] will violate the Subcategorization Principle. Again, then, we will not generate *slept the wicket*. Any head–complement structures in which the complements do not correspond to the SUBCAT list of the head minus its first element will be ruled out by the Subcategorization Principle.

   The situation is very similar within the SUBJ–COMPS framework. Here, we need the following Head–Complement Rule:

(10)   HEAD–COMPLEMENT RULE (SUBJ–COMPS framework)
       [COMPS <>] ⟶ [COMPS L], [ ]*
                       HEAD   COMPS

This can be paraphrased as follows:

(11)   A sign with the feature specification COMPS <> can contain a head
       daughter with the feature specification COMPS L and any number of
       complement daughters.

This will interact with Head Feature Principle and a generalized version of the
Subcategorization Principle, which will affect COMPS, SUBJ and other 'valence'
features. This is called the Valence Principle, and can be formulated as follows:

(12)   VALENCE PRINCIPLE
       In a headed phrase, for any valence feature F, the F value of the head
       is the concatenation of the phrase's F value with the list of SYNSEM
       values of the F daughters.

The category in (5b) will interact with the rule and the two principles to allow
the tree in (13).

(13)

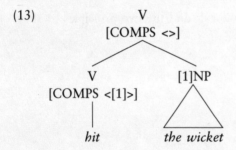

A similar structure with a verb that is [COMPS <>] will violate the Valence
Principle. Any head–complement structures in which the complements do not
correspond to the COMPS list of the head are ruled out by the principle.

As in GPSG, the selection of complements with specific cases is just like the
selection of complements with any other property. In the SUBCAT framework,
a verb that takes an accusative NP complement would have the category in
(14a) and a verb that takes a dative NP complement would have the category
in (14b).

(14)   a.   V[SUBCAT <NP,NP[CASE ACC]>]
       b.   V[SUBCAT <NP,NP[CASE DAT]>]

In the SUBJ–COMPS framework, these verbs would have the following categories:

(15) a. V[COMPS <NP[CASE ACC]>]
      b. V[COMPS <NP[CASE DAT]>]

Again, then, there seems to be no need for any special case-marking conventions.

An important question which we can consider at this point is: what happens with a head that does not take any complements, i.e. which is SUBCAT <NP> in the SUBCAT framework or COMPS <> in the SUBJ–COMPS framework? As they stand, (6) will allow a SUBCAT <NP> head to be the sole constituent of a sign with exactly the same category, and (10) will allow COMPS <> head to be the sole constituent of a sign with the same category. This is clearly unsatisfactory. There are two plausible solutions. One is to use a feature to distinguish between a lexical sign that does not require any complements and the phrasal sign of which it is the sole constituent, and to revise the Head–Complement Rule accordingly. This is the approach taken in Pollard and Sag (1987, 1994). They mark lexical signs as LEX + and phrasal signs as LEX –. The other solution is to restrict the Head–Complement Rule to heads that require at least one complement. This would entail allowing an intransitive verb to combine directly with its subject. It would make HPSG rather like Categorial Grammar.

We noted earlier that the SUBCAT feature takes as its value a list of signs in Pollard and Sag (1987) while the SUBCAT and COMPS features take a list of *synsem* objects as their value in Pollard and Sag (1994). The reason for the revision is quite simple. There appear to be no heads which require a complement with particular phonological properties or particular immediate constituents. Both are expected if we have lists of signs, but neither is expected if we have lists of *synsem* objects. Here, then, we have a good reason for preferring the latter position.

It is clear that GPSG and HPSG have very different approaches to head–complement structures. One might argue that this is the most important difference between the two frameworks. Whereas HPSG has a single ID rule for head–complement structures, GPSG has a large number of ID rules, as many rules as there are different head–complement combinations. The appendix to Gazdar et al. (1985) lists 30 rules for verbal head–complement structures, 8 for nominal head–complement structures, 7 for adjectival head–complement structures, and 3 for prepositional head-complement structures. It is clear that an adequate grammar would need further rules for head–complement structures. The fact that the HPSG approach has a single rule where the GPSG approach has a large number would seem to be one reason for favouring the HPSG approach. However, the objection to the GPSG approach is not just that it involves many more rules but also that it fails to capture the fact that there is a single type of structure here. It seems to me, then, that we have an important reason here for preferring HPSG.

A different reason for preferring the HPSG approach to head–complement structures to the GPSG approach is highlighted in Fodor (1992b). Fodor argues that the GPSG approach is problematic from the standpoint of acquisition. She points out that there are many verbs, e.g. *read*, which optionally take an object. It would be natural for the learner to postulate a separate rule for such verbs of the following form:

(16)   VP $\longrightarrow$ H°[SUBCAT 5], (NP)

The problem is that once the learner has postulated this rule it is not clear what would prevent her from assigning verbs which always take an object, e.g. *hit*, to V[SUBCAT 5] rather than to the correct category, V[SUBCAT 2]. Notice that the two categories are equally complex. Hence, a preference for simple categories will not help. It is not clear, then, how the wrong category is to be avoided. Within the SUBJ–COMPS version of HPSG, a verb like *read* will be V[COMPS <(NP)>], while a verb like *hit* will be V[COMPS <NP>] (as we have seen). The former is more complex than the latter since it includes the information (represented by round brackets) that the object is optional. Thus, if the learner prefers simple categories, she will only assign a verb to the former on the basis of positive evidence. Hence, there is no danger of adopting the wrong category.

Most work in both GPSG and HPSG has assumed that heads combine with their complements 'all at once'. However, it has sometimes been suggested that they combine with their complements 'one at a time', as in Categorial Grammar. (See Nerbonne 1986a, Johnson 1986 and Netter 1992.) This view requires the rule in (17), which we can paraphrase as (18).

(17)   [LEX −] $\longrightarrow$ [COMPS L], [ ]
                        HEAD   COMPS

(18)   A phrasal sign can contain a head daughter with the feature specification COMPS L and a complement daughter.

Another possibility, developed in Pollard (1994), is that heads may combine with all their complements or with a subset of their complements. This requires something like the rule in (19), which we can paraphrase as (20).

(19)   [LEX −] $\longrightarrow$ [COMPS L], [ ]*
                        HEAD   COMPS

(20)   A phrasal sign can contain a head daughter with the feature specification
       COMPS L and any number of complement daughters.

The head will combine with all its complements if the mother has an empty
COMPS list and with a subset of its complements if the mother has a non-empty
COMPS list. We will consider the motivation for these approaches in chapter
12.

   Head–complement structures are a fundamental concern for any theory of
syntax. They are, however, not quite as important for standard versions of Modern PSG as they are for some other frameworks. This is because certain classes
of item that are analysed as heads in some other frameworks are not analysed
as heads in standard versions of Modern PSG. There are two main classes of
items: complementizers and determiners. Both are analysed as heads in P&P and
also in Hudson's (1984, 1990) Word Grammar framework. There is, however,
nothing in Modern PSG that precludes a head analysis of complementizers and
determiners. Borsley (1989b) shows that the idea that complementizers are heads,
and related ideas about clause structure that are developed in Chomsky (1986b),
can be incorporated quite easily into a version of HPSG. Netter (1994) argues
for a head analysis of both complementizers and determiners within a version
of HPSG. Thus, something like the following structures are compatible with
HPSG assumptions:

(21)   C
                   [COMPS <>]
                    ╱   ╲
               C   [1]S
          [COMPS <[1]>]

(22)   D
                   [COMPS <>]
                    ╱   ╲
               D   [1]NP
          [COMPS <1>]

   Examples like the following appear to pose a problem for the assumption that
complementizers and determiners are heads:

(23)   Sandy thinks (that) Kim is foolish.
(24)   Sandy saw (the) pictures of Kim.
(25)   Sandy likes (the) soup.

(23) shows that a complementizer is optional when a clause is the complement of a verb, and (24) and (25) show that a determiner is optional with a plural noun or a singular non-count noun. If complementizers and determiners are heads, it looks as if one must either allow empty complementizers and determiners, as P&P would, or allow verbs like *think* and *see* to take two different complements, a CP or an S in the first case and a DP or a plural or non-count NP in the second case. Netter shows, however, that it is possible to avoid both of these positions. He proposes that functional categories like complementizers and determiners have the same basic categorial status as their complements. Thus, complementizers are verbal and determiners are nominal. Within this approach, one does not need a disjunctive statement to allow certain NPs to appear in the same positions as DPs or to allow both CPs and Ss in certain positions. Thus, this looks like quite a promising approach.[3]

Pollard and Sag (1994: ch. 9), however, argue against the view that determiners are heads. Their argument is essentially quite simple. It focuses on simple nominal expressions consisting of items like *many* and *more* and a noun. They note that if these items are heads of the nominal expressions, it should not be possible to expand them. They cite examples like the following:

(26)   a.   many people
       b.   too many people
       c.   far too many people

In (26a) we have just *many*. In (26b), *many* is modified by *too*. Finally, in (26c), *too* is modified by *far*. Rather similar are the following examples:

(27)   a.   more people
       b.   many more people
       c.   many more than fifty people

In (27a) we have just *more*. In (27b), *more* is modified by *many*. Finally, in (27c), it is also modified by *than fifty*. These examples suggest rather strongly that *many* and *more* are not heads of the nominal expressions. Thus, if they are determiners, we must apparently conclude that determiners are not heads. One might argue, however, that they are not determiners but members of a separate quantifier category. If so, these observations will show nothing about determiners.

Although complements are normally phrases of some kind, it has been suggested in some recent HPSG work that some heads take as complements a lexical item of some kind and whatever complements the lexical item requires. For example, Abeillé and Godard (1994) propose an analysis of this kind for the

French auxiliaries *avoir* and *être*. Simplifying somewhat, we can represent the category they propose for the former as follows:

(28)
$$
\begin{bmatrix}
\text{HEAD } verb \\
\text{SUBJ } <[1]> \\
\text{COMPS } <\begin{bmatrix} \text{HEAD } verb[part] \\ \text{SUBJ } <[1]> \\ \text{COMPS } [2] \end{bmatrix}> \& [2]
\end{bmatrix}
$$

This involves the SUBJ feature, which we will discuss in the next section. '&' denotes concatenation of lists. On this analysis, (29) will have the structure in (30).

(29) Jean a mangé à midi.
  Jean has eaten at 12
  'Jean has eaten at 12.'

(30)

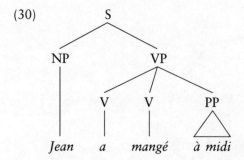

A broadly similar analysis is proposed in Pollard (1994) for the German auxiliary *haben* 'have'. Analyses of this kind, in which a head inherits complements from another head, are commonly said to involve 'argument composition'.

Related to such analyses are analyses in which an auxiliary combines with a lexical verb to form a 'verbal cluster', which then combines with whatever complements the lexical verb takes. Such an analysis is proposed for German in Hinrichs and Nakazawa (1994). They assume categories rather like (28), but they propose two different head–complement rules, one licensing the verbal cluster and one licensing the combination of verbal cluster and complements of the lexical verb. A somewhat different approach to verbal clusters is developed by Rentier (1994a) in connection with Dutch cross-serial dependencies. This involves an extra valence feature GOV selecting lexical complements. Applying this approach to German, we would need the following category for finite forms of *haben*.

(31) $\begin{bmatrix} \text{HEAD } verb[fin] \\ \text{SUBJ } <[1]> \\ \text{COMPS } [2] \\ \text{GOV } < \begin{bmatrix} \text{HEAD } verb\ [part] \\ \text{SUBJ } <[1]> \\ \text{COMPS } [2] \end{bmatrix} > \end{bmatrix}$

Rentier assumes one rule combining a head with the element required by its GOV feature, and another combining a head with its complements and sub-ject. These rules will interact with (31) to give the structure in (33) for the sub-ordinate clause in (32).

(32)   dass Sie ihm   den Wagen   gegeben hat
       that she him-DAT the car-ACC given   has
       'that she gave him the car'

(33)

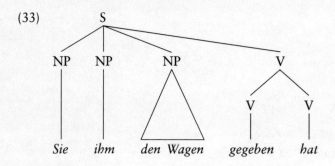

We will see in chapter 12 how this approach permits an analysis of cross-serial dependencies.

There is one further approach to head–complement structures that we should briefly mention. This is the approach developed within the framework known as Japanese Phrase Structure Grammar (JPSG) in Gunji (1987). For JPSG, as for the SUBCAT version of HPSG, a single feature SUBCAT indicates both what complements a head takes and what kinds of subject it requires. Unlike the HPSG feature, however, its value is a set of categories. Dependants are distin-guished from each other by features, a subject being marked [SBJ] and an object [OBJ]. Since both subjects and objects are marked with a postposition, they are analysed as PPs. Given these assumptions, we have the following category for a simple transitive verb.

(34)   V[SUBCAT{PP[SBJ],PP[OBJ]}]

Such categories interact with an ID rule that combines a head with a single dependant. Since the value of SUBCAT is a set, a head can be combined with its dependants in any order. Thus, both of the following are generated.

(35) Ken-ga   Naomi-wo   aisteiriu.
      Ken-NOM Naomi-ACC love
      'Ken loves Naomi.'

(36) Naomi-wo   Ken-ga   aisteiriu.
      Naomi-ACC Ken-NOM love
      'Ken loves Naomi.'

Thus, a set-valued SUBCAT feature provides one way of accounting for certain kinds of word order variation. We should add that a set-valued SUBCAT feature has sometimes been assumed in HPSG work. It is assumed, for example, in Pollard's (forthcoming) analysis of German.

6.3 Subject–predicate structures

We turn now to subject–predicate structures. Normally, a subject and the associated predicate form a clause of some kind. However, not all subject–predicate combinations are constituents for Modern PSG. Hence not all are clauses. We will return to this point in chapter 8. In the present section, we will just be concerned with subject–predicate combinations that are clauses.

We begin by looking at the GPSG approach. Central here is the feature AGR and the Control Agreement Principle (CAP), to which it is subject. AGR encodes the kind of subject that a predicate requires. Thus, for example, a VP which requires a third person singular subject will have the category:

(37) VP[AGR NP[PERS 3,NUMB SING]]

Categories like these interact with an ID rule for subject-initial clauses, which we can represent as follows:

(38) S ⟶ XP, VP

This identifies the subject as a phrase but does nothing to ensure that we have the right type of phrase. This is where the CAP comes in. The CAP refers to the notion controller, which is defined in terms of the semantic interpretations that are associated with local trees. There are two situations in which a category is the controller of a sister category. The simplest case is the following:

(39)   When there are two sisters and one is a functor and the other its argu-
       ment, the argument is the controller of the functor.

We will consider the other situation in which a category is the controller of a
sister category in chapter 8. For GPSG, the VP in a subject-initial sentence is a
functor and the subject is its argument, i.e. it has the following semantic type:

(40)   <NP,S>

It follows that the subject is the controller of the VP. The CAP refers to CON-
TROL features, the most important of which is AGR. We will consider the one
other CONTROL feature in chapter 9. For now, we can formulate the CAP as
follows:

(41)   CONTROL AGREEMENT PRINCIPLE (preliminary version)
       The value of a CONTROL feature in a category is identical to the con-
       troller of the category if it has one.

We will extend the principle in chapter 8. The CAP ensures that the value of
AGR in the VP of a subject-initial clause is identical to the subject. The following tree conforms to the CAP:

(42)

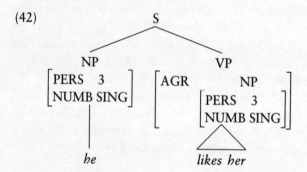

However, a similar tree with a third person plural subject would violate the
CAP. Hence, a sentence like *They likes her* is ruled out.
    Within this approach, subject–verb agreement is the selection by a verb with
a certain form of a subject with certain person and number properties. It is
natural to treat subject case-marking in the same way. It is natural, that is, to
say that finite verbs have a nominative NP as the value of AGR while non-finite
verbs have an accusative NP as the value of AGR. This would account for the
following data:

(43)   a. He/*him will be here.
       b. I will arrange for him/*he to be here.

In fact, however, we cannot say that non-finite verbs have an accusative NP as the value of AGR. This is because of examples like the following:

(44)   He/*him seemed to impress her.

As we will see in chapter 8, the verbs in such examples will have the same value for AGR. Thus, we cannot say that the value of AGR in a non-finite verb involves the specification [CASE ACC]. This suggests that subject case-marking may not be reducible to selection by a verb of a subject with a certain case, and that it may be necessary to invoke tree-based case-marking conventions for subject case-marking.

There are some further points that we should make about this approach. The first is that it involves a redundancy. The rule in (38) stipulates that the subject is a maximal projection. However, the value of AGR will always be a maximal projection of some kind. Hence, the fact that subjects are maximal projections is stated twice. The obvious way to eliminate this redundancy would be to remove the stipulation that subjects are maximal projections from the ID rule for subject-initial clauses, i.e. to reformulate it as follows:

(45)   S $\longrightarrow$ X, VP

As we will see shortly, this makes the GPSG approach closer to the HPSG approach.

The second point is that Gazdar et al. (1985) seem somewhat uncertain about the status of the AGR feature. They assume that it is relevant not only to subject–predicate structures but also to other sorts of structure in which agreement occurs. For example, they suggest (p. 91) that a determiner might have the AGR feature where it agrees with the associated noun. They also assume that it is relevant to all kinds of subject selection whether or not it is associated with any agreement morphology. For example, they assume that verbs that require an expletive *it* subject have the feature specification AGR[NP[*it*]]. It is worth noting here that Hukari (1989) outlines a revised version of the standard GPSG framework in which what subject a head requires is encoded in a category-valued feature SUBJ.

The final point that we should note is that Gazdar et al. (1985) assume, following Borsley (1983, 1984), that VP and S are the same basic category distinguished by just a single feature specification. Both are V^2 and VP is [SUBJ –] while S is [SUBJ +]. We will consider the motivation for this in chapter 8.

We turn now to the HPSG approach to subject–predicate structures. We will look first at the SUBCAT framework, in which what kind of subject a head requires is encoded in the SUBCAT feature. Then we will consider the

SUBJ–COMPS framework, in which it is encoded in the SUBJ feature, and summarize some of the arguments that can be advanced for this approach.

The SUBCAT framework assumes a subject–predicate rule, which we can represent as follows:

(46)   SUBJECT–PREDICATE RULE (SUBCAT framework)
       [SUBCAT <>] ⟶ [SUBCAT <[ ]>], [ ]
                        HEAD   COMPS

Recall that '[ ]' stands for an arbitrary list member. We can paraphrase the rule as follows:

(47)   A sign with the feature specification SUBCAT <> can contain a head daughter with the feature specifications SUBCAT <[ ]> and a complement daughter.

This will interact with the Subcategorization Principle and the Head Feature Principle to allow trees like the following:

(48)

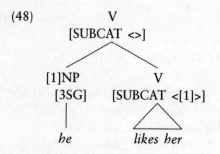

A similar tree with a third person plural subject would violate the Subcategorization Principle. Hence, an example like *They likes her* is ruled out.

The SUBJ–COMPS framework employs the following subject–predicate rule:

(49)   SUBJECT–PREDICATE RULE (SUBJ–COMPS framework)
       [SUBJ <>] ⟶ [SUBJ <[ ]>,COMPS <>], [ ]
                      HEAD   SUBJ

This can be paraphrased as follows:

(50)   A sign with the feature specification SUBJ <> can contain a head daughter with the feature specifications COMPS <> and SUBJ <[ ]> and a subject daughter.

The COMPS <> specification ensures that a head combines with any complements that it requires before it combines with a subject. The rule will interact with the Valence Principle and the Head Feature Principle to allow trees like the following:

(51)

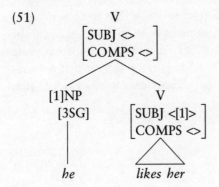

A similar tree with a third person plural subject will violate the Valence Principle.

A number of arguments for the SUBJ–COMPS framework are advanced in Borsley (1987, forthcoming). We will consider just two of them here.

One argument for the framework is that it allows a more restrictive characterization of typical non-heads. Within the SUBCAT framework, typical non-heads are either [SUBCAT <>] categories, e.g. NPs and clauses, or [SUBCAT <[]>] categories, e.g. subjectless infinitives or predicative APs. The following, in which the categories of the bracketed constituents are given in brackets, illustrate:

(52) Sandy impressed [the lecturer]   (N[SUBCAT <>])
(53) Sandy said [she was coming]   (V[SUBCAT <>])
(54) Sandy expected [to be on time]   (V[SUBCAT <NP>])
(55) Sandy was [very late]   (A[SUBCAT <NP>])

In the SUBJ–COMPS framework, typical non-heads are [COMPS <>] categories, as the following illustrate:

(56) Sandy impressed [the lecturer]   (N[SUBJ <>,COMPS <>])
(57) Sandy said [she was coming]   (V[SUBJ <>,COMPS <>])
(58) Sandy expected [to be on time]   (V[SUBJ <NP>,COMPS <>])
(59) Sandy was [very late]   (A[SUBJ <NP>,COMPS <>])

Notice that I refer here to 'typical non-heads'. This is necessary in view of the analyses mentioned in the last section in which auxiliaries take a verb as their complement. If these analyses are right, we cannot say that all non-heads are [COMPS <>]. We can say, however, that typical non-heads are, and the fact that the SUBJ–COMPS framework allows a more restrictive characterization of typical non-heads than the SUBCAT framework provides some motivation for it.

Another argument for the SUBJ–COMPS framework is that it allows one to recognize heads that require a complement but not a subject. Such heads can be analysed as [SUBJ <>,COMPS <[]>]. The SUBCAT framework cannot recognize such heads. In the SUBCAT framework, a head requires a subject if it requires anything at all. However, there appear to be various examples of heads that require a complement but not a subject.

We look first at prepositions. Consider firstly the following:

(60)   Kim was [on the bed]

Here, we have a predicative PP which it is natural to analyse within the SUBCAT framework as P[SUBCAT <NP>]. If the PP has this category, the preposition *on* will have the following category:

(61)   P[SUBCAT <NP,NP>]

Consider now the following:

(62)   Kim relies [on Sandy]
(63)   Kim met Sandy [on Wednesday]

(62) contains an argument PP and (63) an adverbial PP. It seems natural to analyse both as P[SUBCAT <>]. If the PPs have this category, the preposition will have the following category:

(64)   P[SUBCAT <NP>]

However, if it has this category, its complement will really be a subject. There is no reason to think that the complement has a different status in (62) and (63). Thus, this is rather unsatisfactory. Within the SUBJ–COMPS framework, we can assign *on* in (62) to the following category:

(65)   P[SUBJ <>,COMPS <NP>]

This will give us the following tree for the PP in (62):

(66)

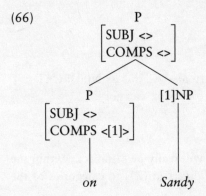

On in (63) would involve a similar category, but with the MOD feature discussed in the next chapter, which indicates what sort of head an adjunct combines with. In contrast, *on* in (60) would involve the following category:

(67) P[SUBJ <NP>,COMPS <NP>]

This would give the following tree for the PP in (60):

(68)

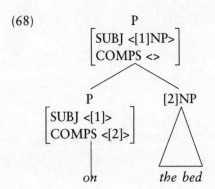

Here, then, the SUBJ–COMPS framework seems to have a clear advantage over the SUBCAT framework.

We have a similar situation with nouns. Consider firstly the following.

(69) They are [followers of the prophet]

Here, we have a predicative NP, which can be analysed within the SUBCAT framework as N[SUBCAT <NP>]. Given this category, the noun will have the following category:

(70) N[SUBCAT <NP,PP[*of*]>]

Consider now (71).

(71)   [Followers of the prophet] wear green.

Here we have an argument NP. It is natural to analyse this as N[SUBCAT <>].
Given this category, the noun will have the following category:

(72)   N[SUBCAT <PP[*of*]>]

With this category, however, the complement will really be a subject. Within the
SUBJ–COMPS framework, we can assign *followers* in (71) to categories of the
following form:

(73)   N[SUBJ <>,COMPS <PP[*of*]>]

This will give us the following tree for the NP in (71):

(74)

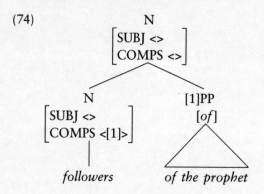

followers   of the prophet

In contrast, *followers* in (69) would involve the following category:

(75)   N[SUBJ <NP>,COMPS <PP[*of*]>]

This would give the following tree for the NP in (69):

(76)

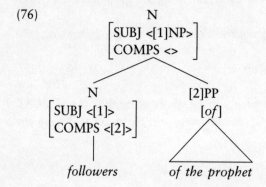

followers   of the prophet

Again, then, the SUBJ–COMPS framework seems preferable to the SUBCAT framework.

There may well be various other examples of heads taking complements but no subject. If complementizers and determiners are heads, they will presumably be heads of this kind. Consider also imperative verbs such as *go* in (77).

(77)   Go to bed!

A natural suggestion is that this involves the category in (78).

(78)   V[SUBJ <>,COMPS <PP[*to*]>]

This would give the following tree for (77).

(79)

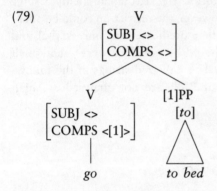

One might suggest a similar approach to the subjectless finite clauses that are a feature of so-called null-subject languages. An example is Italian, where we have sentences like the following:

(80)   Ho   telefonato.
       have-1SG telephoned
       'I have telephoned.'

There is, however, an obvious alternative analysis that one might consider here, one involving an empty subject. In fact, such an analysis is proposed for examples like (80) in Pollard and Sag (1994: ch. 6). However, Pollard and Sag (1994: ch. 9) seek to avoid empty categories. Presumably, then, they would favour an analysis in which subjectless sentences have a verb which takes complements but no subject.

However examples like (80) are to be analysed, it seems that there are quite good reasons for assuming the SUBJ–COMPS version of HPSG. I will assume this version of HPSG in the rest of the book.

For HPSG, as for GPSG, subject–verb agreement is just the selection by a verb of a certain form of a subject with certain person and number properties.[4] As in GPSG, it is natural to treat subject case-marking in the same way. However, as in GPSG, subjects of non-finite verbs are a problem. As we will see in chapter 8, the verbs in examples like (44) will have the same *synsem* object in their SUBJ list. Thus, we cannot assume that non-finite verbs have an accusative NP in their SUBJ list. Again, then, it seems that subject case-marking may not be reducible to selection by a verb of a subject with a certain case and that it may be necessary to assume tree-based case-marking conventions for subject case-marking. This is in fact suggested in connection with German in Pollard (1994).

So far we have only considered clauses with verbal predicates. It is commonly assumed, however, that there are clauses with non-verbal predicates, so-called small clauses. Gazdar et al. (1985) propose a feature co-occurrence restriction (FCR 12) which limits AGR to verbal categories. Hence, they implicitly assume that predicates are always verbal. Clearly, however, the restriction could be abandoned. In HPSG, there is no assumption that predicates are only verbal and small clauses are only to be expected. It should be noted, however, that small clauses play a rather limited role in HPSG. The italicized strings in the following, which are analysed as small clauses in P&P, are not analysed as small clauses in either GPSG or HPSG.

(81)   I found *Kim afraid of spiders*.
(82)   I want *Kim out of town*.
(83)   I consider *Kim the leading candidate for the post*.

We will return to such examples in chapter 8. At least within HPSG, however, the italicized strings in the following are analysed as small clauses:

(84)   With *Kim afraid of spiders*, we don't know what to do.
(85)   With *Kim out of town*, we can do what we like.
(86)   With *Kim the leading candidate for the post*, we're all worried.

Pollard and Sag (1994: 111) also argue that the italicized string in the following is a small clause:

(87)   We feared *Noriega in power*.

They note that the following suggests that this string is a constituent:

(88) What we feared was *Noriega in power*.

If any of these strings are indeed small clauses, it is quite easy to accommodate them within the approaches that we have been considering. Within the SUBJ–

COMPS version of HPSG, all we need to do to accommodate the string in (84) is to assign *afraid* to the following category:

(89)   A[SUBJ <PP[*of*],COMPS <NP>]

This will interact with the head–complement rule and the subject–predicate rule to give the following tree:

(90)

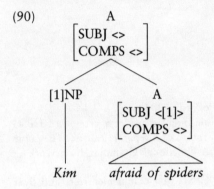

Thus, small clauses are quite easy to accommodate. One question that arises here is: how are nominal small clauses distinguished from argument NPs? Both will be N[SUBJ <>,COMPS <>]. They will in fact be distinguished by the fact that the former will be [PRD +] while the latter will be [PRD –]. [PRD +] groups together NPs, APs, PPs, and progressive and passive VPs. As Pollard and Sag (1987: 64–7) show, there are a variety of contexts in which just these categories appear. These include predicate position in the type of clause that we have in (84)–(86). The following show that progressive and passive VPs can appear in this position:

(91)   With Kim living in Spain, we're sure of a good holiday.
(92)   With Kim sent to London, things are very quiet.

Thus, small clauses do not necessarily have a non-verbal predicate. Rather, they have a [PRD +] predicate.

6.4   Summary

In this chapter, we have looked at two major types of syntactic structure: head–complement structures and subject–predicate structures. In head–complement structures, we emphasized that GPSG and HPSG have very different approaches, and that this is one area where HPSG seems to be an advance on GPSG. We also highlighted the fact that there are different versions of the HPSG approach. We noted that there is some disagreement over what exactly are head–complement structures, and we introduced the notion of 'argument composition'. We also referred briefly to the JPSG approach to head–complement structures. In connection with subject–predicate structures, our main concern was to highlight the case for the SUBJ–COMPS version of HPSG, in which subjects are the realization of a separate SUBJ feature.

Notes

1 The SUBCAT feature was first proposed in Pollard (1984).
2 Pollard and Sag (1987: 118) point out that one might consider a version of HPSG in which every dependant of a head is the realization of a separate feature. They note that this would be very similar to the Lexical Functional Grammar framework of Bresnan (1982b).
3 Warner (1989) proposes within a version of GPSG that complementizers and their S sisters are co-heads. Such an analysis is not available within HPSG given its more restrictive notion of head.
4 Kathol (forthcoming) argues that subject–verb agreement is not just the selection by a verb with a certain form of a subject with certain person and number properties. He proposes that verbs that show agreement have a feature AGR, whose value is a group of agreement features. He argues that this permits a more satisfactory account of the relation between syntax and morphology.

Exercises

1 Provide GPSG ID rules and HPSG COMPS feature specifications for the items in bold in the following examples. Remember to distinguish different types of PP.

(1) Kim **reminded** Sandy of her mother.
(2) Kim **talked** to Sandy about the weather.
(3) It **annoyed** me that Kim was late.
(4) Kim **said** to Sandy that it was late.
(5) Kim **bought** a book for Sandy.
(6) Kim **bet** Sandy five dollars that it would rain.
(7) Kim **provided** Sandy with a good excuse.
(8) Kim would **prefer** it for Sandy to go.

2   Explain how the data in (1)–(8) provide evidence for the idea that the French auxiliary *avoir* takes as its complements not a VP but a past participle and whatever complements the past participle requires. Do the data in (9) provide a problem for this analysis?

(1)   *Jean croyais avoir compris,   mais il   ne   l' avait pas.
       John thought have understood but   he NEG it had   NEG
       'John thought he had understood, but he had not.'

(2)   Jean peut venir, mais il   ne   le veut pas.
       John can come but   he NEG it want NEG
       'John can come but he doesn't want to.'

(3)   *Qu' a-t-elle? Vendu ses livres.
       what has she   sold   her books
       'What has she done? Sold her books.'

(4)   Que veut- elle? Partir
       what wants she   go away
       'What does she want? To go away.'

(5)   *Jean a   fini   son travail, mais Marie n'   a   pas.
       John has finished his work   but   Mary NEG has NEG
       'John has finished his work but Mary hasn't.'

(6)   Si Jean veut   venir, il   peut.
       If John wants come he can
       'If John wants to come he can.'

(7)   *Lu   cet article, non, je n'   ai   pas.
       read this article no   I NEG have NEG
       'Read this article, no, I have not.'

(8)   Aller aux EU, je n'   oserai   jamais.
       go   to USA I NEG will-dare never
       'Go to the USA, I will never dare.'

(9)   Paul a   parlé   avec Marie et   compris   son erreur.
       Paul has spoken with Mary and understood his mistake
       'Paul has spoken with Mary and understood his mistake.'

3   Explain how the structure in (1) but not the structure in (2) provides a natural basis for accounting for the fact that the subject of a non-finite clause introduced by *for* is accusative.

(1)

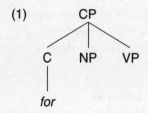

(2)

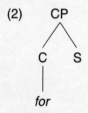

4   Provide full HPSG trees for the bracketed strings in the following:

(1) [Kim amazed Lee]
(2) [Kim laughed at Lee]
(3) [afraid of spiders]
(4) with [Kim in bed]
(5) with [Kim wanted for fraud]

5   Say which of the following sentences from languages with different orders of subject, verb and object can be accommodated with the GPSG and HPSG mechanisms proposed in the chapter and which cannot, and explain why.

(1) Prynodd Megan fuwch.
     bought   Megan cow
     'Megan bought a cow.'
     Welsh

(2) Naomi-ga   kare-wo   mituketa.
     Naomi-NOM he- ACC found
     'Naomi found him.'
     Japanese (Gunji 1987)

(3) Nividy kisoa ho'an ny ankizy   Rakoto.
     bought pig   for   the children Rakoto
     'Rakoto bought some pork for the children.'
     Malagasy (Pullum 1977)

(4) Toto-komo   yonoye kamara
    man-COLLECTIVE ate   jaguar
    'The jaguar ate people.'
    Hixkaryana (Pullum 1980)

(5) Anana   nota apa
    pineapple I   fetch.
    'I fetch pineapple.'
    Apurina (Pullum 1980)

7 Some Further Structures

7.1 Introduction

In the last chapter, we considered what are arguably the most important types of syntactic structure, head–complement structures and subject–predicate structures. In this chapter, we will look at four more important types of structure: specifier–head structures, adjunct–head structures, marker–head structures, and coordinate structures.

7.2 Specifier–head structures

In the last chapter, we looked at the view that determiners are heads and briefly summarized Pollard and Sag's (1994) argument against this view. If they are not heads, the obvious suggestion is that they are specifiers, a category assumed in such works as Chomsky (1970) and Jackendoff (1977) to include determiners and possessives within NPs and degree words within APs. But what exactly are specifiers? We will see that there is evidence that specifiers are a distinctive type of dependent element which cannot be equated with any other type.

Pollard and Sag (1987) equate specifiers with subjects and specifier–head structures with subject–predicate structures. They assume that both specifiers and subjects are realizations of the least oblique member of a SUBCAT list. Thus, they assume trees like the following:

(1)

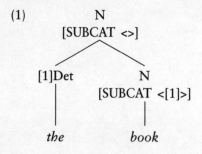

If specifiers could be equated with subjects, we would have trees like the following within the SUBJ–COMPS framework:

(2)

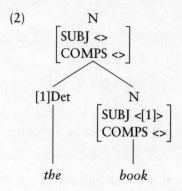

There is, however, quite strong evidence that specifiers cannot be equated with subjects. The evidence comes from heads that have both a specifier and a subject. Consider firstly the following:

(3)   With Sandy a candidate, anything could happen.
(4)   With Sandy Kim's secretary, there are bound to be problems.
(5)   With Kim too drunk to stand up, the party came to an end.

In (3), the noun *candidate* takes both a specifier *a* and a subject *Sandy*. In (4), the noun *secretary* takes both a specifier *Kim's* and a subject *Sandy*. Finally, in (5), the adjective *drunk* takes both a specifier *too* and a subject *Kim*. Consider also the following examples:

(6)   Sandy is a candidate.
(7)   Sandy is Kim's secretary.
(8)   Kim was too drunk to stand up.

These also involve heads taking a specifier and a subject, but the subject is 'raised'. We will return to such examples in chapter 8. The two types of example suggest very strongly that specifiers cannot be equated with subjects.

   It seems, then, that specifiers must be analysed as a separate type of dependent element associated with a separate valence feature. In Borsley (forthcoming) this feature is called SPEC. In Pollard and Sag (1994: ch. 9) it is called SPR, and I will use this name in subsequent discussion. Assuming this feature, we can assign a simple noun like *book* to the following category:

(9)   N[SPR <Det>,COMPS <>]

To utilize such categories we need a Specifier–Head Rule, which we can formulate as follows:

(10) SPECIFIER–HEAD RULE
      [SPR <>] ⟶ [SPR <[ ]>,COMPS <>], [ ]
                        HEAD   SPR

We can paraphrase this as follows:

(11) A sign with the feature specification SPR <> can contain a head daughter with the feature specifications COMPS <> and SPR <[ ]> and a specifier daughter.

The COMPS <> specification on the head ensures that a head will always combine with any complements it requires before it combines with a specifier. The rule will interact with the Valence Principle and the Head Feature Principle to allow trees like the following:

(12)

$$
\begin{array}{c}
N \\
\left[\begin{array}{l} \text{SPR} <> \\ \text{COMPS} <> \end{array}\right]
\end{array}
$$

[1]Det   N
                 $\left[\begin{array}{l} \text{SPR} <[1]> \\ \text{COMPS} <> \end{array}\right]$

the   book

One consequence of introducing the SPR feature is that it is necessary to reformulate the subject–predicate rule as follows:

(13) SUBJECT–PREDICATE RULE (revised version)
      [SUBJ <>] ⟶ [SUBJ <[ ]>,SPR <>,COMPS <>], [ ]
                          HEAD   SUBJ

Here, the SPR <> specification on the head ensures that a head combines with any specifier that it takes before it combines with a subject.

Pollard and Sag (1994) in fact propose a rather more complex analysis of specifiers. For semantic reasons, they propose that specifiers select the associated heads as well as being selected by them. What type of head a specifier selects is encoded in a feature SPEC, whose value is a *synsem* object. This is governed by the SPEC Principle, which we can formulate as follows:

(14) SPEC PRINCIPLE
      If a non-head daughter in a headed structure bears a SPEC value, it is token-identical to the *synsem* value of the head daughter.

Assuming the SPEC feature, we will have the following instead of (12):[1]

(15)

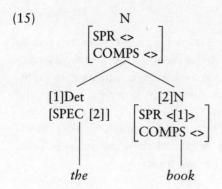

There is one further matter that we should briefly consider here. In P&P, it is assumed that the fillers in filler-gap structures such as *wh*-questions are specifiers of a possibly empty complementizer. Within Modern PSG, it has generally been assumed that fillers are a further type of dependent element. However, as was pointed out in Borsley (1989b), they can be analysed as specifiers of a complementizer in Modern PSG if one is prepared to assume empty complementizers. Thus, the bracketed subordinate clause in (16) could have something like the structure in (17).

(16) Sandy wondered [what Kim was doing]

(17)

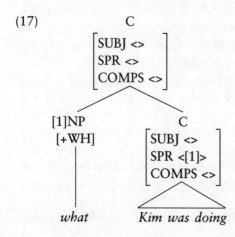

Pollard and Sag (1994) in fact propose an analysis of this kind for fillers in relative clauses although not for fillers in *wh*-questions. We will return to this in chapter 9.[2,3]

7.3 Adjuncts

We turn now to adjuncts. They have been something of a poor relation in syntactic theory. Standard presentations of X-bar theory, for example Chomsky (1986b: 3), ignore their existence. Adjuncts have had some attention in GPSG and rather more within HPSG. It is probably fair to say, however, that it is still unclear what the right analysis is.

A quite widely held view of adjuncts is that they combine with a head–complement phrase of some kind to give a phrase of the same kind. In other words, they appear in structures of the following form:

(18)

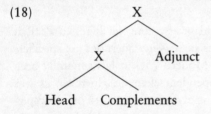

This view is presented in such P&P textbooks as Radford (1988) and Haegeman (1994) and is standard in Categorial Grammar. Essentially this view is adopted in GPSG and later HPSG, i.e. Pollard and Sag (1994).

Within GPSG, it was suggested by Pullum (1985) that head–adjunct structures provide evidence for a default formulation of the Head Feature Convention. In head–adjunct structures head and mother have the same value for the feature BAR, whereas in head–complement structures, subject–predicate structures and specifier–head structures, they have different values. Pullum argues that a default Head Feature Convention permits a straightforward account of the facts if BAR is a HEAD feature. ID rules for head–adjunct structures can say nothing about the value of BAR in the head, and the Head Feature Convention will ensure that it is the same as in the mother. In contrast, ID rules for the other types of structure can specify different values for BAR in the mother and in the head, and this will override the Head Feature Convention.

GPSG assumes many different ID rules for head–adjunct structures. In contrast, HPSG, following the JPSG framework of Gunji (1987), assumes just a single rule interacting with categories for adjuncts which incorporate information about what type of head they combine with. This information is encoded in a HEAD feature MOD (MODIFIED), whose value is a *synsem* object. Within this approach, a preposition that heads an adverbial PP will have something like the following category:

(19)   P[SUBCAT <NP>,MOD VP]

This will interact with the Head–Adjunct Rule, which we can formulate as follows:

(20)   HEAD–ADJUNCT RULE
    [ ] —→ [SYNSEM [1]], [MOD [1]]
          HEAD   ADJUNCT

We can paraphrase this as follows:

(21)   A sign can contain a head daughter and an adjunct daughter with the
    •value of SYNSEM in the head daughter token-identical to the value of
    MOD in the adjunct daughter.

The rule will allow trees like the following:

(22)

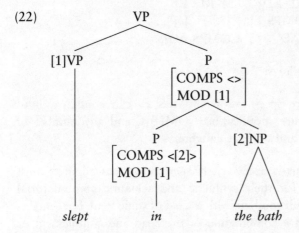

The Valence Principle will ensure that the sign has the same value for SUBJ and COMPS as the head daughter (<> in the latter case). The Head Feature Principle will ensure that the sign has the same value for HEAD as the head daughter. This approach is seen by Pollard and Sag as appropriate to all sorts of adjuncts. We will see in chapter 9 how they extend it to relative clauses.

This approach to adjuncts predicts that complements will precede adjuncts in a head-initial language. There are, however, examples in English and other head-initial languages where an adjunct precedes a complement. Consider, for example, the following:

(23) Sandy said last week that she would be here.
(24) Sandy thought until she met him that Kim was too old.

In (23) *last week* is an adjunct and *that she would be here* is a complement, and in (24) *until she met him* is an adjunct and *that Kim was too old* is a complement. One way to accommodate such examples would be to invoke something like the SLASH mechanism that is assumed in connection with unbounded dependencies. (See chapter 9.) One might, however, see them as evidence that adjuncts can be sisters of complements. This is a position that is developed in early HPSG, i.e. Pollard and Sag (1987), and it is revived in Kasper (1994).

Pollard and Sag (1987) propose that heads include a feature ADJUNCTS whose value is a set of categories and which identifies what type of adjuncts they can combine with. Pollard and Sag (1994) point out that it is very unclear how this approach could be made to work. Kasper (1994) explores the possibility of combining an analysis in which adjuncts and complements are sisters with the view that adjuncts select the heads with which they combine. His approach involves a head–complement–adjunct rule of the following form:

(25) HEAD–COMPLEMENT–ADJUNCT RULE
      [COMPS <>] ⟶ [COMPS L], [ ]*,   [ ]*
                      HEAD   COMPS ADJS

We can paraphrase this as follows:

(26) A sign with the feature specification COMPS <> can contain a head daughter with the feature specification COMPS L and any number of complement daughters and adjunct daughters.

However, much more than this is necessary. Kasper shows that adjuncts must have separate specifications for their syntactic and semantic combinatorial potential. Syntactically, they will combine with a head of some kind, but semantically they may combine with a combination of the head and complement or with the combination of head, complement and adjunct. We can illustrate with the following example:

(27) Kim saw Sandy every day for a month.

We can paraphrase this as follows:

(28) It was for a month that Kim saw Sandy every day.

Thus, *every day* combines semantically with *saw Sandy* and *for a month* combines semantically with *saw Sandy every day*. To accommodate such facts, Kasper proposes that MOD takes as its value not a *synsem* object but a MOD object with separate SYNTAX and SEMANTICS attributes. To utilize these attributes, he proposes one principle governing the syntax of adjuncts and one governing their semantics. The analysis is a rather complex one and one might feel that it is not entirely satisfactory. We will mention an alternative approach in chapter 12.

One rather important element that may well be an adjunct is *not*. Within P&P, it has been generally assumed since Pollock (1989) that it is one of a number of functional heads. It is clear, however, that it is unlike ordinary heads.[4] Consider the following data:

(29)   Kim has not $\begin{Bmatrix} \text{read} \\ \text{*reading} \end{Bmatrix}$ the book

(30)   Kim is not $\begin{Bmatrix} \text{*read} \\ \text{reading} \end{Bmatrix}$ the book

In (29) we have a past participle and not a present participle because we have the auxiliary *have*, and in (30) we have a present participle and not a past participle because we have the auxiliary *be*. It looks, then, as if it is not *not* but the participle that heads the complement of the auxiliary. If *not* is not a head the obvious assumption is that it is an adjunct. Examples like the following, in which it combines with an adverb and a quantifier, provide further support for this assumption.

(31)   It was a not entirely pointless suggestion.
(32)   Not every paper was rejected.

Of course, we have not actually provided an analysis of *not*, but it does look as if an adjunct analysis may be the right one.

In this section, we have concentrated on verbal adjuncts. Nominal adjuncts such as attributive adjectives and relative clauses are also of considerable interest. We will say something about the latter in chapter 9. For some interesting discussion of the former, see Arnold and Sadler (1992).

7.4   Markers

GPSG implicitly assumes that there is a further class of non-heads distinct from complements, subjects, specifiers and adjuncts, and this is explicitly assumed in HPSG. In HPSG, these are called markers. The most important example of markers are complementizers, which, as we noted earlier, are not analysed as heads within standard versions of GPSG and HPSG.

Pollard and Sag (1994) cite examples like the following in support of the view that complementizers are non-heads:

(33)   I demand that he leave/*leaves immediately.

Here, *demand* seems to determine the form of the verb within the complement clause. This suggests that the verb is the head of the complement. It will be if *that* is a marker, but it would not be if *that* were a head. If one assumes that complementizers are heads, one would have to assume that there are two *that*'s, one selected by verbs like *say*, *think* and *know* and taking an indicative complement and the other selected by verbs like *demand* and taking a subjunctive complement. One might feel that this is a rather unsatisfactory approach.

Pollard and Sag suggest that conjunctions and certain prepositions are markers as well. Such an analysis is quite plausible for prepositions with no semantic content such as *of* in (34) and *on* in (35).

(34)   Kim is afraid of spiders.
(35)   Kim relies on Sandy.

Heinz and Matiasek (1994) analyse similar prepositions in German as markers.

Pollard and Sag propose that markers are distinguished by a feature MARKING, which they share with their mother, and that they select the heads that they combine with through the SPEC feature, which we referred to in connection with specifiers. For the complementizer *that*, we will have something like the following category:

(36)   [SPEC S[*fin* ∨ *base*, MARKING *unmarked*], MARKING *that*]

This interacts with the following Head–Marker Rule:

(37)   HEAD–MARKER RULE
       [MARKING [1]] ⟶ [ ],   [MARKING [1]]
                        HEAD   MARKER

It can be paraphrased as follows:

(38)   A sign with some value for the MARKING feature can contain a head daughter and a marker daughter with the same value for the MARKING feature.

There is no need to mention the SPEC feature in the rule since it is governed by the SPEC principle referred to in section 7.2. There is also no need to stipulate that head and mother have the same value for HEAD and the various valence features; the former is ensured by the Head Feature Principle and the latter by the Valence Principle. Given the category in (36) and the Head–Marker Rule, we will have structures like the following:

(39)

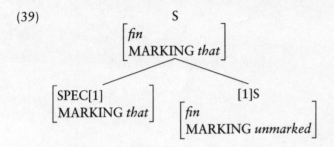

Marker–head structures are an important feature of HPSG. They are, however, a controversial feature. As we have noted, it has been proposed within HPSG that complementizers are not markers but heads, and one might propose that all prepositions are heads as well. An interesting point to note is that markers, like heads, precede their sisters in English. It is natural to ask what happens in other languages. If markers really are a separate type of element, one would expect to find languages in which they are linearized differently from heads. If there are no such languages, the existence of a separate class of markers will be called into question.

7.5 Coordinate structures

We turn finally to coordinate structures, a type of structure which figures prominently in the GPSG literature but which has had much less attention in HPSG.[5]

On the face of it, there are at least three types of coordinate structure to consider, exemplified by the following:

(40)   both Kim and Sandy
(41)   Kim, Sandy and Lee
(42)   Kim and Sandy and Lee

In (40) we have two conjuncts, the first introduced by *both* and the second by *and*. In (41) and (42) we have three conjuncts. In (41) the first two have no marking and the third is introduced by *and*, while in (42) the first has no marking and the second and third are introduced by *and*. In (41) further unmarked conjuncts could be added at the beginning, and in (42) further marked conjuncts could be added at the end. If we assume that a coordination-introducing particle like *both* is a specialized conjunction we can say that these examples instantiate structures of the following form:

(43)

(44)

(45)

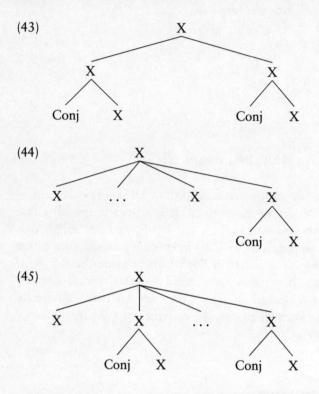

One point that we should note straightaway is that these structures are misleading in one important respect. They suggest that the conjuncts and the coordinate structure must be the same category. Contrary to what has often been assumed, this is not the case. This is stressed and its implications discussed in Sag et al. (1985). We can illustrate with the following examples:

(46)   Sandy is a linguist and proud of it.
(47)   Kim was drunk and shouting at everybody.

Clearly, a satisfactory approach to coordination must be able to accommodate such examples.

Although we have three different structures here, the second and third structures can be plausibly seen as instances of a single type of structure. Both involve a single constituent and a set of one or more constituents, and either the single constituent (44) or each member of the set of constituents (45) is 'marked' by a conjunction. It looks, then, as if there may be just two types of coordination.

This view is made explicit in the GPSG analysis of Gazdar et al. (1985). Gazdar et al. propose four ID rules, or more precisely three ID schemata and one ID rule. They propose one schema for coordination with just two conjuncts (binary coordination) and one for coordination with an unlimited number of conjuncts (iterating coordination). They are as follows:

(48)   BINARY COORDINATION SCHEMA
       X $\longrightarrow$ H[CONJ α_0], H[CONJ α_1]
       where $\alpha \in$ {*<both, and>*, *<either, or>*, *<NIL, but>*}

(49)   ITERATING COORDINATION SCHEMA
       X $\longrightarrow$ H[CONJ α_0], H[CONJ α_1]$^+$
       where $\alpha \in$ {*<and*, NIL>, *<NIL, and>*, *<neither, nor>*, *<or*, NIL>, *<NIL, or>*}

'+' in (49) stands for any number except none. Both (48) and (49) are schemata because a number of possible values are specified for the variables. Each corresponds to as many rules as the number of possibilities that are specified. The Binary Coordination Schema allows the following three possibilities (the Xs are not necessarily identical):

(50)   a.   *both* X_1 *and* X_2
       b.   *either* X_1 *or* X_2
       c. X_1 *but* X_2

The Iterating Coordination Schema allows the following five possibilities (again, the Xs are not necessarily identical):

(51)   a. $X_1 \ldots X_{n-1}$ *and* X_n
       b. X_1 *and* $X_2 \ldots X_n$
       c.   *neither* X_1 *nor* $X_2 \ldots$ *nor* X_n
       d. $X_1 \ldots X_{n-1}$ *or* X_n
       e. X_1 *or* $X_2 \ldots X_n$

(51a) and (51d) correspond to (44), and (51b) and (51e) correspond to (45). (51c) does not correspond to any of the trees in (43)–(45). One point to note is that the Iterating Schema allows coordinate structures with just two conjuncts as well as coordinate structures with more than two. In particular, it allows coordinate structures of the following form:

(52) a. X_1 *and* X_2
      b. X_1 *or* X_2

Thus, not all coordinate structures with just two conjuncts are the product of the Binary Coordination Schema. Gazdar et al. propose two ID rules for conjuncts, one for conjuncts with no conjunction and another for conjuncts with a conjunction.[6] They are as follows:

(53) X[CONJ NIL] $\longrightarrow$ H

(54) X[CONJ α] $\longrightarrow$ {[SUBCAT α]}, H
      where $\alpha \in$ {*and, both, but, neither, nor, or*}

Notice that (53) embodies the assumption that conjuncts with no conjunction involve a non-branching structure. One might see this as a weakness of the analysis. To ensure the right order of conjuncts, Gazdar et al. propose the following schema:

(55) COORDINATION LP SCHEMA
      [CONJ α_0] > [CONJ α_1]
      where α_0 is in {*both, either, neither,* NIL}
      and α_1 is in {*and, but, nor, or*}

This ensures (a) that a conjunct marked with *both* precedes one marked with *and*, (b) that a conjunct marked with *either* precedes one marked with *or*, (c) that a conjunct marked with *neither* precedes one marked with *nor*, and (d) that an unmarked conjunct precedes one marked with *and* or *or* or *but*.

One might ask here whether the two coordination schemata are really necessary. Ojeda (1988) shows that they can be combined if one allows immediate precedence rules. He proposes the following coordination schema:

(56) COORDINATION SCHEMA
      X $\longrightarrow$ H[CONJ α_0], H[CONJ α_1]$^+$
      where $\alpha \in$ {<*and,* NIL>, <NIL, *and*>, <*or,* NIL>, <NIL, *or*>,
      <*neither, nor*>, <*both, and*>, < *either, or*>, <NIL, *but*>}

This will allow a [CONJ *both*] category to have more than one [CONJ *and*] sister, a [CONJ *either*] category to have more than one [CONJ *or*] sister, and a [CONJ NIL] category to have more than one [CONJ *but*] sister. Ojeda excludes these possibilities with the following immediate precedence schema:

(57) COORDINATION ILP SCHEMA
      [CONJ α_0] << [CONJ α_1]
      Where $\alpha \in$ <*both, and*>, <*either, or*>, <NIL, *but*>}

This schema requires a [CONJ *both*] category to immediately precede any [CONJ *and*] sister, a [CONJ *either*] category to immediately precede a [CONJ *or*] sister, and a [CONJ NIL] category to immediately precede a [CONJ *but*] sister. It will be violated if a [CONJ *both*] category has more than one [CONJ *and*] sister, if a [CONJ *either*] category has more than one [CONJ *or*] sister, and if a [CONJ NIL] category has more than one [CONJ *but*] sister. Thus, it is possible to assume a single coordination schema if one is prepared to allow immediate precedence rules.

We noted earlier that conjuncts need not be the same category. The two coordination schemata do not require the conjuncts and the coordinate structure to be the same category. In fact, they impose no restriction at all on the conjuncts. Restrictions are imposed by the Head Feature Convention. Gazdar et al. propose that conjuncts are heads, and hence that coordinate structures are multi-headed structures. They bring multi-headed structures within the scope of the HFC by reformulating it as follows:

(58) HEAD FEATURE CONVENTION (revised version)
      The HEAD feature specifications that are common to a set of heads are identical to those of their mother unless some rule or principle requires otherwise.

The 'unless' clause identifies this as a default principle. We can illustrate the effects of this by considering the coordinate structures in (46) and (47). For Gazdar et al., these will have the following structures (I ignore the CONJ feature):

(59)

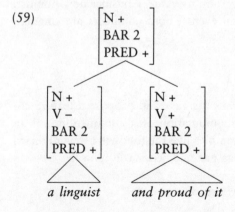

$\begin{bmatrix} N+ \\ BAR\ 2 \\ PRED+ \end{bmatrix}$

$\begin{bmatrix} N+ \\ V- \\ BAR\ 2 \\ PRED+ \end{bmatrix}$ $\begin{bmatrix} N+ \\ V+ \\ BAR\ 2 \\ PRED+ \end{bmatrix}$

a linguist   *and proud of it*

(60)

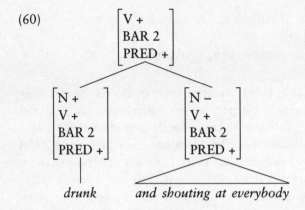

For Gazdar et al., nominal categories are [N +, V −] and adjectival categories are [N +, V +]. Hence, when a nominal category is coordinated with an adjectival category, the result is a category that is [N +] but unspecified for V. A verbal category is [N −, V +]. Consequently, when an adjectival category is coordinated with a verbal category the resulting category is [V +] but unspecified for N.

NP coordination raises additional problems. Consider first person. Here, the generalization is that a coordinate structure is first person if one of the conjuncts is first person and second person if one of the conjuncts is second person (and none is first person). We have data like the following:

(61)   You and I understand ourselves well.
(62)   Kim and you talked about yourselves all evening.
(63)   Sandy and I looked at ourselves in the mirror.

As noted in chapter 3, Sag et al. (1985) use unary features to provide an account of these facts. Their approach, however, is criticized in Warner (1988). He argues that a more satisfactory analysis is possible in a framework in which whether or not a feature is a HEAD feature depends on its value. Consider now number. Coordinate structures are normally plural even if both conjuncts are singular. The following illustrates:

(64)   Kim and Sandy were/*was late.

Sag et al. (1985) assume that this is always the case and propose a feature co-occurrence restriction ensuring that the combination of a conjunction and an NP is plural. It is clear, however, from examples like the following (from Pollard and Sag 1994: 70) that NP coordinations are not necessarily plural:

(65)   Steak and okra appears to bother him.

Such examples suggest that the number of a coordinate structure is determined by whether or not it is understood as denoting a single entity or more than one entity and hence that we are concerned here not with syntax but with semantics or pragmatics.

We now turn briefly to HPSG. Coordination has in fact had considerably less attention in HPSG than it received in GPSG. Unlike in GPSG, it is not assumed that conjuncts are heads. This means that a special principle is necessary to constrain the relation between coordinate structures and conjuncts. Pollard and Sag (1994: 203) propose the following principle:

(66) COORDINATION PRINCIPLE
      In a coordinate structure, the CATEGORY and NON-LOCAL value of each conjunct daughter is subsumed by (is an extension of) that of the mother.

Essentially, this ensures that conjuncts have all the feature specifications of the coordinate structure but allows them to have additional feature specifications. As Pollard and Sag note, something like this is necessary not only for examples like (46) and (47), but also for less esoteric examples like the following:

(67) Francis arrived late today but will be on time tomorrow.

Here, the first conjunct is [AUX −] and the second [AUX +]. Pollard and Sag (1994: ch. 4, fn. 30) point out that there is a problem here. As we noted in chapter 3, they assume that categories in linguistic expressions must be fully specified. This approach to coordinate structures assumes that they can have partially specified categories. Hence, it is incompatible with this requirement. They leave the problem unresolved.[7, 8]

An important problem for any account of coordination is so-called non-constituent coordination, coordination in which the components are not constituents on standard assumptions.[9] The following is a typical example:

(68) Kim gave a book to Sandy and a record to Lee.

Here, we seem to have the coordination of two pairs of constituents. One response to this problem developed within Categorial Grammar in, for example, Dowty (1988) and within P&P in Larson (1988a) is to claim that the conjuncts are constituents after all. This response has also been developed within GPSG in Schachter and Mordechai (1983). An alternative response is to claim that such examples involve conjoined VPs, the second of which lacks a verb. This response is developed in Sag et al. (1985). However, as Hudson (1989) points out, the distribution of *both* argues against this approach. It can be inserted after but not before *gave* in (68), as the following illustrate:

(69)   Kim gave both a book to Sandy and a record to Lee
(70)   *Kim both gave a book to Sandy and a record to Lee

This suggests that the first conjunct must be *a book to Sandy* not *gave a book to Sandy* and hence that examples like (68) do not involve conjoined VPs. Clearly, there is an important problem here.[10]

7.6   Summary

In this chapter, we have looked at four more important types of syntactic structure. First, we considered specifier–head structures, which for standard versions of Modern PSG do not subsume subject–predicate structures. Then we looked at adjuncts, which remain a relatively understudied type of structure. Next we considered marker–head structures, a type of structure whose existence some would question. Finally, we looked at coordinate structures, a type of structure which has figured prominently in Modern PSG, especially GPSG.

Notes

1 Netter (1994) points out that Pollard and Sag's (1994) analysis of specifiers involves structures which cannot be represented by directed acyclic graphs. This is because the value of SPEC in the specifier is the head and the value of SPR in the head is the specifier. One might regard this as a weakness.
2 Nerbonne et al. (1989) propose that the bracketed expressions in the following are NPs with a phonologically empty head which takes a specifier and optionally a PP complement headed by *of*:

   (i)   Scarves were on sale. Al bought [several] made in China.

   (ii) Al knew [several of the girls]

   Some recent HPSG work, e.g. Pollard and Sag (1994: ch. 9) and Sag and Fodor (1994), has sought to avoid empty categories. If empty categories are unacceptable, Nerbonne et al.'s analysis must be rejected.
3 For an analysis of Swedish NPs which makes crucial use of Pollard and Sag's analysis of specifiers, see Börjars (1994). For an HPSG analysis of Greek NPs, see Kolliakou (1995).
4 The assumption that *not* is a head is criticized from within P&P by Baker (1991) and Ernst (1992). Warner (1993a, 1993b) proposes within HPSG that *not* is an extra complement. The idea that it is sometimes an extra complement is implicit in Gazdar, Pullum and Sag (1982).

5 There have been a number of attempts in the P&P literature to show that coordinate structures are instantiations of types of structure that occur elsewhere. For some critical discussion, see Borsley (1994).

6 Warner (1989) proposes within a version of GPSG that a conjunction and its sister are co-heads.

7 Proudian and Goddeau (1987) develop an approach to coordinate structures within early HPSG, in which conjuncts are heads as in GPSG. They propose that the mother of a pair of heads is the unification[+] of the heads. The unification[+] of a pair of feature values is the unification if one exists, otherwise it is the distinguished value CONFL. A feature can only have this value in a position where it is not required to have any specific value.

8 For further discussion of coordination from an HPSG standpoint, see Cooper (1990: ch. 5).

9 In chapter 6, we mentioned the proposal that the French auxiliary *avoir* takes as its complements a past participle and whatever complements the past participle requires. Given this proposal, an example like the following from exercise 2 of chapter 6 will be a further instance of non-constituent coordination.

(i) Paul a   parlé   avec Marie et   compris   son erreur.
Paul has spoken with Mary and understood his mistake
'Paul has spoken with Mary and understood his mistake.'

10 An important feature of a number of languages, e.g. Russian and Polish, is what is known as comitative coordination, coordination involving what looks like a preposition meaning 'with'. The following Russian example illustrates:

(i) Anna   s   Petej   napisali pis'mo.
Anna(NOM) with Peter(INST) wrote-PL letter
'Anna and Peter wrote a letter.'

A GPSG analysis of such examples is presented in McNally (1993). A rather different GPSG analysis of Polish comitative coordination is presented in Dyla (1988).

Exercises

1   Provide HPSG analyses, using the SPR and COMPS features, for the items in bold in the following examples. Assume that *so* is a Deg (degree word) and *three miles* and *three minutes* MPs (measure phrases).

(1) this **story** about Kim
(2) so **fond** of spiders
(3) the **fact** that he was late
(4) three miles **from** the village
(5) the **attempt** to break the record

(6) the **presentation** of the cup to the winner
(7) so **certain** that he was right
(8) three minutes **before** Kim arrived

2   The following examples might be used to provide an argument against the view that determiners are heads and in favour of the view that they are specifiers. Explain how.

(1) This man was late.
(2) *This men were late.
(3) This man and woman were late.

3   Given standard HPSG assumptions about NPs, it is not easy to ensure the correct distribution of prenominal adjectives. One might assume that the value of MOD in a prenominal adjective is N[SPR<[ ]>] or that is N[SPR<>]. Show how neither assumption will account for the following data:

(1) the old men
(2) old men
(3) *old the men

4   How, given the view of coordinate structures outlined in 7.5, could one account for the following data and especially the contrast between (1c) and (2c)?

(1) a. Kim is a linguist.
     b. Kim is trying to understand Chomsky.
     c. Kim is a linguist and trying to understand Chomsky.

(2) a. Kim has a new car.
     b. Kim has gone for a drive.
     c. *Kim has a new car and gone for a drive.

5   The following examples show that Welsh verbs and prepositions show agreement with the first conjunct of a coordinate.

(1) a. Gwelais i ac Emrys ddraig.
         saw-1SG I and Emrys dragon
         'I and Emrys saw a dragon.'

     b. Gwelodd Emrys a   fi ddraig.
         saw   Emrys and I dragon
         'Emrys and I saw a dragon.'

(2) a. Mae Gwyn yn edrych amdanaf i ac   Emrys.
       is   Gwyn in look   for-1SG I and Emrys
       'Gwyn is looking for me and Emrys.'

   b. Mae Gwyn yn edrych am Emrys a   fi
      is   Gwyn in look   for Emrys and I
      'Gwyn is looking for Emrys and me.'

Discuss the implications of this for the view of coordinate structures presented in 7.5.

8 Raising and Control

8.1 Introduction

A central concern of syntactic theory since Rosenbaum (1967) has been the analysis of what I will refer to here as raising and control sentences. These are labels that are very widely used, although the second type are sometimes known as equi sentences and the term 'control sentence' is sometimes applied to both types. (1) is a typical raising sentence and (2) a typical control sentence.

(1)   Kim seemed to impress Sandy.
(2)   Kim hoped to impress Sandy.

As is clear from these examples, some raising and control sentences are superficially very similar. However, they differ in a variety of ways. Raising and control sentences have figured prominently in both GPSG and HPSG. Their approaches share certain assumptions but they also differ in important ways. In this chapter, we will begin by introducing some basic data and some basic assumptions. Then we will look at the GPSG[1] and HPSG[2] approaches. Finally we will consider some further data.

8.2 Preliminaries

What are the main properties of raising and control sentences? Both types of sentence involve a predicative expression, typically an infinitival VP, with no overt subject in the sense of a constituent with which it combines to form a clause, but with some expression which is understood as its subject although it does not combine with it to form a clause. I will call the expression which is understood as subject a raised subject in raising sentences and a controller in control sentences. Both the raised subject in (1) and the controller in (2) are subjects. It is clear that controllers can also be objects or objects of a preposition. Relevant examples are (3) and (4), in which *Sandy* is the controller.

(3) Kim persuaded Sandy to go home.
(4) Kim appealed to Sandy to go home.

It is assumed in Modern PSG, as in certain other frameworks such as Lexical Functional Grammar, that raised subjects can also be objects. The following is a relevant example:

(5) Kim expected Sandy to go home.

This, however, is a controversial assumption that is rejected in P&P. For P&P, the string *Sandy to go home* is a clause. Hence, *Sandy* is an ordinary subject and not a raised subject. As we will see in chapter 11, the P&P view is incompatible with standard PSG approaches to passives. For a defence of the PSG view and criticism of the P&P view, see Postal and Pullum (1988) and Pollard and Sag (1994: ch. 3).

How do raising and control sentences differ? There are two main differences. The most obvious one is that a raised subject can be any category at all as long as it is compatible with the predicative expression, while a controller can only be a normal, non-expletive NP. Thus, we have the contrasts like the following:

(6) a. It seemed to be easy to impress Kim.
     b. There seemed to be a fly in the soup.

(7) a. *It hoped to be easy to impress Kim.
     b. *There hoped to be a fly in the soup.

(8) a. Kim expected it to be easy to impress Sandy.
     b. Kim expected there to be a fly in the soup.

(9) a. *Kim persuaded it to be easy to impress Sandy.
     b. *Kim persuaded there to be a fly in the soup.

Another difference involves the paraphrases that typical raising and control sentences have. (1) and (2) have the following paraphrases:

(10) It seemed that Kim impressed Sandy.
(11) Kim hoped that he would impress Sandy.

(10) has an expletive subject, whereas (11) has the same subject as (2). (3) and (5) have the following paraphrases:

(12)   Kim persuaded Sandy that she should go home.
(13)   Kim expected that Sandy would go home.

(12) has two complements, whereas (13) has just a single complement.

For P&P, both raising and control complements are clauses with empty subjects. For Modern PSG, following Brame (1975, 1976), they are VPs or other subjectless categories. Thus, (1) has something like the structure in (14), and (5) has the structure in (15).

(14)

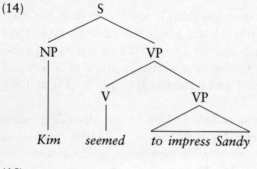

(15)

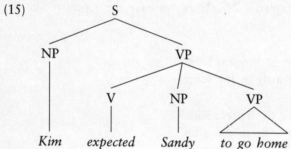

(2) has a structure like (14), and (3) a structure like (15). A satisfactory analysis of raising and control sentences must ensure that the constituent that functions as subject of the predicative expression conforms to the expression's subject requirements and that the controller in a control sentence is a normal NP. It should also provide a basis for explaining the different types of paraphrases that raising and control sentences have.

8.3   The GPSG approach

We turn now to the GPSG approach to raising and control sentences outlined in Gazdar et al. (1985). As we will see, central to the GPSG approach is the Control Agreement Principle (CAP), which we introduced in chapter 6.

We can look first at sentences like (5) in which the raised subect is an object, and sentences like (3) in which the controller is an object. In such examples, the predicative expression and the expression which is understood as its subject are sisters although they do not combine to form a clause. Recall that for GPSG, what sort of subject a predicative expression requires is encoded in the AGR feature. Thus, we need to ensure that the NP complement is identical to the value of AGR on the VP complement. In other words, we need to ensure that sentences like (3) and (5) involve local trees of the following form, where α stands for the features that distinguish different types of NPs:

(16)

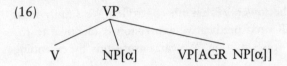

$$\text{V} \qquad \text{NP}[\alpha] \qquad \text{VP}[\text{AGR NP}[\alpha]]$$

The CAP employs a notion of controller which is different from but related to that introduced in this chapter. In chapter (6) we formulated it as follows:

(17)   CONTROL AGREEMENT PRINCIPLE (preliminary version)
       The value of a CONTROL feature in a category is identical to the controller of the category if it has one.

Gazdar et al. (1985) propose that verbs like *persuade* and *expect* combine semantically first with their VP complement and then with their NP complement. In other words, they have the following semantic type:

(18)   <VP,<NP,<NP,S>>>

They propose that the NP is the controller of the VP in this situation. We can express this as follows:

(19)   When a verb, an NP, and a predicative expression are sisters and the verb combines semantically first with the predicative expression and then with the NP, the NP is the controller of the predicative expression.

Given this, the NP in (16) will be the controller of the VP, and the CAP will ensure that the NP is identical to the value of AGR on the VP, as required. Thus, it will allow *Kim expected there to be a problem* while ruling out **Kim expected there to like Lee.*

We can turn now to sentences like (1), in which the raised subject is a subject, and sentences like (2), in which the controller is a subject. In such examples, we need to ensure that the value of AGR in the main VP is identical to the value of AGR in the VP complement. In other words, we need to ensure that we have the following structure:

(20)

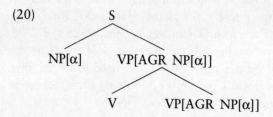

Notice that in this structure, the lower VP has no controller. We simply need to ensure that the value of AGR on a predicative expression is identical to the value of AGR in its mother in this situation. We can ensure this by extending the CAP as follows:

(21)   CONTROL AGREEMENT PRINCIPLE (revised version)
       The value of a CONTROL feature in a category is identical to the controller of the category if it has one. If there is no controller, it is identical to the value of the mother's CONTROL feature.

This will allow *There seemed to be a problem* while ruling out *There seemed to like Kim*. An important point to note here is that the two different types of raising sentence involve two different clauses of the CAP. One might agree with Jacobson (1987b) that this is a weakness of the GPSG approach.

So far, we have seen how the GPSG analysis ensures that the constituent that functions as subject of the predicative expression conforms to the expression's subject requirements. As we have said, a satisfactory analysis must also ensure that the controller in a control sentence is a normal NP. This is ensured by the ID rules with which control verbs are associated. *Persuade* is associated with the ID rule in (22) and *hope* with the ID rule in (23).

(22)   VP $\longrightarrow$ H°, NP VP[INF,AGR NP[NORM]]
(23)   VP $\longrightarrow$ H°, VP[INF,AGR NP[NORM]]

These stipulate that the VP complement requires a normal NP as its subject and thus rule out (7) and (9), repeated here for convenience.

(7)   a.   *It hoped to be easy to impress Kim.
       b.   *There hoped to be a fly in the soup.

(9)   a.   *Kim persuaded it to be easy to impress Sandy.
       b.   *Kim persuaded there to be a fly in the soup.

In contrast, *expect* is associated with the ID rule in (24) and *seem* with the ID rule in (25).

(24) VP $\longrightarrow$ H°, NP VP[INF]
(25) VP $\longrightarrow$ H°, VP[INF]

These allow the VP complement to require any kind of subject and hence allow the examples in (6) and (8).

(6) a. It seemed to be easy to impress Kim.
    b. There seemed to be a fly in the soup.

(8) a. Kim expected it to be easy to impress Sandy.
    b. Kim expected there to be a fly in the soup.

We can now consider the different types of paraphrases that raising and control sentences have. Gazdar et al. (1985) propose that *seem* and *expect* correspond to the same semantic constant in both raising and non-raising sentences but that they combine with a semantic combinator f_R in raising sentences. This converts an <S,S> into a <VP<NP,S>> and an <S,<NP,S>> into <VP,<NP,<NP,S>>>. Similarly, they propose that *hope* and *persuade* correspond to the same semantic constant in control and non-control sentences, but that they combine with a semantic combinator f_E in control sentences. This converts an <S,<NP,S>> into a <VP,<NP,S>> and an <S,<NP,<NP,S>>> into <VP,<NP,<NP,S>>>. Thus, we have the following semantic types:

(26) seem′   <S,S>
      expect′   <S,<NP,S>>
      f_R(seem′)   <VP,<NP,S>>
      f_R(expect′)   <VP,<NP,<NP,S>>>
      hope′   <S,<NP,S>>
      persuade′   <S,<NP,<NP,S>>>
      f_E(hope′)   <VP,<NP,S>>
      f_E(persuade′)   <VP,<NP,<NP,S>>>

The two semantic combinators are associated with meaning postulates which ensure that a raising sentence has the same interpretation as a related non-raising sentence and that a control sentence has the same interpretation as a related non-control sentence.

Any theory of control must accommodate the verb *promise* in examples like the following:

(27) Kim promised Sandy to go home.

Here, the subject *Kim* and not the object *Sandy* is the controller of the infinitive. Gazdar et al. (1985) point out that this is expected if *promise* has the following semantic type:

(28)   <NP,<VP,<NP,S>>>

With this semantic type, the object will not control the VP complement, as it does with *persuade*. Gazdar et al. argue that this analysis of *promise* can account for Visser's generalization, the generalization that subject control verbs do not passivize. The following illustrates:

(29)   *Sandy was promised to leave (by Kim).

They propose that passive participles are derived from active verbs by a lexical rule, which makes the penultimate argument of a verb the final argument if and only if it is an NP or an S. (See chapter 11.) Given the semantic type in (28), the penultimate argument of *promise* is a VP. Hence, the rule will not apply. A problem for this explanation arises from the behaviour of *promise* when it is not a control verb. Here, corresponding to the active sentences in (30) we have the passives in (31):

(30)   a.   Sandy promised Kim a good reference.
       b.   Sandy promised Kim that he would be allowed a holiday.

(31)   a.   Kim was promised a good reference (by Sandy).
       b.   Kim was promised (by Sandy) that he would be allowed a holiday.

This suggests that the goal argument of *promise* is the penultimate argument when it is not a control verb. If this is right, however, it seems dubious to claim that the goal argument of *promise* is the antepenultimate argument when it is a control verb.

One further matter that we should consider is the rather similar distribution of controlled infinitives and clauses. Examples like the following provide a partial illustration:

(32)   a.   Kim expects to be here.
       b.   Kim expects that Sandy will be here.

(33)   a.   Kim wondered whether to leave.
       b.   Kim wondered whether Sandy should leave.

(34)   a.   Kim arranged to see Sandy.
       b.   Kim arranged for Lee to see Sandy.

(35)   a.   The man to talk to is here.
       b.   The man for you to talk to is here.

Such data suggest that controlled infinitives and clauses form a natural class, as suggested in Borsley (1983, 1984). GPSG treats them as such by assigning both VP and S to the category V^2 and distinguishing them with the feature SUBJ, VP being [SUBJ −] and S being [SUBJ +]. This does not by itself provide an account of the above data, but it provides a plausible basis for such an account.

8.4   The HPSG approach

We now consider the HPSG approach to raising and control sentences. We begin with raising sentences.

For HPSG, the central property of raised subjects is that they are not semantic arguments of the heads of which they are syntactic dependants. They also have all the syntactic and semantic properties of the unexpressed subject of a predicative complement. *Seem* will have the schematic sign in (36).

(36) $\begin{bmatrix} \text{SUBJ} <[1]> \\ \text{COMPS} <\text{VP}[\textit{inf}, \text{SUBJ} <[1]>] : [2]> \\ \text{CONTENT} \begin{bmatrix} \text{RELATION } \textit{seem} \\ \text{SOA–ARG } [2] \end{bmatrix} \end{bmatrix}$

Following standard practice, I use 'A:B' here for a category A whose semantic content is B. (36) shows that the complement is the only semantic argument, and the subject not an argument, and that the subject has all the properties of the unexpressed subject of the predicative complement. Since the subject is not a semantic argument, it can be an expletive if that is what the complement requires. Thus, this allows *There seemed to be a problem* but not *There seemed to like Kim*. *Expect* will have the schematic sign in (37).

(37) $\begin{bmatrix} \text{SUBJ} <\text{NP}_{[1]}> \\ \text{COMPS} <[2]\text{NP},\text{VP}[\textit{inf},\text{SUBJ} <[2]>] : [3]> \\ \text{CONTENT} \begin{bmatrix} \text{RELATION } \textit{expect} \\ \text{EXPECTER } [1]\textit{ref} \\ \text{SOA-ARG } [3] \end{bmatrix} \end{bmatrix}$

This shows that the subject and predicative complement are semantic arguments but that the object is not a semantic argument, and that the object has all the syntactic and semantic properties of the unexpressed subject of the predicative complement. Since the object is not a semantic argument, it can be an expletive if that is what the predicative complement requires. Hence, this allows *Kim expected there to be a problem* but not **Kim expected there to like Lee*.

Pollard and Sag (1994) propose that the structure-sharing in signs like (36) and (37) is a consequence of what they call the Raising Principle. We noted in chapter 6 that they assume both SUBJ and COMPS features and a SUBCAT feature. If we assume all three features, we can formulate the principle as follows:

(38)   RAISING PRINCIPLE
       Let E be a lexical entry whose SUBCAT list L contains an element X not specified as expletive. Then X is lexically assigned no semantic role in the content of E if and only if the COMPS list also contains a Y[SUBJ <X>].

The reference to an element in a SUBCAT list covers both subjects and complements. Thus, this essentially says that a non-expletive subject or complement can be assigned no semantic role only if it functions as the subject of a predicative complement.

We turn now to control sentences. Unlike raised subjects, controllers are assigned a semantic role and they share only an index with the unexpressed subject of the predicative complement. *Hope* will have the following schematic sign:

(39) $\begin{bmatrix} \text{SUBJ} <NP_{[1]}> \\ \text{COMPS} <VP[\textit{inf},\text{SUBJ} <NP_{[1]}>] : [2]> \\ \text{CONTENT} \begin{bmatrix} \text{RELATION } \textit{hope} \\ \text{EXPERIENCER } [1]\textit{ref} \\ \text{SOA-ARG } [2] \end{bmatrix} \end{bmatrix}$

Notice that we have the generalized role EXPERIENCER here. Since the subject is a semantic argument, it cannot be an expletive. Thus, the examples in (7), repeated here for convenience, are correctly ruled out.

(7)   a.   *It hoped to be easy to impress Kim.
       b.   *There hoped to be a fly in the soup.

Persuade in (3) will have the schematic sign in (40).

(40)
$$
\begin{bmatrix}
\text{SUBJ } <\text{NP}_{[1]}> \\
\text{COMPS } <\text{NP}_{[2]},\text{VP}[inf,\text{SUBJ } <\text{NP}_{[2]}>] : [3]> \\
\text{CONTENT }
\begin{bmatrix}
\text{RELATION } persuade \\
\text{INFLUENCE } [1]ref \\
\text{INFLUENCED } [2]ref \\
\text{SOA-ARG } [3]
\end{bmatrix}
\end{bmatrix}
$$

Again, we have generalized roles, INFLUENCE and INFLUENCED, here. Since the object is a semantic argument, it cannot be an expletive. Thus, the examples in (9) are correctly excluded.

(9) a.   *Kim persuaded it to be easy to impress Sandy.
   b.   *Kim persuaded there to be a fly in the soup.

Pollard and Sag argue that which NP is the controller in a control sentence is not an arbitrary matter. Rather, it is predictable from the meaning of the sentence. They propose that there are three main classes of control verbs: (1) those that express a relation of *influence*, e.g. *persuade, order, permit, advise*; (2) those that express a relation of *commitment*, e.g. *promise, agree, try, intend, refuse*; and (3) those that express a relation of *orientation*, e.g. *hope, want* and *need*. Which NP is the controller is predicted for these three classes by what they call Control Theory, which can be formulated within the revised version of HPSG as follows:

(41)   CONTROL THEORY
    If the CONTENT of an unsaturated phrase is the SOA-ARG in a *psoa* whose relation is a control relation, then the SUBJ element of the phrase is coindexed with the INFLUENCED, COMMITTOR, or EXPERIENCER value in that *psoa*, according as the control relation is of sort *influence*, *commitment*, or *orientation*, respectively.

Control Theory is just one part of the HPSG analysis of control sentences. As we will see in chapter 10, some of the properties of control sentences are accounted for by a condition on anaphors. We will also see there how HPSG accounts for Visser's generalization.

Pollard and Sag (1994) pay considerable attention to certain apparent counterexamples to Control Theory exemplified by the following:

(42)   Kim promised Sandy to be allowed to attend the party.

Here, the controller is the object *Sandy* and not the subject *Kim*, as Control Theory would appear to predict. This contrasts with the following, where the controller is the subject as expected:

(43)   Kim promised Sandy to attend the party.

Pollard and Sag point out that it is not only where the complement is passivized that an apparently unexpected controller occurs. They cite the following:

(44)   Grandma promised the children to be able to stay up for the late show.

They argue that such cases of controller-shift arise from what they call 'coercion', the reinterpretation of a constituent to fit into a context into which its standard interpretation does not fit. They suggest that coercion is involved in an example like the following:

(45)   They promised us to be on time.

Here, to fit into its context, the infinitival complement has to be interpreted as 'to act in a way that would ensure that they were on time'. In this case, coercion does not produce controller-shift. It does, however, in (42) and (44). In (42), the infinitival complement is interpreted as 'to cause Sandy to be allowed to attend the party'. Thus, the normal controller is understood as the causer, but is not interpreted as subject of the complement. In (44), the infinitival complement is interpreted as 'to cause the children to be able to stay up for the late show'. Again, then, the normal controller is understood as the causer, but not as the subject of the complement. Pollard and Sag suggest that the process of coercion in (42) and (44) is the result of a lexical rule, which we can formulate as follows:

(46)   COERCION LEXICAL RULE

$$
\begin{bmatrix}
\text{COMPS} < \dots, \text{VP[SUBJ <NP}_{[1]}\text{>]} : [2], \dots > \\
\text{CONTENT} \begin{bmatrix} \text{RELN } \textit{commitment} \vee \textit{influence} \\ \text{SOA-ARG } [2] \end{bmatrix}
\end{bmatrix} \implies
$$

$$
\begin{bmatrix}
\text{COMPS} < \dots, \text{VP[SUBJ <NP>]} : [3], \dots > \\
\text{CONTENT|SOA} \begin{bmatrix} \text{RELN } \textit{i-cause} \\ \text{INFLUENCE } [1] \\ \text{SOA-ARG } [3] \end{bmatrix}
\end{bmatrix}
$$

This rule applies to lexical signs interpreted as a relation of the sort *commitment* or the sort *influence*, and derives a lexical sign with a more complex CONTENT value, in which the interpretation of the infinitival complement is an argument not of the basic relation but of the relation *i-cause* which has the index of the normal controller as its other argument. Applied to the basic lexical sign for *promise* in (47), this will give the lexical sign in (48):

(47) $$\begin{bmatrix} \text{SUBJ} <\text{NP}_{[1]}> \\ \text{COMPS} <(\text{NP}_{[4]}),\text{VP[SUBJ} <\text{NP}_{[1]}>] : [2]> \\ \text{CONTENT} \begin{bmatrix} \text{RELN } promise \\ \text{COMMITTOR [1]} \\ \text{COMMISSEE [4]} \\ \text{SOA-ARG [2]} \end{bmatrix} \end{bmatrix}$$

(48) $$\begin{bmatrix} \text{SUBJ} <\text{NP}_{[1]}> \\ \text{COMPS} <(\text{NP}_{[4]}),\text{VP[SUBJ} <\text{NP}>] : [3]> \\ \text{CONTENT} \begin{bmatrix} \text{RELN } promise \\ \text{COMMITTOR [1]} \\ \text{COMMISSEE [4]} \\ \text{SOA-ARG} \begin{bmatrix} \text{RELN } i\text{-}cause \\ \text{INFLUENCE [1]} \\ \text{SOA-ARG [3]} \end{bmatrix} \end{bmatrix} \end{bmatrix}$$

Nothing in (48) specifies how the unexpressed subject of the infinitival complement should be interpreted. However, the condition on anaphors that we will consider in chapter 10 will ensure that the unexpressed subject is coindexed with a less oblique argument of verb. This will normally be the object, as in (42) and (44), but it need not be, as (49) illustrates:

(49) Jim promised Mary to be allowed to get himself a new dog.

Pollard and Sag note that this is difficult to contextualize because it involves imagining a complex situation where Jim causes himself to be allowed to get a new dog, but it is clearly grammatical.

An important proposal in Pollard and Sag (1994) is that certain infinitives are preceded by an empty complementizer. They point out that there are a number of environments in which a clause must have a complementizer, notably sentence fragments, subject position, and focus position in pseudo clefts. The following illustrate:

(50) What did they prefer?
      For Kim to be reassigned.
      *Kim to be reassigned.

(51) What did they believe?
      That they will be reassigned.
      *They will be reassigned.

(52) a. That Dana was unhappy was obvious.
      b. *Dana was unhappy was obvious.
      c. For Pat to resign would be unfortunate.
      d. *Pat to resign would be unfortunate.

(53) a. What they promised was that Kim would be reassigned.
      b. *What they promised was Kim would be reassigned.
      c. What they preferred was for Kim to be reassigned.
      d. *What they preferred was Kim to be reassigned.

They go on to point out that infinitives also appear in these environments provided that they require a non-expletive subject. We have examples like the following:

(54) What did they prefer?
      To be reassigned.

(55) To resign would be difficult.

(56) What they preferred was to be reassigned.

They propose that these infinitives contain an empty complementizer, essentially an empty counterpart of *for*, in other words that they involve something like the following structure:[3]

(57)   VP[*inf,for*]

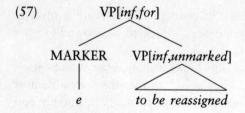

       MARKER   VP[*inf,unmarked*]
         |
         e   to be reassigned

The empty complementizer will have the following category:

(58) [MARKING *for*, SPEC VP[*inf*,SUBJ <NP_{ref}>]]

Notice that this category embodies the assumption that the infinitive with which the empty complementizer combines is one that requires a referential subject. This accounts for the impossibility of the following examples:

(59) What did they prefer?
      *To rain.

(60) *To rain would be difficult.

(61) *What they preferred was to rain.

Pollard and Sag (1994: 140–2) also argue that their analysis provides a natural explanation for certain contrasts between raising and control sentences discussed in Jacobson (1990). Firstly, there is the fact that null-complement anaphora is often possible with control verbs but is not possible with raising verbs. We have a contrast between the control sentences in (62) and (63) and the raising sentences in (64) and (65).

(62) Sandy read the article but Kim refused/forgot.

(63) They persuaded/asked/told/ordered Kim to leave but I don't think they've persuaded/asked/told/ordered Sandy yet.

(64) *Sandy seems/happens/appears/tends to be obnoxious but I don't think that Kim seems/happens/appears/tends.

(65) *They consider/believe/report Sandy to be clever but I don't think they consider/believe/report Kim.

Pollard and Sag argue that the ungrammatical examples are ruled out by the Raising Principle. On the assumption that null-complement anaphora is a lexical process that removes an infinitival complement from a COMPS list, they contain a verb with a SUBCAT list containing a non-expletive element X which is assigned no semantic role and no Y[SUBJ <X>] in the COMPS list. Secondly, there is the fact that control verbs but not raising verbs often allow an NP or a PP complement. The following illustrate:

(66) Sandy $\begin{Bmatrix} \text{tried} \\ \text{attempted} \\ \text{wants} \end{Bmatrix}$ something.

(67)   *Sandy $\begin{Bmatrix} \text{seems} \\ \text{happens} \\ \text{tends} \end{Bmatrix}$ something.

These also violate the Raising Principle since their NP complements are SUBJ <>.

8.5   Some further data

We have now considered how GPSG and HPSG accommodate standard raising and control structures. In this final section, we will consider some further data. In particular, we will consider some non-standard raising structures. We will concentrate on how they can be analysed within HPSG.

In standard raising structures, the predicative expression is an infinitival VP. However, there are various raising structures in which the predicative expression is something other than an infinitival VP. Firstly, there are examples where the predicative expression is a bare VP complement. Modals like *may* are an important example. Examples like the following suggest that *may* is a raising word:

(68)   a.   It may be easy to impress Kim.
       b.   There may be a fly in the soup.

The idea that modals are raising words goes back to Ross (1969). It is assumed within GPSG in Gazdar et al. (1982) and within HPSG in Warner (1993a, 1993b). It is also assumed within P&P in Koopman and Sportiche (1991). Within HPSG, the obvious suggestion is that *may* involves the following schematic sign:

(69) $\begin{bmatrix} \text{SUBJ} <[1]> \\ \text{COMPS} <\text{VP}[\textit{base},\text{SUBJ} <[1]>] : [2]> \\ \text{CONTENT} \begin{bmatrix} \text{RELATION } \textit{may} \\ \text{SOA-ARG} [2] \end{bmatrix} \end{bmatrix}$

Much like the modals but non-finite is infinitival *to*. Examples like the following suggest that it is a raising word:

(70)   a.   It essential for it to be easy to impress Kim.
       b.   It is essential for there to be a fly in the soup.

Again, this is the view that is taken in Gazdar et al. (1982) and Warner (1993a, 1993b), and in Koopman and Sportiche (1991).[4]

With both modals and *to*, the raised subject is a subject. There also seem to be raising structures where the predicative expression is a bare VP and the raised subject is an object. Consider the following:

(71) They made it appear easy to impress Kim.

Examples like this suggest that *make* involves the following schematic sign:

(72)
$$\begin{bmatrix} \text{SUBJ} <NP_{[1]}> \\ \text{COMPS} <[2]NP,VP[\textit{base},\text{SUBJ} <[2]>] : [3]> \\ \text{CONTENT} \begin{bmatrix} \text{RELATION } \textit{make} \\ \text{MAKER } [1]\textit{ref} \\ \text{SOA-ARG } [3] \end{bmatrix} \end{bmatrix}$$

Further non-standard raising structures arise with the auxiliaries *have* and *be*. Again the idea that these are raising words goes back to Ross (1969) and is developed in GPSG by Gazdar et al. (1982) and in HPSG by Warner (1993a, 1993b). Examples like the following suggest that *have* is a raising word:

(73) a. It has been easy to impress Kim.
b. There has been a fly in the soup.

Apart from being an auxiliary, the important fact about *have* is that the predicative expression is a past participle VP. Here, then, we will have the following schematic sign:

(74)
$$\begin{bmatrix} \text{SUBJ} <[1]> \\ \text{COMPS} <VP[\textit{past-part},\text{SUBJ} <[1]>] : [2]> \\ \text{CONTENT} \begin{bmatrix} \text{RELATION } \textit{have} \\ \text{SOA-ARG } [2] \end{bmatrix} \end{bmatrix}$$

Turning to *be*, examples like the following suggest that it is a raising word:

(75) It is raining.
(76) It is said that Kim is ill.
(77) It is obvious that Sandy is a spy.

These examples show that *be* can take a number of different predicative complements. It can also take a PP or an NP complement. These are presumably predicative as well. Here, then, we can propose the following schematic sign:

(78)
$$
\begin{bmatrix}
\text{SUBJ} <[1]> \\
\text{COMPS} <\text{XP[PRD +,SUBJ} <[1]>] : [2]> \\
\text{CONTENT} \begin{bmatrix} \text{RELATION } be \\ \text{SOA-ARG } [2] \end{bmatrix}
\end{bmatrix}
$$

A further point to note about *be* is that there are cases where the complement is a raising structure or a control structure, for example (79) and (80), respectively.

(79)   Kim is likely to impress Sandy.
(80)   Kim is eager to impress Sandy.

To provide for such examples within HPSG, all we need to do is to assign *likely* and *eager* to signs like those assigned to *seem* and *try*, respectively.

Be is not the only raising word that allows a present participle VP as its complement. Others are the aspectual verbs *begin*, *continue* and *stop*. The following illustrate:

(81)   It $\begin{Bmatrix} \text{began} \\ \text{continued} \\ \text{stopped} \end{Bmatrix}$ raining.

For these verbs we need signs like the following:

(82)
$$
\begin{bmatrix}
\text{SUBJ} <[1]> \\
\text{COMPS} <\text{VP[}pres\text{-}part\text{,SUBJ} <[1]>] : [2]> \\
\text{CONTENT} \begin{bmatrix} \text{RELATION } begin \\ \text{SOA-ARG } [2] \end{bmatrix}
\end{bmatrix}
$$

Be is also not the only raising word that allows a non-verbal complement. The following illustrate some other raising words with this property:

(83)   It seemed easy to make an impression.
(84)   We found it easy to make an impression.

Here, we need the following lexical signs:

(85)
$$\begin{bmatrix} \text{SUBJ} <[1]> \\ \text{COMPS} <\text{AP[SUBJ} <[1]>] : [2]> \\ \text{CONTENT} \begin{bmatrix} \text{RELATION } seem \\ \text{SOA-ARG} [2] \end{bmatrix} \end{bmatrix}$$

(86)
$$\begin{bmatrix} \text{SUBJ} <\text{NP}_{[1]}> \\ \text{COMPS} <[2]\text{NP,AP[SUBJ} <[2]>] : [3]> \\ \text{CONTENT} \begin{bmatrix} \text{RELATION } find \\ \text{FINDER } [1]ref \\ \text{SOA-ARG} [3] \end{bmatrix} \end{bmatrix}$$

One point that we should note here is that the combination of raised subject and adjectival predicate in (84) would be analysed in P&P as a small clause. As we shall see in chapter 11, the P&P view is incompatible with standard PSG approaches to passives.[5]

We can now look briefly at non-canonical control structures. These seem to be less common than non-canonical raising structures. Thus, while we have both *Kim seems to be clever* and *Kim seems clever*, we only have *Kim tries to be clever* and not **Kim tries clever*. There are, however, some control structures with an ING VP. Consider the following:

(87)   Kim considered resigning.
(88)   Kim remembered going there.

Both seem to be control sentences. For *consider* in (87), we might propose the following schematic sign:

(89)
$$\begin{bmatrix} \text{SUBJ} <\text{NP}_{[1]}> \\ \text{COMPS} <\text{VP[}pres\text{-}part\text{,SUBJ} <\text{NP}_{[1]}>] : [2]> \\ \text{CONTENT} \begin{bmatrix} \text{RELATION } consider \\ \text{EXPERIENCER } [1]ref \\ \text{SOA-ARG} [2] \end{bmatrix} \end{bmatrix}$$

Pollard and Sag (1994: 133) suggest that the following are control sentences:

(90)   Kim felt hot.
(91)   Kim looked ill.

This suggests that we need a schematic sign like the following:

(92) $\begin{bmatrix} \text{SUBJ} <\text{NP}_{[1]}> \\ \text{COMPS} <\text{AP[SUBJ} <\text{NP}_{[1]}>] : [2]> \\ \text{CONTENT} \begin{bmatrix} \text{RELATION } feel \\ \text{EXPERIENCER } [1]ref \\ \text{SOA-ARG } [2] \end{bmatrix} \end{bmatrix}$

8.6 Summary

In this chapter, we have looked at raising and control sentences, considering first the GPSG approach and then the HPSG approach. This is an area where the two frameworks differ quite considerably. However, in both, it is an area in which semantics is very important. We will say more about the HPSG approach to control in chapter 10.

Notes

1 GPSG ideas on control and raising sentences are presented in Gazdar et al. (1985: ch. 5.3, ch. 6.2). See also Klein and Sag (1985).
2 HPSG ideas about control and raising sentences are presented in Pollard and Sag (1994: ch. 3, ch. 7) and Sag and Pollard (1991).
3 Some recent HPSG work, e.g. Pollard and Sag (1994: ch. 9) and Sag and Fodor (1994), has sought to eliminate empty categories. If empty categories are to be eliminated the empty complementizer analysis in (57) will have to be rejected.
4 It is assumed in both GPSG and HPSG that infinitival *to* is not just a raising word but a raising verb. This view was first advanced in Pullum (1982a).
5 The history of English auxiliaries is discussed and analysed in HPSG terms in Warner (1993a), and one aspect of this history is explored in more detail in Warner (1995).

Exercises

1   Consider the implications of the following examples for either GPSG or HPSG ideas about raising sentences.

(1)   It looks like there is going to be a storm.
(2)   There looks like there is going to be a storm.
(3)   *There looks like it is going to rain.

2   As we noted in chapter 3, the feature specification defaults (FSDs) assumed in GPSG include the following:

(1)   [NFORM] ⊃ [NFORM NORM]

Show how examples like the following create a problem for this FSD given a simple interpretation of how defaults function.

(2)   It seems to be raining.
(3)   There seems to a problem.

3   Provide HPSG analyses for the items in bold in the following examples. Decide first whether they are control or raising sentences. In connection with *seems*, recall the discussion of *appears* in chapter 4. Assume that *as* in (3) and (4) is a marker.

(1)   Kim **seemed** to Sandy to be unwell.
(2)   Kim **relied** on Sandy to be there.
(3)   Kim **sees** Sandy as a threat.
(4)   Kim **strikes** Sandy as a genius.
(5)   Kim **allowed** Sandy to go home.

4   Provide schematic HPSG signs for *took* in each of the following examples. Decide first whether *Kim* in (2) and (3) is a controller or a raised subject.

(1) It took three hours for Kim to read the paper.
(2) It took Kim three hours to read the paper.
(3) Kim took three hours to read the paper.

5   What problems do the following examples pose for views of control and coordination developed within GPSG and HPSG?

(1)   Kim expects to be here and that Lee will be here.
(2)   Kim arranged to see Sandy and for Lee to see Sandy.

9 Unbounded Dependencies

9.1 Introduction

Unbounded dependencies of the kind that are found in *wh*-questions such as the bracketed string in (1) and relative clauses such as the bracketed string in (2) were once seen as providing important evidence for a transformational approach to syntax (see, for example, Bresnan 1978).

(1) I wonder [who Kim talked to]
(2) This is the man [Kim talked to]

Not surprisingly, therefore, proponents of both GPSG and HPSG have been concerned to show that they can provide an elegant account of such dependencies. As was noted in chapter 1, this was in fact one of the central concerns of the earliest work in Modern PSG, Gazdar's 1979 papers, which laid the foundations of GPSG, and the demonstration in these papers that GPSG could provide an interesting account of unbounded dependencies was responsible for much of the early impact of the framework. This is an area in which GPSG and HPSG have quite similar analyses.[1] In this chapter, we will look first at the basic approach that the two frameworks adopt to unbounded dependencies. Then we will consider how they handle island constraints. Finally, we will look at some further unbounded dependency constructions.

9.2 The basic approach

A typical unbounded dependency involves a 'gap' in the sense that a normally obligatory constituent is missing, and some structure higher in the tree which licenses the gap in the sense that the gap would not be possible if the structure were not present. In some cases, the higher structure contains a constituent in a non-argument position which is interpreted as if it were in the position of the gap. We can call such a constituent a filler and the dependency a filler-gap dependency. In other cases, there is no such constituent. The *wh*-questions in (3) illustrate the first type, and the relatives in (4) illustrate the second type.

(3) a. Who did she talk to?
     b. *Did she talk to?
     c. *Who did she talk to him?

(4) a. This is the man she talked to.
     b. *She talked to.
     c. *This is the man she talked to him.

The (b) examples show that a normally obligatory constituent is missing in the (a) examples. The (c) examples show that a constituent must be missing. The motivation for the term 'unbounded dependency' comes from data like the following:

(5) a. Who does she regret that she talked to?
     b. Who did she say she regrets that she talked to?
     c. Who do you think she says she regrets that she talked to?

These examples show that the gap in an unbounded dependency construction can be indefinitely far from the higher licensing structure. One further point to note at the outset is that the filler and the gap in filler-gap dependencies generally have the same categorial status. The following illustrate:

(6) a. Who does she trust?
     b. *On whom does she trust?

(7) a. On whom does she depend?
     b. *Who does she depend?

As Kaplan and Bresnan (1982) note, there are examples where a clausal filler is associated with an NP gap, for example the following:

(8) That he might be wrong, he didn't think of.

These, however, are very much exceptions. In this section, we will concentrate on filler-gap dependencies. We will consider some unbounded dependencies in which there is no filler constituent in section 9.4.

As we have noted, GPSG and HPSG have very similar approaches to unbounded dependencies, which derive from Gazdar (1981a, 1981b), and we can introduce them together. As we noted in chapter 3, both employ a feature called SLASH to encode the fact that a constituent contains an unbounded dependency gap of some kind.[2] This appears within every category between the gap and the licensing higher structure. For GPSG, this is a category-valued feature. In most HPSG work its value is a set of LOCAL feature structures, although in Sag and Fodor (1994) it is a list of such structures. In GPSG, SLASH is one of a number of FOOT features. The others are a WH feature, which occurs in *wh*-questions and relatives, and a RE feature, which is central to the GPSG analysis of reflexives. Both are category-valued. In HPSG, SLASH is one of a number of NON-LOCAL features. The others are a WH feature, which occurs in *wh*-questions, and a REL feature, which occurs in relatives. The former takes as its value a set of nominal objects, and the latter takes a set of indices. For GPSG, the bracketed subordinate clause in (9) will have something like the structure in (10).

(9)   I wonder [who Kim talked to]

(10)

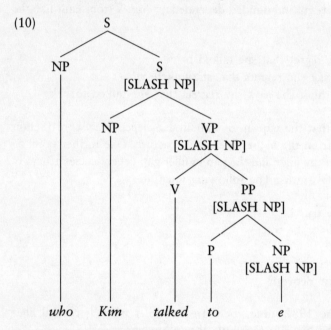

For HPSG, we would have a similar structure, but the value of SLASH would be a set with a single member. We will look at reasons for assuming a set-valued feature later.[3]

Structures like these have three distinct parts: the bottom consisting of an empty category of the form X[SLASH X] or X[SLASH {X}], the middle consisting of local trees with a SLASH feature specification on a daughter and on its mother, and the top, in which a SLASH feature appears on a daughter but not on its mother. We will consider each part in turn.

The standard versions of GPSG and HPSG have rather similar approaches to the bottom of unbounded dependencies. Both assume specialized empty categories, which are often referred to, following transformational grammar, as 'traces', and both assume that traces are restricted to complement positions. For GPSG, traces are empty categories of the form X[SLASH X]. They are introduced into trees by ID rules that are the product of a metarule called SLASH Termination Metarule 1, which takes the following form:

(11)   SLASH TERMINATION METARULE 1
       X ⟶ W, XP
              ⇓
       X ⟶ W, XP[NULL +]

This will, for example, derive (12b) from (12a).

(12)   a.   PP ⟶ H° [SUBCAT 20], NP
       b.   PP ⟶ H° [SUBCAT 20], NP[NULL +]

A feature specification default ensures that only categories in local trees licensed by rules that are the output of STM1 are [NULL +], and a feature co-occurrence restriction ensures that categories that are [NULL +] have a specification for SLASH. They take the following form:

(13)   FSD 3: ~[NULL]
(14)   FCR 19: [NULL +] ⊃ [SLASH]

FCR 19 ensures that the NP[NULL +] licensed by (12b) will have a specification for the feature SLASH. In addition to these elements, GPSG assumes an empty category of the following form:

(15)   α[NULL +,SLASH α]

This ensures that the value of SLASH in a [NULL +] category will be identical to the basic category. The Foot Feature Principle, which we will look at shortly, ensures that the mother of the empty category has the same SLASH feature specification. Thus, (12b) will license the following local tree:

(16)

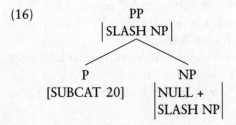

GPSG assumes, following Flickinger (1983), that metarules only apply to lexical ID rules. This entails that STM1 can only assign [NULL +] to an XP on the right-hand side of a lexical ID rule. The result is that unbounded dependency gaps can only appear as sisters to a lexical category. We will consider the implications of this in the next section.

We turn now to HPSG. The version of HPSG presented in chapters 1–8 of Pollard and Sag (1994) assumes an empty category of the following form:

(17) [LOCAL [1], NON-LOCAL|SLASH {[1]}]

This is subject to a principle called the Trace Principle, which we can formulate as follows:

(18) TRACE PRINCIPLE
      A trace must appear in the COMPS list of a head.

This requires this empty category to be a complement. As we have said, we will look at the implications of this restriction in the next section.

A rather different approach to the bottom of unbounded dependencies is proposed in chapter 9 of Pollard and Sag (1994). This revives the view of the earliest work in HPSG and some work in GPSG that the bottom of an unbounded dependency involves not an empty category but a missing category. (This is also the position of Categorial Grammar.) It involves a lexical rule called the Complement Extraction Lexical Rule, which we can formulate as follows:

(19) COMPLEMENT EXTRACTION LEXICAL RULE
      X[COMPS <...,[LOCAL [1]],...>] $\Longrightarrow$
      X[COMPS <......>,SLASH {[1]}]

This will, for example, derive (20b) from (20a).

(20) a. P[COMPS <[LOCAL NP]>]
      b. P[COMPS <>,SLASH {NP}]

(20a) will provide for an ordinary preposition taking an NP object, while (20b) will provide for a preposition whose object has been 'extracted'. This approach is defended at some length in Sag and Fodor (1994).[4]

The middle of an unbounded dependency consists of local trees with [SLASH X] or [SLASH {X}] in a category and in its mother. In other words, we have local trees of the form in (21) in GPSG and similar local trees with '{X}' in HPSG.

(21)

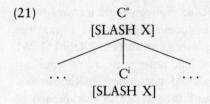

It looks, then, as if we need to allow local trees of the form in (21) while ruling out local trees of the form in (22) or (23) in GPSG and similar local trees with '{X}' in HPSG.

(22)

(23)

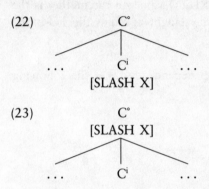

We could do this by stipulating that if a SLASH feature appears in some category it must appear in its mother and if it appears in some category it must appear in a daughter. However, this is too simple, most obviously because we do have local trees of the form (22) at the top of an unbounded dependency. The question, then, is: how can we generally exclude local trees like (22) and its HPSG counterpart while allowing such trees at the top of an unbounded dependency?

GPSG addresses this problem by distinguishing features in local trees that are present in the licensing rule and features that are not. The former are said to be 'inherited' while the latter are said to be 'instantiated'. The difference between the local tree at the top of an unbounded dependency and the local trees in the middle is that the SLASH feature is inherited in the former but instantiated in the latter. It is possible then to propose a condition on instantiated FOOT features as follows:

(24) FOOT FEATURE PRINCIPLE
The set of instantiated FOOT features in a category is the unification of the instantiated FOOT features in its daughters.

One point that we should note is that this formulation allows a SLASH feature specification in a category to appear in more than one of its daughters. We will see in the next section that this is important.

HPSG addresses the problem by allowing heads to incorporate features which encode the fact that certain NON-LOCAL features in a daughter should not appear in the mother. More precisely, it distinguishes two sorts of NON-LOCAL features, INHERITED and TO-BIND features. The latter appear in a head category and encode the fact that the former should not appear in the mother. Given these features, the Non-Local Feature Principle can be formulated as follows:

(25)   NON-LOCAL FEATURE PRINCIPLE
       For each non-local feature, the INHERITED value on the mother is the union of the INHERITED values on the daughters minus the TO-BIND value on the head daughter.

Within this approach, the top of a filler-gap dependency takes the following form:

(26)

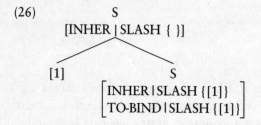

Here, the TO-BIND SLASH feature on the head ensures that the value of the INHERITED SLASH feature is not shared by the mother. Like the GPSG approach, this approach allows more than one daughter to have the same value for SLASH as the mother.[5]

As we noted earlier, SLASH is not the only feature that obeys the Foot Feature Principle in GPSG or the Non-Local Feature Principle in HPSG. This means that the distribution of SLASH is in part attributable to a principle which is independently motivated. This adds significantly to the attractiveness of the approach.

To provide for the top of a filler-gap dependency all that is needed within GPSG is an ID rule combining an S[SLASH X] with an X to form an S, and all that is needed in HPSG is an ID rule combining an S[SLASH {X}] with an X. The GPSG rule can be formulated as follows:

(27)   S ⟶ S[SLASH], X

Nothing in this rule requires the value of the SLASH feature on the S daughter to be identical to its sister. For GPSG, an inherited SLASH is a CONTROL feature. Hence, the necessary identity is a consequence of the Control Agreement Principle. Within HPSG, the top of a filler–gap dependency requires the following Filler–Head Rule:

(28) FILLER–HEAD RULE
      [ ] $\longrightarrow$ [LOCAL [1]],
            FILLER

      S[*fin*,INHER I SLASH {[1], . . . },TO-BIND I SLASH {[1]}]
      HEAD

One might suppose that the identity between the filler's LOCAL feature and a member of the SLASH set should follow from some general principle. It is clear, however, that it cannot follow from the obvious candidate, the Valence Principle, since this requires identity of SYNSEM values and not identity of LOCAL values.[6]

As we noted in chapter 7, the top of a filler–head dependency is a specifier–head structure in P&P. Standard versions of GPSG and HPSG do not share this assumption. However, as demonstrated in Borsley (1989b), it is quite easy to incorporate the P&P approach into HPSG, and, as we will see in section 9.4, Pollard and Sag (1994) propose that the top of a filler-gap dependency in certain relative clauses is a specifier–head structure.

A further important fact about the top of a filler-gap dependency is illustrated by the following:

(29) a. Which book has he read?
      b. *Which book he has read?

(30) a. No book has he read.
      b. *No book he has read.

(31) a. This book he has read.
      b. *This book has he read.

(32) a. I wonder which book he has read.
      b. *I wonder which book has he read.

(33) a. the book which he has read
      b. *the book which has he read

These show that the sentence is required to be auxiliary-initial in root interrogatives and in sentences with a negative topic and to be subject-initial in embedded

interrogatives, sentences with a positive topic, and relative clauses. This means
that additional constraints must be imposed on the top of a filler-gap dependency. For some discussion of how this might be done, see Green and Morgan
(1996).

As we noted earlier, HPSG assumes a set-valued (or list-valued) SLASH feature. Apart from this, the HPSG analysis is very similar to the GPSG analysis.
In particular, the Non-Local Feature Principle is very similar to the Foot Feature
Principle. The main motivation for a set-valued feature comes from unbounded
dependencies in the Scandinavian languages. Consider, for example, the following Norwegian example from Maling and Zaenen (1982):

(34) Dette er de diktene som   laererin spurte oss [hvem vi trodde
      These are the poems COMP teacher asked us   who we thought
         hadde skrevet]
         had   written
      'These are the poems that the teacher asked us who we thought had
      written.'

Here, the bracketed subordinate clause involves two unbounded dependencies.
Rather similar on the face of it are examples like the following:

(35) Which violin would this sonata be easy [to play on]

Here, the bracketed infinitive appears to involve two unbounded dependencies.
It should be noted, however, that Hukari and Levine (1991a) argue within a
version of GPSG that the dependency associated with 'tough' adjectives like *easy*
is not an ordinary unbounded dependency and that it should be analysed in
terms of a separate feature GAP. If this is right, there may be no motivation
in English for a set-valued SLASH feature. We return to this matter in section
9.4.[7,8]

9.3   Island constraints

Although unbounded dependencies are unbounded, they are not unrestricted.
They are subject to a number of restrictions, traditionally known as island constraints. Island constraints have been an important concern within Modern PSG
just as they have within most other frameworks. Within Modern PSG, they can
be accommodated by imposing constraints on the SLASH feature.

It has long been recognized that subjects are islands. We can illustrate with
the following data:

(36) a. Which man do you think stories about Kim really annoy?
      b. *Which man do you think stories about really annoy Kim?
      c. Which man do you think stories about really annoy?

In (36a), we have a gap as object of *annoy*. In (36b), we have a gap as object of *about* within the subject NP. Its ungrammaticality illustrates the Subject Condition. Finally, in (36c), we have gaps in both positions, the first being a so-called parasitic gap, a gap which is only possible because there is a 'real' gap in the same structure. These examples involve the following local tree:

(37)   S

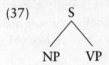

        NP   VP

It looks, then, as if we need to ensure that the SLASH feature appears on the NP daughter only if it appears on the VP daughter. We will see shortly how GPSG and HPSG ensure this.

More recently, it has been suggested that adjuncts too are islands. Data like the following support this view:

(38) a. Which book did he criticize without reading the introduction?
      b. *Which book did he criticize the introduction without reading?
      c. Which book did he criticize without reading?

In (38a), we have an unbounded dependency gap as object of *criticize*. In (38b), we have a gap as object of *reading*, within an adjunct PP. Its ungrammaticality illustrates the so-called Adjunct Island Condition. Finally, in (38c), we have gaps in both positions, the second being a parasitic gap. All three examples involve something like the following local tree:

(39)   VP

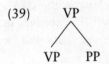

        VP   PP

On the face of it, then, we need to ensure that the SLASH feature appears on the PP daughter only if it also appears on the VP daughter.

A central feature of GPSG is a unified account of subject and adjunct islands. What subjects and adjuncts have in common for GPSG is that both are sisters of a phrasal head. The idea, then, is that SLASH must appear in a phrasal head if it appears in its sister. This idea is implemented by analysing SLASH as a HEAD feature as well as a FOOT feature. This entails that if SLASH appears in a category it will also appear in its head unless the head is lexical, in which case the following feature co-occurrence restriction overrides the HFC:

(40)   FCR 6: [SUBCAT] ⊃ ~[SLASH]

This approach allows SLASH to appear in the sister of a phrasal head as long as it appears in the head itself. Thus, it allows parasitic gaps in subjects and adjuncts.

This is an interesting approach to some important phenomena. Pollard and Sag (1994) argue, however, that it is both too weak and too strong. They point out (p. 188), following Pollard (1985b), Hukari and Levine (1987) and Jacobson (1987b), that it is too weak if one assumes a ternary branching structure for auxiliary-initial clauses, in other words if one assumes that a sentence like (41) has the structure in (42):

(41)   Did Kim annoy Sandy?

(42)

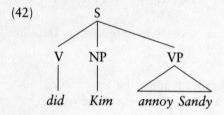

The following examples show that subjects of auxiliary-initial clauses affect unbounded dependencies in the same way as subjects of subject-initial clauses:

(43)   a.   Which man did stories about Kim really annoy?
       b.   *Which man did stories about really annoy Kim?
       c.   Which man did stories about really annoy?

All these examples will involve the structure in (41), and nothing in the GPSG approach will ensure that a SLASH feature appears in the VP if it appears in the NP since the VP is not a phrasal head. Hence, all three sentences will be generated.

A more careful consideration of adjuncts suggests that the GPSG approach is also too strong. Pollard and Sag (1994: 191) cite a variety of acceptable examples with an ordinary gap inside an adjunct. Consider, for example, the following:

(44)   a.   That's the symphony that Schubert died without finishing.
       b.   Which room does Julius teach his class in?
       c.   This is the blanket that Rebecca refuses to sleep without.

Similar examples are cited in Hukari and Levine (1995b). What such examples suggest is that adjuncts are simply not islands in the way that subjects are and hence that it is a mistake to seek a unified account.

Pollard and Sag account for the islandhood of subjects with what they call the Subject Condition. We can formulate it as follows:

(45) SUBJECT CONDITION
The single element in the SUBJ list of a lexical head may have a non-empty SLASH feature only if a member of its COMPS list has a non-empty SLASH feature.

This approach accounts for the islandhood of subjects of all types of clauses. It also accounts for the islandhood of certain objects. The following data from Pollard and Sag (1994: 189) illustrate:

(46) a. *Who did you consider friends of angry at Sandy?
b. Who did you consider friends of Sandy angry at?
c. Who did you consider friends of angry at?

Here we have sentences with a raised subject in object position. The verb *consider*, where it takes a raised subject as its object, will have the following schematic sign:

(47)
$$
\begin{bmatrix}
\text{SUBJ } <NP_{[1]}> \\
\text{COMPS } <[2]NP, AP[SUBJ <[2]>] : [3]> \\
\text{CONTENT } \begin{bmatrix} \text{RELATION } consider \\ \text{CONSIDERER } [1]ref \\ \text{SOA-ARG } [3] \end{bmatrix}
\end{bmatrix}
$$

This makes it clear that the unexpressed subject of the second complement has all the syntactic and semantic properties of the first complement. Hence, if the first complement has a non-empty SLASH feature, so will the unexpressed subject of the second complement. This will be the case in both (46a) and (46c). Thus, in both cases the head of the second complement *angry* will have a SUBJ list whose single member has a non-empty SLASH feature, but only in (46c) will a member of its COMPS list have a non-empty SLASH feature. Hence, of these two, only (46c) is grammatical.

We turn now to coordinate structures. Here, we have data like the following:

(48) a. *Who do you think Sandy admires and Kim respects Lee?
b. *Who do you think Sandy admires Lee and Kim respects?
c. Who do you think Sandy admires and Kim respects?

Such data suggest that an unbounded dependency cannot cross the boundary of a coordinate structure unless it affects both conjuncts. In the latter case, we have a so-called across-the-board dependency. The facts have been well-known since Ross (1967), who introduced the term Coordinate Structure Constraint in connection with them, but they have received relatively little attention in TG, including P&P. However, they were a central concern of early GPSG.

It was assumed in early GPSG that all the conjuncts in a coordinate structure must be identical. If this were correct, the facts in (48) would be an automatic consequence. The (a) and (b) examples involve the coordination of an S and an S[SLASH NP] while the (c) example involves the coordination of two instances of S[SLASH NP]. Thus, if conjuncts were necessarily identical, the (a) and (b) examples would be ruled out and only the (c) example would be allowed. It is clear, however, as we saw in 7.5, that conjuncts are not necessarily identical. Thus, a more subtle account is necessary. In the standard version of GPSG, the facts are attributed to the dual nature of SLASH as both a FOOT and a HEAD feature. As a FOOT feature it must appear within the coordinate category if it appears within any of the conjunct categories, and as a HEAD feature it must appear within all conjunct categories if it appears within the coordinate category. Thus, if SLASH appears in any conjunct, it must appear in all of them. This is the desired result. However, one point to note about this approach is that it links the islandhood of conjuncts to the islandhood of subjects. Both are a consequence of the dual nature of SLASH. The approach predicts that conjuncts will be islands in a language if and only if subjects are. As Pollard and Sag (1994: 197) point out, following Sells (1984), Swedish is a counterexample here. Conjuncts are islands, but subjects are not. This suggests that it is mistake to seek to link the islandhood of conjuncts and the islandhood of subjects.

Pollard and Sag propose instead that the islandhood of conjuncts is a consequence of the Coordination Principle, which we introduced in chapter 7 and which we repeat here.

(49) COORDINATION PRINCIPLE

In a coordinate structure, the CATEGORY and NON-LOCAL value of each conjunct daughter is subsumed by (is an extension of) that of the mother.

This ensures *inter alia* that conjuncts and their mother have the same value for SLASH. Hence, it rules out (48a) and (48b) while allowing (48c).

Thus, HPSG has an account of the Coordinate Structure Constraint. It should be noted, however, that there are certain counterexamples to the constraint. The following from Goldsmith (1985) illustrate:

(50) a. How many courses can we expect our graduate students to teach and
         still finish a dissertation on time?
     b. How many lakes can we destroy and not arouse public sympathy?
     c. Sam is not the sort of guy you can just sit there and listen to.

In (50a) and (50b) there is an unbounded dependency gap in the first conjunct
only, and in (50c) there is an unbounded dependency gap in the second conjunct only. Lakoff (1986) argues that extraction is possible from just one conjunct
provided certain pragmatic conditions are met. It may be, then, that syntactic
theory should not restrict extraction from conjuncts and that the unacceptability
of examples like (48a) and (48b) is a matter for pragmatic theory.

Rather different from the phenomena considered so far are the so-called
complementizer-trace facts, illustrated by the following:

(51) a. *Who do you think that did this?
     b. *Who did you ask whether did this?
     c. *Who did you arrange for to see Lee?

Such examples suggest that unbounded dependency gaps cannot appear in subject position in a clause introduced by a complementizer. Both GPSG and HPSG
have proposed that they are ungrammatical because a gap never appears in subject position. As we saw earlier, traces can only be sisters of a lexical category
in GPSG and can only be complements in HPSG. These restrictions entail that
traces cannot appear in subject position (at least in subject-initial clauses.) Both
frameworks seem to face a problem in examples like the following, which have
traditionally been seen as involving a gap in subject position:

(52) Who [did this]
(53) I wonder who you think [did this]

However, both frameworks claim that the bracketed strings in such examples
are VPs and not Ss with a subject gap, in other words that they have the following structures:

(54)

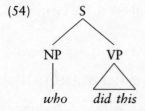

(55)

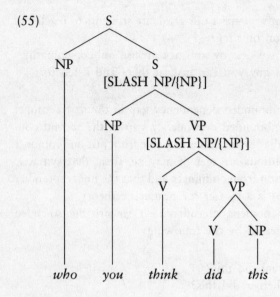

To allow structures like (55), GPSG needs additional ID rules and HPSG needs additional lexical signs.

To allow structures like (55), GPSG needs to associate *think* with the rule in (57) as well as the rule in (56):

(56)   VP ⟶ H°, S
(57)   VP[SLASH NP] ⟶ H°, VP

The latter can be derived from the former by the following metarule:

(58)   SLASH TERMINATION METARULE 2
       X ⟶ W, S[FIN]
              ⇓
       X[SLASH NP] ⟶ W, VP

Within GPSG, the lowest SLASH in (55) must have the same value as the AGR feature in its VP daughter. This is ensured by the Control Agreement Principle since both are CONTROL features. (See 8.3.)

To allow structures like (55), HPSG needs to assign *think* to the category in (60) as well as the category in (59):

(59)   V[SUBJ <NP>,COMPS <S[*unmarked*]>]
(60)   V[SUBJ <NP>,COMPS <VP[SUBJ <LOC[1]>]>, INHER|SLASH {[1]}]

The latter can be derived from the former by the following lexical rule:

(61)   SUBJECT EXTRACTION LEXICAL RULE
       X[COMPS < . . . S[*unmarked*] . . . >] $\implies$
       X[COMPS <VP[SUBJ <LOC[1]>]>,INHER|SLASH {[1]}]

Although examples like those in (51) are ungrammatical in English and many other languages, such examples are grammatical in some languages. A notable example is Icelandic, where we have sentences like the following:

(62)   Hver heldur þu að væri kominn till Reykjavikur?
       who think you that was come   to Reykjavik
       'Who do you think came to Reykjavik?'

This suggests that the impossibility of subject gaps in English should not be attributed to a fundamental constraint such as the restriction of metarules to lexical ID rules. Such examples are no problem for HPSG since one can simply claim that the Trace Principle is language-specific. There are, however, English examples which are problematic for both GPSG and HPSG. The crucial examples, which are discussed in Culicover (1993), are exemplified by the following:

(63)   Who do you think that under those circumstances would do this?

Such examples show that unbounded dependency gaps can appear in subject position in a clause introduced by a complementizer if the clause contains a preposed adverbial. It seems, then, that we must allow gaps in subject position even in English. This leaves the ungrammaticality of examples like those in (51) unexplained. One possibility is that it is the adjacency of the complementizer and the gap that is unacceptable, but it is far from clear how this could be formalized.

Examples like (63) show that gaps cannot be restricted to complement position. There is independent evidence for this conclusion from examples involving adjuncts, such as the following:

(64)   When did Pat eat dinner?
(65)   When do you think Pat ate dinner?

Pollard and Sag (1994: 176–81) consider the possibility of claiming that such examples do not involve real unbounded dependencies, but they reject it. Further evidence that such examples involve real unbounded dependencies is presented in Hukari and Levine (1995a). Thus, they provide further evidence that gaps are not limited to complement position.

To conclude this section, we note one other island constraint, proposed in Fodor (1992b): the Obliqueness Extraction Constraint. This draws on the HPSG assumption that dependants are ordered in terms of obliqueness. We can formulate it as follows:

(66) OBLIQUENESS EXTRACTION CONSTRAINT
      If two arguments are ordered other than by increasing obliqueness, then
      the more oblique is an island.

Fodor attributes the ungrammaticality of the following to this constraint:

(67) *Who did you say to that you wanted to work with Kim?
(68) *Who did you shout to to bring the beer?
(69) *Who did you learn from how to play the oboe?

In (67), the contrast between *say something to him*, **say to him something*
suggests that the PP complement is more oblique than the clausal complement.
In (68), the contrast between *shout something to him*, **shout to him something*
suggests that the PP complement is more oblique than the infinitival complement. Finally, in (69), the contrast between *learn something from him*, **learn
from him something* suggests that the PP complement is more oblique than the
infinitival complement. Unlike (67)–(69) is the following:

(70) Who were you relying on to bring the beer?

Here, the contrast between *rely on him for something*, **rely for something on
him* suggests that the PP complement is less oblique than the infinitival complement. Hence, (70) is predicted to be grammatical. Fodor also draws attention
to the following contrast:

(71) *Who did you appear to to be polite?
(72) Who did you appeal to to be polite?

Pollard and Sag (1987: ch. 7) argue that the PP complement is more oblique
than the infinitival complement with *appear* but that the opposite is true with
appeal. Given this, we expect the contrast between (71) and (72).

9.4 Some further constructions

In this section, we will consider some further unbounded dependency constructions. We will look in particular at relative clauses, *tough* constructions, resumptive pronouns, and right node raising.

In English, some relative clauses involve a filler and some do not.[9] We will look first at examples involving a *wh*-filler. Consider, for example, the following:

(73)   the man who we talked to

One thing that we need here is an analysis of relative pronouns. Pollard and Sag propose that the CONTENT of a relative pronoun is an index. This is plausible given that relative pronouns seem to correspond to logical bound variables. Thus, we could translate (73) into a quasi-logical notation as follows:

(74)   the x ((x is a man) & (we talked to x))

The index that is the CONTENT of a relative pronoun also appears in its REL set. This ensures that a *wh*-phrase containing a relative pronoun will have the same index in its REL set. Thus, we have schematic signs of the following form:

(75) $\begin{bmatrix} \text{HEAD } noun \\ \text{CONTENT } npro[\text{INDEX } [1]] \\ \text{INHER} \,|\, \text{REL } \{[1]\} \end{bmatrix}$

Consider now the following examples:

(76)   the man who we think knows/*know the answer
(77)   the men who we think know/*knows the answer

These show that the N′ that the relative clause modifies must agree in number with the relative pronoun. This means that the index in the CONTENT of the modified N′ must be identical to the relative index. As noted earlier, Pollard and Sag adopt the P&P view that relative *wh*-phrases occupy the specifier position of a null complementizer, or, as they prefer to call it, a relativizer. Among other things, this ensures the necessary identity of indices. It has the following schematic sign:

(78) $\begin{bmatrix} \text{MOD N′}[\text{TO-BIND}\,|\,\text{REL}\{[1]\}] : \begin{bmatrix} \text{INDEX } [1] \\ \text{RESTR } [3] \end{bmatrix} \\ \text{SPR}<[\text{LOC}[2], \text{INHER}\,|\,\text{REL}\{[1]\}]> \\ \text{COMPS } <\text{S}[\text{SLASH } \{[2]\}] : [5]> \\ \text{CONTENT} \begin{bmatrix} \text{INDEX } [1] \\ \text{REST } \{[5]\} \cup [3] \end{bmatrix} \\ \text{TO-BIND}|\text{SLASH } \{[2]\} \end{bmatrix}$

There are a variety of points to note here. The complement is an S with a single member SLASH set. The specification TO-BIND | SLASH {[2]} ensures that the mother has an empty SLASH set. The specifier's LOCAL feature is required to be identical to the single member in the SLASH set. It is also required to be INHER | REL {[1]}. Hence, it is a relative *wh*-phrase. The N' which the relative clause modifies is required to be TO-BIND | REL {[1]}. This ensures that the combination of N' and relative clause is [INHER | REL { }]. The CONTENT of the relativizer consists of the index from the REL set and the restrictions from the modified N' and the complement. Interacting with the Content Principle of chapter 5, this ensures that the combination of N' and relative clause has the appropriate CONTENT value. Finally, notice that the relative index is identical to the index in the CONTENT of the modified N'. This ensures that the modified N' agrees with the relative pronoun. Given this sign, the combination of noun and relative clause in (73) will have the following structure:

(79)

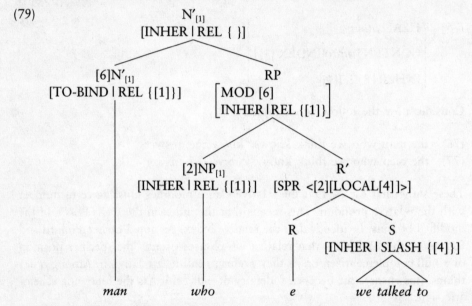

One point we should note here is that (78) will violate the Raising Principle introduced in chapter 8 given the natural assumption that the specifier appears in the SUBCAT list. Given this assumption, the SUBCAT list will contain a non-expletive element which is assigned no semantic role and does not function as the subject of a predicative complement. This is noted by Pollard and Sag (1994: 216, fn. 3). They suggest that the Raising Principle should be reformulated to allow such a case, but they do not offer a reformulation.

Pollard and Sag suggest that (78) undergoes the Subject Extraction Lexical Rule in (61) to give an empty relativizer that takes a finite VP complement. They propose that this is involved in examples like the following:

(80)   the man [who knows the answer]

However, if we abandon the Trace Principle and allow traces in subject position, such examples can involve the empty relativizer in (78).

We have now dealt with *wh*-relatives, but we also need an account of non-*wh*-relatives such as the following:

(81)   the man [that knows the answer]
(82)   the man [that we talked to]
(83)   the man [we talked to]

Pollard and Sag (1994: 220) propose, following Gazdar (1981a), that *that* in (81) is not a complementizer, as has often been assumed, but a nominative relative pronoun. In other words, it is a non-*wh*-filler. It involves the following schematic sign:

(84) $\begin{bmatrix} \text{HEAD } \textit{noun}\,[\textit{nom}] \\ \text{CONTENT } \textit{npro}[\text{INDEX } [1]] \\ \text{INHER | REL } \{[1]\} \end{bmatrix}$

With this sign, (81) will have the same sort of analysis as (80). This analysis works. However, one might well feel that the idea that relative *that* is a pronoun is dubious given that it is invariant, unlike demonstrative *that* which has the plural form *these*. Pollard and Sag (1994: 22) propose that the relative clauses in (82) and (83) involve a second null relativizer with the following sign:

(85) $\begin{bmatrix} \text{MOD N'[TO-BIND|REL }\{[1]\}] : \begin{bmatrix} \text{INDEX } [1] \\ \text{RESTR } [3] \end{bmatrix} \\ \text{COMPS } <\text{S}[\textit{fin},\text{SLASH }\{[4]\}] : [5]> \\ \text{CONTENT } \begin{bmatrix} \text{INDEX } [1] \\ \text{REST } \{[5]\} \cup [3] \end{bmatrix} \\ \text{INHER | REL } \{[1]\} \\ \text{TO-BIND | SLASH } \{[4]\text{NP}_{[1]}\} \end{bmatrix}$

An important point here is that the complement's value for the MARKING attribute is left unspecified. Hence, its value may be either *unmarked* or *that*. Given (85), the combination of noun and relative clause in (82) and (83) will have the following structure:

(86)

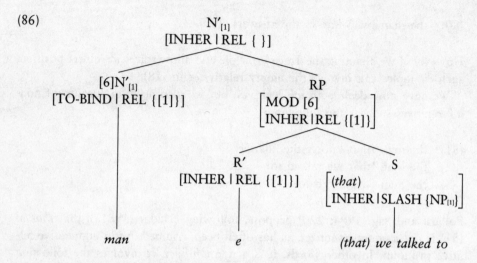

A final point that we should note is that Sag (forthcoming) has proposed an analysis of relative clauses which does not involve any null relativizers. Thus, the analysis that we have just outlined is one that he at least no longer subscribes to.[10]

We turn now to the 'tough' construction, in which an adjective takes an infinitival complement containing an NP gap and a subject which is associated with it. The following illustrate:

(87)   Kim would be easy to bribe.
(88)   The problem would be difficult for anyone to solve.

In this construction, the subject in a sense acts as a filler. Notice, however, that unlike a standard filler, it can differ in case from the gap. Consider, for example, the following:

(89)   He would be easy to bribe.

Here, the subject is clearly nominative, but the gap is in an accusative position, as (90) shows:

(90)   It would be easy to bribe him.

'Tough' constructions are discussed in Gazdar et al. (1985: ch. 7.5) and Pollard and Sag (1994: ch. 4.3). Both note that they have proved quite problematic for transformational grammar. Both propose that 'tough' adjectives take a complement with a gap. Pollard and Sag (1994) assume a category of the following form:

(91) $\begin{bmatrix} \text{HEAD } adj \\ \text{SUBJ } <NP_{[1]}> \\ \text{COMPS } <VP[inf,\text{SLASH } \{[2]NP[acc] : ppro_{[1]}, \ldots \}]> \\ \text{TO-BIND}|\text{SLASH } \{[2]\} \end{bmatrix}$

An important feature of this category is that the subject and the NP in the value of SLASH only share an index and hence are not required to have the same case. Pollard and Sag (1994: 196) point out that the possibility of case disagreement is problematic for Gazdar et al.'s approach.

Hukari and Levine (1991a) highlight the fact that 'tough' dependencies differ from standard unbounded dependencies in two important ways. Firstly, for many speakers, they cannot cross the boundary of a finite clause. Thus, they have contrasts like the following:

(92)   *Kim is tough for me to believe that Sandy would ever marry.

(93)   Who do you believe that Sandy would never marry?

Secondly, it is possible to have a tough dependency and a standard unbounded dependency in the same constituent, but not two standard unbounded dependencies. The following illustrate:

(94)   Which fiddle would this jig be easy to play on?

(95)   *Which fiddle did you ask which jig Kim played on?

These contrasts lead Hukari and Levine to propose that 'tough' dependencies are a reflection not of the SLASH feature but of a separate GAP feature. As we noted in section 9.2, if they are right, then the SLASH may never have more than a single member set as its value in English.

Hukari and Levine also point out that there is evidence that the subject and the gap share more than just an index in 'tough' sentences. They note, for example, that the subject can be a clause if the gap is in a position where a clause can appear. The following illustrate:

(96)   That I was sick would have been very difficult for me to pretend when I really wasn't.

(97)   That we be there on time would have been very difficult for Robin to demand (of us).

It looks as if the subject and the gap have to share all features apart from case. Hukari and Levine ensure this by making the Control Agreement Principle a default principle, which can be overridden in specific cases. It is far from clear how the facts should be handled in a framework like HPSG, which does not allow default principles. It may be, however, that they should be seen as evidence for a tree-based approach to case, something which was mentioned in 6.3.[11]

We turn now to resumptive pronouns (RPs). These are an important feature of unbounded dependencies in many languages. They have had relatively little attention within Modern PSG, but it seems likely that Modern PSG has the mechanisms to accommodate the sort of phenomena that occur.

A particularly well-studied RP language is Irish. Here, according to McCloskey (1979, 1990), RPs and not gaps appear just in case the bottom of the unbounded dependency is within certain constituents and the top outside. One such constituent is an interrogative clause. We have data like the following from McCloskey (1990: 209):

(98) a. ne dánta sin   nach bhfuil fhios   againn [cén áit
          the poems DEM NEG is   knowledge at-us   what place
             ar   cumadh   iad]
          COMP were-composed them
          'those poems that we do not know where they were composed'

      b. *ne dánta sin   nach bhfuil fhios   againn [cén áit
          the poems DEM NEG is   knowledge at-us   what place
             ar   cumadh]
          COMP were-composed
          'those poems that we do not know where they were composed'

These are identical except that (98a) contains an RP while (98b) just has a gap. Assuming a transformational framework, McCloskey proposes that unbounded dependencies with a gap result from movement while unbounded dependencies with an RP are base-generated. In other words, he proposes that there are two different types of unbounded dependency here. One way to incorporate this approach into HPSG would be to propose a new feature, RSLASH say, for unbounded dependencies involving an RP. This would be broadly similar to SLASH but less constrained.

Some other languages have RPs which seem less straightforward than those of Irish. Among these are the Scandinavian languages, discussed within an early version of GPSG in Maling and Zaenen (1982). One thing that is clear about these languages is that RPs cannot be accommodated by introducing an additional feature. This is because there is evidence that RPs have the same basic status as gaps. One thing that suggests this is that it is possible to have across-the-board dependencies with a gap in one conjunct and an RP in the other. The following, Swedish, example illustrates:

(99) Där borta går en man som jag ofta träffar men inte vet   vad
      there away goes a man that I   often meet but not know what
      han heter.
      he   is-called
      'There goes a man that I often meet but don't know what he is called.'

It looks, then, as if these languages involve a single SLASH feature and a single value realized in different ways in different circumstances. This is an important area for future research.

We look finally at so-called right node raising (RNR), the phenomenon exemplified by the following examples:

(100) Kim likes and Sandy adores Indian food.
(101) Kim suspects and Sandy is sure that Lee was there.

Gazdar (1981a) proposes that such examples simply involve an across-the-board rightward unbounded dependency. On this view, (100) will have the following structure in GPSG and a similar structure with a set-valued SLASH in HPSG:

(102)

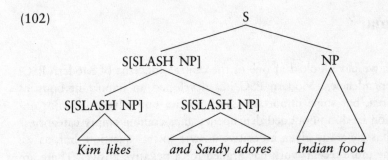

There is evidence, however, that RNR does not involve SLASH. Most importantly, it does not obey certain island constraints. Thus, while (103) in which the second gap is within a relative clause is ungrammatical, (104) is perfectly acceptable.

(103) *What does Sandy buy and Lee know a man who sells?
(104) Sandy buys and Lee knows a man who sells pictures of Elvis Presley.

Data like these have led syntacticians like McCawley (1982), Levine (1985) and Ojeda (1988) to propose that RNR sentences involve not an unbounded dependency but a constituent with two mothers. On this view, (100) has something like the following structure:

(105)

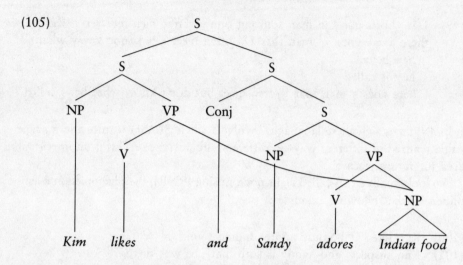

However, Postal (1993) argues at length that RNR sentences do involve an unbounded dependency, albeit one with distinctive properties. Thus, there are important unresolved issues here.[12]

9.5 Summary

In this chapter, we have looked at one of the central concerns of Modern PSG: unbounded dependencies. Modern PSG has developed an important body of ideas in this area, but some important issues remain unresolved. A major unresolved question is: do unbounded dependency gaps contain empty categories? Modern PSG has generally given a positive answer to this question, but, as we have seen, some more recent work has argued for a negative answer. There are also unresolved questions about the treatment of island constraints, and about the phenomena considered in section 9.4. It is likely, then, that unbounded dependencies will continue to be a major concern of Modern PSG.

Notes

1 GPSG ideas about unbounded dependencies are presented in Gazdar et al. (1985: ch. 7). HPSG ideas are set out in Pollard and Sag (1994: ch. 4).
2 The SLASH feature was first proposed in Bear (1981). Instead of categories with the SLASH feature, the earliest GPSG work, e.g. Gazdar (1981a, 1981b, 1982), employs ordered pairs of categories written as α/β. The name SLASH derives from this notation.

3 An approach to unbounded dependencies which is rather like the SLASH approach is the 'gap-threading' approach of Pereira (1981). See Pereira and Shieber (1987: ch. 4.2.7) and Alshawi (1992: ch. 4.6).

4 Sag and Fodor (1994) argue that various kinds of data which have been seen as providing evidence for empty categories in unbounded dependencies do not in fact do so, and also that there is no psycholinguistic evidence for empty categories in unbounded dependencies.

5 In a number of languages, either verbs or complementizers that intervene between a filler and the associated gap display distinctive behaviour. For a survey see Hukari and Levine (1995a), and for an HPSG analysis of one case, Chamorro, see Goldberg (1985).

6 Gazdar (1982: 9) suggests that the fact that the filler c-commands the gap in a filler-gap dependency is an automatic consequence of the GPSG approach to such dependencies. Levine (1989b) points out that it is quite possible within GPSG to accommodate a dependency in which the filler does not c-command the gap.

7 *Wh*-questions in German and some other languages often show 'partial *wh*-movement'. The *wh*-phrase is in a position lower than its semantic scope and an expletive *wh*-element marks its scope. The following illustrates:

(i) Was glaubst du [wen Hans gesehen hat]?
     what believe you who-ACC Hans seen has
     'Who do you believe Hans saw?'

For an HPSG analysis of such sentences, see Kathol (1995b: ch. 6).

8 Dutch unbounded dependency constructions are discussed in Rentier (1994b).

9 Pollard and Sag (1994: ch. 5) provide analyses of two other types of relative clause construction: relative–correlative constructions and internally headed relatives. In the former, the relative clause appears in sentence-initial or sentence-final position. The following Hindi example from Andrews (1975) illustrates:

(i) [Mere pas jo lərka rəhta hai] vəh mera chota bhaii hai.
     me near which boy lives AUX he my little brother is
     'The boy who lives next door is my brother.'

In the latter, what in familiar languages would be the head of the relative clause appears within the relative clause. The following, from Donno Sɔ (a variety of Dogon, a language of Mali), illustrates:

(ii) [ya indɛ mi we gɔ] yimaa boli.
      yesterday person 1SG see-PN-ø DEF die-PSP go-PN-3SG
      'The person I saw yesterday is dead.'

10 One weakness of the Pollard and Sag approach to relative clauses is that it provides two analyses for an example like the following:

(i) the man that we think did it

Here we have a relative clause introduced by *that* with a gap in a subordinate subject position. This will have one analysis in which *that* is a nominative relative pronoun and one in which it is a complementizer preceded by the second null relativizer.

11 For further discussion of the 'tough' construction, see Grover (1994).

12 Unbounded dependencies also occur in comparatives, as the following illustrate:

(i)   Kim is taller than Sandy is.
(ii) Kim is taller than they say Sandy is.
(iii) Kim is taller than I think they say Sandy is.

For an analysis within early GPSG, see Gazdar (1980).

Exercises

1 Chung and McCloskey (1983) point out that the view that what look like clauses with a subject gap are really VPs, combined with the GPSG view of SLASH as a category-valued feature, predicts (apparently correctly) the grammaticality of the examples in (1) and the ungrammaticality of the examples in (2). Explain how these predictions arise.

(1) a. That's one trick that I've known a lot of people who've been taken in by.
     b. Isn't that the song that Paul and Stevie were the only ones who wanted to record?
     c. This is the paper that we really need to find someone who understands.

(2) a. *That's one trick that I know a lot of people that the police have taken in with.
     b. *Isn't that the song that Paul and Stevie were the only ones that George would let record?
     c. *This is the paper that we really need to find someone that we can intimidate with.

2 The following examples suggest that the bare VP treatment of subject gaps is incompatible with the Subject Condition. Explain how.

(1) Which linguist do students of think deserves a Nobel prize?

(2) Kim is the kind of author that even good friends of believe should be closely watched.

3 The HPSG Subject Condition in (45) correctly allows the sentence in (1), but incorrectly rules out the sentence in (2). Explain how.

(1) There are certain heroes that Kim finds long stories about very easy to listen to.

(2) There are certain heroes that long stories about are always very easy to listen to.

4   Although the (a) examples in the following are grammatical, the (b) examples are ungrammatical (at least with the same interpretation).

(1) a. Which man did you see?
    b. *Which did you see man?

(2) a. How tall was Kim?
    b. *How was Kim tall?

(3) a. How quickly did he run?
    b. *How did he run quickly?

Explain how these data are predicted by GPSG and a version of HPSG assuming traces and the Trace Principle. What conclusions might be drawn from the fact that all of the following Polish examples are grammatical?

(4) a. Którego mężczyzną widziałeś?
        which man   saw-2SG

    b. Którego widziałeś mężczyzną?
        which saw-2SG man
        'Which man did you see?'

(5) a. Jaki wysoki jest Jan?
        how tall   is Jan

    b. Jaki Jan jest wysoki?
        how Jan is   tall
        'How tall is Jan?'

5   The Middle English examples in (1)–(6) (from Grimshaw 1974) and the Norwegian examples in (7)–(10) (from Maling 1978) suggest that relative clauses with and without a *wh*-element may involve different mechanisms in some languages. Explain how, and discuss what mechanisms might be proposed within GPSG or HPSG.

(1) this bok which (that) I see

(2) *this bok which (that) I make mencioun of

(3) this bok of which I make mencioun

(4)   this bok that I see

(5)   this bok that I make mencioun of

(6)   *this bok of that I make mencioun

(7)   Det er melodien, som ingen visste, hvem skrev?
      'This is the song that no-one knew who wrote?'

(8)   *Hva visste ingen hvem skrev?
      'What did no-one know who wrote?'

(9)   Det er melodien, som Jan spurte, hvem skrev?
      'This is the song that Jan asked who wrote.'

(10) *Hva spurte Jan hvem skrev?
      'What did Jan ask who wrote?'

10 Anaphora

10.1 Introduction

Restrictions on the distribution and interpretation of so-called bound anaphors, i.e. reflexives and reciprocals, have been a major concern of generative grammar since Lees and Klima (1963) and especially since the emergence of P&P.[1] Any theory of grammar must be able to explain why (1) is grammatical but not (2).

(1) John admires himself.
(2) *John thinks Mary admires himself.

The most important question here is: what sort of principle accounts for the properties of typical anaphors? As we will see, GPSG and HPSG give quite different answers to this question. Another question is: how broad is the scope of the principle? We will see that the HPSG principle is rather narrower in its scope than the GPSG principle. A final question is: does the principle account for any other phenomena? We will see that the HPSG principle accounts for certain properties of control sentences.

   Since the 1960s it has been widely assumed that so-called disjoint reference phenomena, such as the fact that *John* and *him* cannot be coreferential in the following examples, involve principles like that involved in bound anaphora.

(3) John likes him.
(4) He likes John.

This idea is central to the binding theory of P&P. As we will see, it is also an important feature of HPSG.

10.2 The GPSG approach

The first GPSG analysis of anaphora was sketched in Gazdar and Sag (1981). The basic approach was developed somewhat in a non-standard version of

GPSG in Pollard and Sag (1983), and it is developed further in Hukari (1989). It is the latter's analysis that we will look at here.

Like the earlier analyses, Hukari's is based on a category-valued FOOT feature RE(flexive). This appears in a reflexive pronoun and in the categories dominating it. Reflexive pronouns have categories of the following form, where α stands for person, number and gender features:

(5) NP[α,RE NP[α]]

For example, *himself* has a category which we can abbreviate as follows:

(6) NP[3SGM,RE NP[3SGM]]

This will appear as a tree like the following:

(7)   PP[3SGM,RE NP[3SGM]]

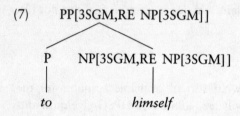

P   NP[3SGM,RE NP[3SGM]]

to   *himself*

The Foot Feature Principle ensures that the PP has the same value for the feature RE as the NP. Central to the analysis are two feature co-occurrence restrictions, both constraining the category-valued feature SUBJ, which indicates what sort of subject a head requires, like the AGR feature of standard GPSG. They are as follows:

(8) FCR 1: [VP ∨ [PRD +]] ⊃ SUBJ
(9) FCR 2: ~ [SUBJ & RE]

The first of these ensures that both VPs and [PRD +] categories, predicative APs, NPs and PPs, are specified for SUBJ. The second ensures that a category that is specified for SUBJ cannot be specified for RE. The result is that neither a VP nor a [PRD +] category can be specified for RE. The Foot Feature Principle is an absolute principle. Hukari reformulates it so that it can be overridden by FCRs. He treats the agreement between a reflexive and its antecedent as a consequence of a condition on semantic binding, which is operative when a category contains a specification for RE and its mother does not. This ensures that either the subject of the mother category or another daughter is the antecedent of the reflexive, and that reflexive and antecedent have the same person, number and gender. The two possibilities are illustrated in the following:

(10)   John showed Mary a picture of himself.
(11)   John showed Mary a picture of herself.

These will have the following structures:

(12)

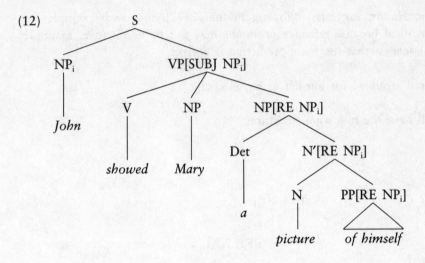

(13)

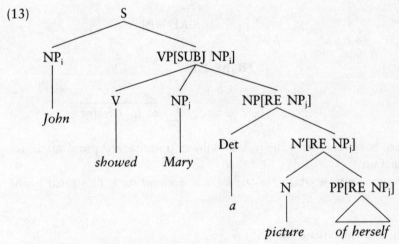

There is no possibility within this analysis of a reflexive within an embedded VP having an antecedent within the matrix clause. Thus, (2), repeated here for convenience, is correctly excluded:

(2)   *John thinks Mary admires himself.

A notable feature of Hukari's analysis is that it predicts that a reflexive in an embedded subject position can have an antecedent in the matrix clause. Examples like the following seem to pose a problem here:

(14)   *John thinks that himself is clever.

However, Hukari suggests, following Brame (1977), that such examples are ungrammatical because reflexive pronouns may not be nominative. Examples like (15) suggest that the basic prediction is correct.

(15)   Fred arranged for himself to be selected.

This will have the following structure:

(16)

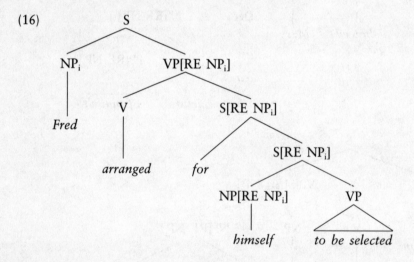

We will see, however, that reflexives in subject position are problematic for Hukari's analysis.

An important contrast which Hukari seeks to account for is illustrated by the following:

(17)   Mary likes pictures of herself.
(18)   *Mary likes John's pictures of herself.
(19)   Mary likes John's pictures of himself.

These suggest that a reflexive within an NP can have an antecedent outside the NP if the NP contains no possessive NP, but must have the possessive

NP as its antecedent if it does. To account for these data, Hukari analyses possessive NPs as subjects. Thus, (17) has the structure in (20) and (19) has that in (21).

(20)

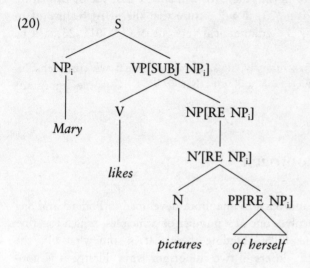

(21)

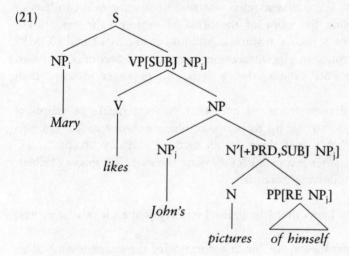

This is an interesting account. Notice, however, that it is incompatible with the arguments in 7.2 that specifiers are not subjects.

A further point to note about Hukari's analysis is that it will interact with the GPSG approach to control sentences to accommodate data like the following:

(22)   John persuaded Mary to defend herself/*himself.
(23)   John promised Mary to defend himself/*herself.

In these examples, the SUBJ feature of the non-finite verb will agree with the reflexive. If the Control Agreement Principle applies to SUBJ as it does to AGR in the standard version of GPSG, the SUBJ feature of *to* will agree with the SUBJ feature of the non-finite verb. In (22) the CAP will ensure that the SUBJ feature of *to* agrees with *Mary* and in (23) it will ensure that the SUBJ feature of *to* agrees with *John*. Thus, only the grammatical versions of (22) and (23) will be generated.

Thus, Hukari's analysis has many virtues. However, when we consider Pollard and Sag's HPSG analysis, we will see that it also has some important weaknesses.

10.3   The HPSG approach

We turn now to the HPSG approach to anaphora developed in Pollard and Sag (1992; 1994: ch. 6). This involves one of a number of principles, which together make up what they call the HPSG binding theory. It is somewhat like the binding theory of P&P but it differs in two important ways. Firstly, it is non-configurational in the sense that it refers not to tree structures but to lists of *synsem* objects forming the value of the SUBCAT feature. The main argument for assuming the SUBCAT feature in addition to the SUBJ and COMPS features is that it permits an elegant account of anaphora. Secondly, it is narrower in scope than P&P binding theory. It is also narrower in scope than Hukari's approach.

Pollard and Sag present strong evidence that many instances of anaphora thought within P&P to fall within the scope of binding theory in fact fall outside its scope. They show that there are all sorts of perfectly acceptable examples violating the rather intricate P&P binding theory of Chomsky (1986a). Consider firstly the following example:

(24)   John and Mary knew that [the journal had rejected each other's papers]

On Chomsky's binding theory, the binding domain for the anaphor *each other* is the bracketed clause. The antecedent *John and Mary* is outside this domain but the sentence is perfectly acceptable. In (24), the anaphor does have a c-commanding antecedent, so it is bound. There are, however, various examples in which there is no c-commanding antecedent, and in which therefore the anaphor is not bound. Consider the following:

(25)   John suggested that tiny gilt-framed pictures of each other would amuse the twins.

Here, the antecedent *the twins* is within the subordinate VP. Hence, it does not c-command *each other* within the subordinate subject. The following is rather similar except that the antecedent is not the whole object but just part of it:

(26) John suggested that tiny gilt-framed pictures of each other would make ideal gifts for the twins.

A further interesting example is the following:

(27) The agreement that Iran and Iraq reached guaranteed each other's trading rights in the disputed waters until the year 2010.

Here the antecedent *Iran and Iraq* is inside a relative clause within the subject while the anaphor is within the object. In all the above examples, there is at least an antecedent within the same sentence as the anaphor. There are, however, examples where this is not the case. Pollard and Sag cite the following:

(28) Mary still hadn't decided about birthday presents for the twins. Tiny gilt-framed pictures of each other would be nice but there was also that life-size stuffed giraffe.

Here, the antecedent *the twins* is in one sentence while the anaphor is within another.

It seems, then, that many anaphors fall outside the scope of binding theory. Pollard and Sag propose that an anaphor falls within the scope of binding theory just in case the head of which it is a dependant has a less oblique referential dependant. To implement this idea they formulate binding theory in terms of SUBCAT lists. Before we can introduce the theory, we must introduce a number of basic assumptions and definitions.

As noted in chapter 5, the CONTENT value of an NP is a feature structure of sort *nominal-object* (*nom-obj*), which has the subsorts *nonpronoun* (*npro*) and *pronoun* (*pro*), the latter divided into the subsorts *personal-pronoun* (*ppro*) and *anaphor* (*ana*). Nominal objects have the attributes INDEX and RESTRIC-TION, and the value of the former is a structure of sort *index*. *Index* has the subsorts *referential*, *it* and *there*, and the agreement features PERSON, NUM-BER and GENDER. Within these assumptions, we have the following nominal objects for *they*, *herself* and expletive *it*:

(29) *they*

$$\begin{bmatrix} \text{INDEX} & {}_{ref}\begin{bmatrix} \text{PER } \textit{3rd} \\ \text{NUM } \textit{plur} \end{bmatrix} \\ {}_{ppro}\text{RESTRICTION } \{ \ \} \end{bmatrix}$$

herself

$$\begin{bmatrix} \text{INDEX} & {}_{ref}\begin{bmatrix} \text{PER } 3rd \\ \text{NUM } sing \\ \text{GEND } fem \end{bmatrix} \\ {}_{ana}\text{RESTRICTION } \{\ \} \end{bmatrix}$$

it

$$\begin{bmatrix} \text{INDEX} & {}_{it}\begin{bmatrix} \text{PER } 3rd \\ \text{NUM } sing \end{bmatrix} \\ {}_{ppro}\text{RESTRICTION } \{\ \} \end{bmatrix}$$

We turn now to some basic definitions. Firstly, we define local o-command as follows:

(30) Let Y and Z be referential *synsem* objects with distinct LOCAL values. Then Y locally o-commands Z just in case Y is less oblique than Z.

Next we define o-command:

(31) Let Y and Z be referential *synsem* objects with distinct LOCAL values. Then Y o-commands Z just in case Y locally o-commands X dominating Z.

Now we define (local) o-binding:

(32) Y (locally) o-binds Z just in case Y and Z are coindexed and Y (locally) o-commands Z. If Z is not (locally) o-bound, then it is said to be (locally) o-free.

With these definitions in place, we can introduce the HPSG binding theory.

(33) HPSG BINDING THEORY
Principle A. A locally o-commanded anaphor must be locally o-bound.
Principle B. A personal pronoun must be locally o-free.
Principle C. A nonpronoun must be o-free.

Here, as in the P&P binding theory, we have three conditions, one constraining anaphors, one constraining personal pronouns, and one constraining nonpronominal NPs.

We now consider how Principle A accounts for some basic examples. Consider first the following:

(34)   John knows Bill likes himself.

Here, the embedded verb *likes* will have a SUBCAT list which we can abbreviate as follows:

(35)   <NP : *npro*, NP : *ana*>

I use 'A : *b*' here to mean an A whose CONTENT is of sort *b*. Given Principle A, the two NPs must be coindexed. Hence, *Bill* must be the antecedent of *himself*. We look next at the following:

(36)   John knows Bill relied on himself.

Pollard and Sag assume that PPs containing a 'case-marking' preposition have the same CONTENT value as the NP they contain. Thus, *relied* here has the following SUBCAT list:

(37)   <NP : *npro*, PP[on] : *ana*>

Principle A requires the NP and the PP to be coindexed. Again, then, *Bill* must be the antecedent of *himself*. The analysis of case-marking PPs permits a straightforward account of examples like the following, which seem to pose a further problem for the P&P binding theory:

(38)   I talked to Mary about herself.

Here, *Mary* does not c-command *herself*. Hence, it is problematic for the P&P assumption that reflexives require a c-commanding subject. However, *talked* will have the following SUBCAT list:

(39)   <NP : *npro*, PP[to] : *ppro*, PP[about] : *ana*>

Principle A requires the two PPs to be coindexed. Hence, *Mary* must be the antecedent of *herself*.

Like Hukari, Pollard and Sag assume that reflexives are impossible as subjects of finite clauses because they may not be nominative. However, their position on reflexives as subjects of non-finite clauses is different from Hukari's. As we have seen, such reflexives are constrained by Hukari's principles, but they fall outside the scope of Pollard and Sag's Principle A. Examples like the following suggest that Hukari's theory is too restrictive here:

(40)   John thinks that it is essential for himself to be selected.

On Hukari's theory, this should be ungrammatical since *himself* does not have an antecedent within the next higher clause.

We should now consider how Pollard and Sag's approach handles the data in (17)–(19), repeated here for convenience:

(17)   Mary likes pictures of herself.
(18)   *Mary likes John's pictures of herself.
(19)   Mary likes John's pictures of himself.

In (17), *pictures* will have the following SUBCAT list:

(41)   <PP[*of*] : *ana*>

Given this, the reflexive will be unaffected by Principle A. In (18) and (19), however, *pictures* will have the following SUBCAT list:

(42)   <NP : *npro*, PP[*of*] : *ana*>

Given this, the reflexives in (18) and (19) will fall within the scope of Principle A, and as a result (18) will be ruled out.

Pollard and Sag pay considerable attention to the interaction of anaphora with expletives. They consider, for example, the following:

(43)   They made sure that it was clear to themselves that this needed to be done.

(44)   John knew that there were pictures of himself in the post office.

Both examples are problematic for Hukari's analysis since they involve a reflexive within an embedded VP whose antecedent is in the matrix clause. There is no problem, however, for Pollard and Sag's analysis. *Clear* in (43) will have the SUBCAT list in (45) and *were* in (44) will have that in (46).

(45)   <NP$_{it}$, PP[*to*] : *ana*, S'>
(46)   <NP$_{there}$, NP : *ana*, XP[PRD +]>

In both cases, there is a member of the SUBCAT list that is less oblique than the reflexive. In both, however, the less oblique member is non-referential. Hence, it does not locally o-command the reflexive and as a result such examples fall outside the scope of Principle A. Rather different is the following example:

(47)   *John knew that it would rain on himself.

Pollard and Sag suggest that this example is ungrammatical because weather *it* is not an expletive but a referential NP, a position they associate with Bolinger (1973). Given this assumption, the PP in (47) will be locally o-commanded and we will have a violation of Principle A.

We must now say something about what Pollard and Sag call 'exempt anaphors', anaphors which fall outside the scope of binding theory. Pollard and Sag argue that restrictions on them stem from processing and pragmatic considerations. They suggest that processing considerations lead hearers to prefer the nearest antecedent provided it has the right semantic properties. Consider firstly (48).

(48)   Bill remembered that Tom saw a picture of himself in the post office.

Here, it seems that the antecedent for *himself* must be *Tom* and not *Bill*. Consider next (49):

(49)   ? Bill remembered that *The Times* had printed a picture of himself in the Sunday edition.

Here, the nearest NP *The Times* is not a possible antecedent for the reflexive and hence *Bill* must be the antecedent. Pollard and Sag suggest that examples in which the nearest NP is a quantified NP are even better than (49). They cite, for example, (50).

(50)   Bill thought that nothing could make a picture of himself in *The Times* acceptable to Sandy.

Turning to pragmatic factors, Pollard and Sag suggest, following among others Kuno (1972, 1975, 1983, 1987), that 'point of view' plays an important role. More precisely, they suggest that reflexives are preferred where they refer to the individual whose viewpoint is presented. They contrast (51) and (52).

(51)   John was going to get even with Mary. That picture of himself in the paper would really annoy her, as would the other stunts he had planned.

(52)   *Mary was quite taken aback by the publicity John was receiving. That picture of himself in the paper had really annoyed her, and there was not much she could do about it.

They suggest that the narrator takes John's point of view in (51), but takes Mary's in (52). This, they suggest, explains why it is acceptable to refer to John with a reflexive in (51) but not in (52).

We must now look briefly at Principles B and C of binding theory. Principle B accounts, for example, for the fact that *him* in (53) can have *John* but not *Bill* as its antecedent:

(53)   John knows Bill likes him.

Likes here will have the following SUBCAT list:

(54)   <NP : *npro*, NP : *ppro*>

Principle B will prevent the two NPs from being coindexed and hence will prevent *Bill* from being the antecedent of *him*. It will allow *John* to be the antecedent of *him*. Principle C accounts for the fact that neither *he* in the following can have *Fred* as its antecedent:

(55)   He knows he likes Fred.

Here, *likes* will have the following SUBCAT list:

(56)   <NP : *npro*, NP : *ppro*>

Given this, Principle C will prevent *Fred* from being coindexed with the lower *he*. It will also prevent *Fred* from being coindexed with the higher *he* since this o-commands the complement clause which dominates *Fred*.

A further point to note about Pollard and Sag's analysis is that it will interact with the HPSG approach to control sentences to accommodate examples like (22) and (23), repeated here for convenience.

(22)   John persuaded Mary to defend herself/*himself.
(23)   John promised Mary to defend himself/*herself.

The lexical sign for *to* will ensure that its SUBJ feature has the same value as the SUBJ feature of the following verb. In (22), the lexical sign for *persuade* will ensure that its object is coindexed with the unexpressed subject of *to*, and in (23), the lexical entry for *promise* will ensure that its subject is coindexed with the unexpressed subject of *to*. Hence, only the grammatical versions of (22) and (23) will be allowed.

A natural question to ask about Pollard and Sag's binding theory is: does it require the SUBCAT feature or could it be reformulated in terms of SUBJ and

COMPS? The answer is that it depends on how unbounded dependencies are analysed. Consider first the following:

(57) I described John to himself.

Here, the antecedent of *himself* is *John*. *Described* will have the SUBCAT list in (58) and the COMPS list in (59).

(58) <NP : *ppro*, NP : *npro*, PP[*to*] : *ana*>
(59) <NP : *npro*, PP[*to*] : *ana*>

In both cases, the antecedent is contained in the list. Hence, it does not seem to matter which list binding theory refers to. Consider now the following:

(60) Which man did you describe to himself?

Here, the filler *which man* is the antecedent of *himself*. *Described* will have the same SUBCAT list here as in (57). If unbounded dependencies involve an empty category, it will also have the same COMPS list. However, if unbounded dependencies do not involve an empty category, it will have the following COMPS list:

(61) <PP[*to*] : *ana*>

The antecedent is not present in this COMPS list. Hence, if unbounded dependencies do not involve an empty category, binding theory must refer to SUBCAT. However, if unbounded dependencies do involve an empty category, it might be possible to reformulate binding theory in terms of SUBJ and COMPS.

10.4 More on control

As we noted at the outset, an important question about bound anaphors is: does the principle that accounts for their properties also account for some other phenomena? In P&P, it is generally assumed that the binding theory condition on anaphors accounts for the impossibility of examples like *John seems is clever* and *John is believed is clever* through its effect on so-called NP-traces. In some P&P work, notably Bouchard (1984) and Koster (1986), it is assumed that the binding theory condition on anaphors accounts for some properties of control sentences. HPSG also makes this assumption.

Pollard and Sag (1994; Sag and Pollard 1991) are particularly concerned with what they call Manzini's generalization, a generalization which derives from Manzini (1983). We can formulate this as follows:

(62)   A controlled complement must have a controller within the minimal clause that contains that complement.

Contrasts like the following illustrate this generalization:

(63)   a.   John promised Mary to shave himself.
       b.   *John said that Sue promised Mary to shave himself.

(64)   a.   Mary asked John to shave himself.
       b.   *John said that Mary asked Sue to shave himself.

Pollard and Sag argue that the generalization is a consequence of the fact that the unexpressed subject of a controlled complement is an anaphor subject to Principle A. To implement this idea they first extend the definition of local o-command as follows:

(65)   Y locally o-commands Z if Y o-commands some X that subcategorizes for Z.

This entails that a less oblique dependant locally o-commands the unexpressed subject of a controlled complement. Pollard and Sag then reformulate Control Theory as follows:

(66)   CONTROL THEORY
       If the CONTENT of an unsaturated phrase is the SOA-ARG in a *psoa* whose relation is a control relation, then the SUBJ element of the phrase is
       (i)   reflexive; and
       (ii)   coindexed with the INFLUENCER, COMMITTOR, or EXPERIENCER value in that *psoa*, according as the control relation is of sort *influence*, *commitment*, or *orientation*, respectively.

Given (65), the unexpressed subject of a controlled complement will normally be locally o-commanded by some other dependant of the control verb. Since it is reflexive it must be locally o-bound. Examples like (63b) and (64b) involve a reflexive which is not locally o-bound. This, then, is Pollard and Sag's explanation for Manzini's generalization. A notable feature of this explanation is that it predicts an important class of exceptions to Manzini's generalization. The following are typical examples:

(67) John knew that to shave himself in public would upset/irritate/annoy Mary.

(68) John knew that it would upset/irritate/annoy Mary to shave himself in public.

In these examples, there is no less oblique referential dependant. In (67) there is no less oblique dependant at all, and in (68) the less oblique dependant is not referential. It seems, then, that we have a satisfying account both of Manzini's generalization and of a major class of exceptions to it.[2]

Pollard and Sag argue that this approach to control also provides an account of Visser's generalization, the generalization that subject control verbs like *promise* do not passivize.[3] Recall that we considered the GPSG explanation in chapter 8. The following illustrates the generalization:

(69) *Mary was promised to leave by him/John.

Here, Control Theory requires the unexpressed subject of the predicative complement to be coindexed with the object of *by*. Principle A requires this unexpressed subject to be coindexed with a less oblique dependant. The only possibility is the subject. However, if it is coindexed with the subject, the object of *by* will also be coindexed with the subject and there will be a violation of Principle B if the object is *him* and a violation of Principle C if it is *John*. One point to note about this explanation of Visser's generalization is that unlike the GPSG explanation it has no problem with the fact that *promise* can passivize where it takes two NP complements, i.e. the fact that we have examples like (70):

(70) Mary was promised a good time by him/John.

Here, nothing will coindex the subject with the object of *by*.

10.5 Summary

In this chapter, we have looked at how restrictions on the distribution and interpretation of bound anaphors have been accommodated within GPSG and HPSG. We have seen that rather different approaches have been developed within the two frameworks. The HPSG approach is narrower in its scope than the GPSG approach, but we have seen that there is evidence that this is appropriate. We have seen that the HPSG approach is allied to an account of disjoint reference phenomena. We have also seen that the HPSG condition on anaphors also accounts for certain features of control.

Notes

1   In addition to their anaphoric use, reflexives have an emphatic use illustrated by the following:

(i)   I myself was there.
(ii) I saw John himself yesterday.

For some discussion within GPSG, see Verheijen (1986).

2   Pollard and Sag propose that some verbs take a VP complement with an unexpressed subject which is a pronominal. They propose that *help* in the following is such a verb:

(i)   Rene helped (to) trim the sail.

Interacting with binding theory, this assumption accounts for the fact that the complement does not have a controller within the minimal clause that contains it and thus is an exception to Manzini's generalization.

3   It has sometimes been suggested that the impossibility of passivization with verbs whose subject is a raised subject, illustrated by the following, is another manifestation of Visser's generalization.

(i)   Sandy struck Kim as unreliable.
(ii) *Kim was struck as unreliable by Sandy.

However, Pollard and Sag suggest that this is impossible because only verbs that assign a semantic role to their subject allow passivization. This constraint is illustrated by the following:

(i)   It rained on our party.
(ii) *Our party was rained on by it.

Exercises

1   It has sometimes been suggested that adjuncts should be analysed as extra complements, more oblique than standard complements. Explain how the contrast in the following sentences argues against this view given Pollard and Sag's approach to anaphora.

(1)   I hired him$_i$ because John$_i$ was the best man for the job.
(2)   *I persuaded him$_i$ that John$_i$ was the best man for the job.

2   An important fact about anaphora is that topicalized pronouns and reflexives behave as if they were 'in situ'. Thus, *him* cannot be interpreted as coreferential to *he* in (1), and (2) is grammatical.

(1)   Him he really can't stand.
(2)   Himself, he really admires.

Explain how this is a consequence of Pollard and Sag's approach to anaphora. Explain also how it correctly allows *Claire* to be interpreted as coreferential with *her* in the following:

(3)   I wonder which of Claire's friends we should let her invite to the party.

3   On the HPSG approach to raising sentences, the raised subject and the unexpressed subject of the predicative complement share all their syntactic and semantic properties. This means, among other things, that if the raised subject is a nonpronoun the unexpressed subject will be too. Given this fact, what does binding theory say about the following examples? (Recall the argument in chapter 4 that the PP complement of *appear* is more oblique than the VP complement.)

(1)   They seemed to each other to be excellent linguists.
(2)   They struck each other as excellent linguists.

4   Huang (1993) points out that while either *John* or *Bill* can be antecedent of *himself* in (1) only *Bill* can be antecedent of *himself* in (2).

(1)   Those pictures of himself John thinks Bill will buy.
(2)   How proud of himself does John think Bill will be?

Show how Pollard and Sag's analysis combined with the analysis of modals and *be* presented in chapter 8 predicts this.

5   The following examples provide a partial illustration of the interaction of anaphora and coordination. Discuss whether Pollard and Sag's analysis makes the right predictions here.

(1)   *John and Mary talked about himself/herself for hours.
(2)   John and Mary talked to Bill about himself for hours.
      (*himself = Bill*)
(3)   John talked to Mary and Bill about himself for hours.
      (*himself = John*)
(4)   John talked about Mary and himself for hours.
(5)   John said Mary and himself were going on holiday.
(6)   John said Jane talked about Mary and himself for hours.

11   Valency Alternations

11.1   Introduction

A major concern for any theory of syntax is valency alternations, where members of some class of lexical heads systematically appear with more than one set of dependants. The classic example is the active–passive alternation. Both GPSG and HPSG have given considerable attention to such alternations. Both have a favoured approach, but other approaches to the phenomena are compatible with the assumptions of Modern PSG and a number of alternative approaches have been proposed.

In this chapter, we will look first at the standard GPSG and HPSG approach to passives. Then, we will look briefly at some other valency alternations. Finally, we will consider some alternative approaches to passives.

11.2   Passives

Undoubtedly the most widely studied valency alternation is the active–passive alternation. To accommodate the alternation, GPSG uses both a metarule and a lexical rule. HPSG requires just a lexical rule.

We can illustrate the active–passive alternation by comparing the active sentences in (1) with their passive counterparts in (2).

(1) a. Mary annoyed John.
     b. The government sent John to China.
     c. Mary told John the truth.

(2) a. John was annoyed (by Mary).
     b. John was sent to China (by the government).
     c. John was told the truth (by Mary).

The passives in (2) are in fact not the simplest passives because they contain *be*, which, as noted in chapter 8, is essentially a raising verb. Rather simpler are the bracketed passive small clause examples in the following:

(3) a.   With [John annoyed (by Mary)] ...
     b.   With [John sent to China (by the government)] ...
     c.   With [John told the truth (by Mary)] ...

The examples in (2) and (3) suggest that passives lack an object and have a subject interpreted in the same way as the object of their active counterparts, and optionally a PP containing an NP interpreted in the same way as the subject of their active counterparts.[1]

Central to the GPSG approach is a metarule, a rule deriving ID rules from ID rules of the kind introduced in chapter 4. For GPSG, the active VPs in (1) require the rules in (4) and the passive VPs in (2) and (3) require the rules in (5).

(4) a.   VP $\longrightarrow$ H°, NP
     b.   VP $\longrightarrow$ H°, NP, PP[*to*]
     c.   VP $\longrightarrow$ H°, NP, NP

(5) a.   VP[PASS +] $\longrightarrow$ H°, (PP[*by*])
     b.   VP[PASS +] $\longrightarrow$ H°, PP[*to*], (PP[*by*])
     c.   VP[PASS +] $\longrightarrow$ H°, NP, (PP[*by*])

The latter can be derived from the former by a metarule of the following form:

(6) PASSIVE METARULE
     VP $\longrightarrow$ W, NP
           $\Downarrow$
     VP[PASS +] $\longrightarrow$ W, (PP[*by*])

This adds [PASS +] to the left-hand side of an appropriate rule and replaces an NP on the right-hand side by a PP[*by*] in brackets.

While this metarule is the most prominent feature of the GPSG analysis, GPSG also needs a lexical rule to derive passive participles with appropriate semantic properties from related active verbs. This rule applies to verbs with a semantic type of the form in (7), where β is NP or S, and adds the semantic combinator f_P, which produces a semantic type of the form in (8).

(7) $<\alpha_1, <\ldots <\alpha_n, <\beta, <NP,S>>> \ldots >>$
(8) $<NP, <\alpha_1, <\ldots <\alpha_n, <\beta,S>> \ldots >>>$

Thus, f_p has the effect of cyclically permuting the verb's arguments. Hence, we have the following semantic types for the active and passive forms in (1)–(3):

(9) **annoy′**   <NP,<NP,S>>
     send′   <PP,<NP,<NP,S>>>
     tell′   <NP,<NP,<NP,S>>>
     f_P(**annoy′**)   <NP,<NP,S>>
     f_P(**send′**)   <NP,<PP,<NP,S>>>
     f_P(**tell′**)   <NP,<NP,<NP,S>>>

This lexical rule is an essential component of the GPSG analysis. As Kilbury (1986) observes, it seems rather unsatisfactory that the analysis needs both a metarule and a lexical rule.

One problem for the GPSG analysis is that not all verbs with an NP complement can be passivized. The following illustrate:

(10) a. The film lasted three hours.
      b. *Three hours was lasted by the film.

(11) a. The baby weighed seven pounds.
      b. *Seven pounds were weighed by the baby.

(12) a. Mary had a solution to the problem.
      b. *A solution to the problem was had (by Mary).

Thus, having an NP complement is not a sufficient condition for passivization. One solution to this problem would be to identify the NP complements that permit passivization with some feature, for example [OBJ +], and to add this to the NP in the input to the passive metarule.

Another problem for the GPSG analysis is that passivization is sometimes possible when there is no NP complement. Consider the following:

(13) a. Everyone believes that John is a fool.
      b. That John is a fool is believed by everyone.

(14) a. Everyone considers under the bed to be a good place to hide.
      b. Under the bed is considered by everyone to be a good place to hide.

Thus, having an NP complement is not a necessary condition for passivization. Interestingly, Gazdar et al. (1985) seem to recognize this in their formulation of the lexical rule, which, as we noted, applies where β is NP or S. (14) shows, however, that it is not just Ss which can permit passivization. An obvious solution is to mark all constituents which permit passivization as [OBJ +] and to replace NP[OBJ +] with XP[OBJ +] in the input to the metarule.

Whereas the GPSG approach involves both a metarule and a lexical rule, the HPSG approach involves just a lexical rule. For HPSG, the active verbs in (1) will have the schematic signs in (15) and the passive verbs in (2) and (3) will have those in (16).

(15) a.
$$\begin{bmatrix} \text{HEAD } verb \\ \text{SUBJ } <\text{NP}_{[1]}> \\ \text{COMPS } <\text{NP}_{[2]}> \\ \text{CONTENT } \begin{bmatrix} \text{RELN } annoy \\ \text{ANNOYER } [1] \\ \text{ANNOYED } [2] \end{bmatrix} \end{bmatrix}$$

b.
$$\begin{bmatrix} \text{HEAD } verb \\ \text{SUBJ } <\text{NP}_{[1]}> \\ \text{COMPS } <\text{NP}_{[2]},\text{PP}[to]_{[3]}> \\ \text{CONTENT } \begin{bmatrix} \text{RELN } send \\ \text{SENDER } \quad [1] \\ \text{SENT } \quad\quad [2] \\ \text{RECIPIENT } [3] \end{bmatrix} \end{bmatrix}$$

c.
$$\begin{bmatrix} \text{HEAD } verb \\ \text{SUBJ } <\text{NP}_{[1]}> \\ \text{COMPS } <\text{NP}_{[2]},\text{NP}_{[3]}> \\ \text{CONTENT } \begin{bmatrix} \text{RELN } tell \\ \text{TELLER } \quad\quad [1] \\ \text{TOLD } \quad\quad\quad [2] \\ \text{INFORMATION } [3] \end{bmatrix} \end{bmatrix}$$

(16) a.
$$\begin{bmatrix} \text{HEAD } verb[pass] \\ \text{SUBJ } <\text{NP}_{[2]}> \\ \text{COMPS } <(\text{PP}[by]_{[1]})> \\ \text{CONTENT } \begin{bmatrix} \text{RELN } annoy \\ \text{ANNOYER } [1] \\ \text{ANNOYED } [2] \end{bmatrix} \end{bmatrix}$$

b.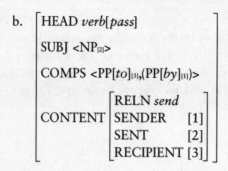

$$\begin{bmatrix} \text{HEAD } verb[pass] \\ \text{SUBJ } <\text{NP}_{[2]}> \\ \text{COMPS } <\text{PP}[to]_{[3]},(\text{PP}[by]_{[1]})> \\ \text{CONTENT} \begin{bmatrix} \text{RELN } send \\ \text{SENDER} \quad [1] \\ \text{SENT} \qquad [2] \\ \text{RECIPIENT } [3] \end{bmatrix} \end{bmatrix}$$

c.

$$\begin{bmatrix} \text{HEAD } verb[pass] \\ \text{SUBJ } <\text{NP}_{[2]}> \\ \text{COMPS } <\text{NP}_{[3]},(\text{PP}[by]_{[1]})> \\ \text{CONTENT} \begin{bmatrix} \text{RELN } tell \\ \text{TELLER} \qquad [1] \\ \text{TOLD} \qquad\quad [2] \\ \text{INFORMATION } [3] \end{bmatrix} \end{bmatrix}$$

Lexical entries for passive verbs can be derived from lexical entries for active verbs with a lexical rule. This will change the syntactic category of verbs while leaving their CONTENT unchanged. Ignoring phonology, we might formulate the rule as follows:

(17) PASSIVE LEXICAL RULE (preliminary version)

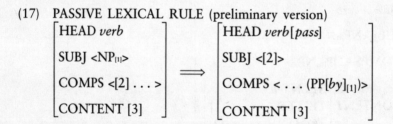

$$\begin{bmatrix} \text{HEAD } verb \\ \text{SUBJ } <\text{NP}_{[1]}> \\ \text{COMPS } <[2] \dots > \\ \text{CONTENT } [3] \end{bmatrix} \Longrightarrow \begin{bmatrix} \text{HEAD } verb[pass] \\ \text{SUBJ } <[2]> \\ \text{COMPS } < \dots (\text{PP}[by]_{[1]})> \\ \text{CONTENT } [3] \end{bmatrix}$$

This replaces the active subject with the least oblique complement and introduces a PP[*by*] complement with the same index and hence the same interpretation as the active subject. As it stands, it will allow the ungrammatical passives in (10)–(12). One solution would be to mark those complements that permit passivization as [OBJ +]. Another solution would be to mark those verbs that can undergo the rule with a distinguishing feature.

In fact this account is rather too simple. We noted in chapter 10 that HPSG handles anaphora with a condition on SUBCAT lists. Consider now the following data:

(18) a. John annoyed himself.
      b. *Himself annoyed John.

(19) a. John was annoyed by himself.
      b. *Himself was annoyed by John.

These data show that active and passive verbs must have different SUBCAT lists. The active verb in (18) will have the category in (20) while the passive verb in (19) will have the category in (21).

(20)
$$\begin{bmatrix} \text{HEAD } verb \\ \text{SUBJ } <[1]NP_{[2]}> \\ \text{COMPS } <[3]NP_{[4]}> \\ \text{SUBCAT } <[1],[3]> \\ \text{CONTENT } \begin{bmatrix} \text{RELN } annoy \\ \text{ANNOYER } [2] \\ \text{ANNOYED } [4] \end{bmatrix} \end{bmatrix}$$

(21)
$$\begin{bmatrix} \text{HEAD } verb[pass] \\ \text{SUBJ } <[3]NP_{[4]}> \\ \text{COMPS } <([5]PP[by]_{[2]})> \\ \text{SUBCAT } <[3],[5]> \\ \text{CONTENT } \begin{bmatrix} \text{RELN } annoy \\ \text{ANNOYER } [2] \\ \text{ANNOYED } [4] \end{bmatrix} \end{bmatrix}$$

We can derive (21) from (20) with the following lexical rule:

(22) PASSIVE LEXICAL RULE (revised version)

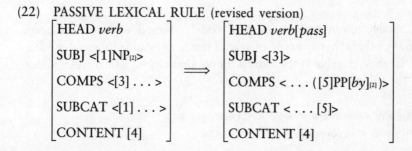

In addition to the changes carried out by the earlier rule, this rule removes the first item from the SUBCAT list and adds the PP[*by*] to the end of the list.[2]

The analysis that we have just sketched embodies the assumption that a passive subject has all the syntactic and semantic properties of the related active object. This is almost but not quite true. Active objects have accusative case, while passive subjects in finite clauses have nominative case. The following illustrate:

(23) Mary annoyed him/*he.
(24) He/*him was annoyed (by Mary).

One solution to this problem would be to abandon the assumption that case-marking is just the selection by a head of a subject or a complement with a specific case, and to introduce certain tree-based case-marking conventions. We noted in 6.3 that this might be necessary for subjects. It may be that it is necessary for complements as well.

There are various possible objections to the HPSG approach. It seems clear, however, that it is preferable to the GPSG approach.

Both the GPSG and the HPSG analysis of passives embody the assumption that passive subjects correspond to active objects. Thus, they require the post-verbal NP in the examples in (25) to be an object and not, as in P&P, a subject, given that they have the passive counterparts in (26).

(25) a. We considered John irritating.
      b. We expected Mary to make a good impression.

(26) a. John was considered irritating.
      b. Mary was expected to make a good impression.

We will see in section 11.4 that there is an alternative approach to passives which does not have this property.

11.3 Other valency alternations

While the passive alternation is the most widely studied valency alternation, there are many others that a theory of syntax needs to be able to accommodate.

Perhaps the most notable is the extraposition alternation, which we can illustrate with the following:

(27) That John was late annoyed everyone.
(28) It annoyed everyone that John was late.

In (27) we have a clausal subject, and in (28) we have an expletive *it* subject and an extra clausal complement. Again the GPSG analysis involves both a lexical rule and a metarule deriving additional ID rules, and the HPSG analysis involves just a lexical rule.

For GPSG, the VP in (27) requires the rule in (29) and the VP in (28) requires the rule in (30).

(29) VP[AGR S] $\longrightarrow$ H°, NP
(30) VP[AGR NP[*it*]] $\longrightarrow$ H°, NP, S

The latter can be derived from the former by the following metarule:

(31) EXTRAPOSITION METARULE
    XP[AGR S] $\longrightarrow$ W
        $\Downarrow$
    XP[AGR NP[*it*]] $\longrightarrow$ W, S

GPSG also needs a lexical rule to derive verb forms with the appropriate semantic translations to appear in sentences like (28). Again, the fact that the GPSG approach needs both a metarule and lexical rule seems a weakness.

Turning to HPSG, we will have the following categories for the verbs in (27) and (28).

(32)   V[SUBJ <S>,COMPS <NP>]
(33)   V[SUBJ <NP$_{it}$>,COMPS <NP,S>]

The latter can be derived from the former by the following lexical rule:

(34)   EXTRAPOSITION LEXICAL RULE
    V[SUBJ <S>,COMPS < ... >] $\implies$
    V[SUBJ <NP$_{it}$>,COMPS < ... S>]

This rule replaces the S in the value of SUBJ by NP$_{it}$ and adds the S to the end of the COMPS list. Like the passive lexical rule, it will leave the semantic content of the affected verbs unchanged.

One point to note about extraposition is that it is not limited to verbs. It is also found with adjectives. The following illustrate:

(35)   That John is a fool is obvious to everyone.
(36)   It is obvious to everyone that John is a fool.

For GPSG, these will involve the following ID rules:

(37) A'[AGR S] $\longrightarrow$ H°, PP[*to*]
(38) A'[AGR NP[*it*]] $\longrightarrow$ H°, PP[*to*], S

Note that the left-hand side categories are A' and not AP. This suggests that XP should be replaced by X in the extraposition metarule. For HPSG, these examples will involve the following lexical categories:

(39) A[SUBJ <S>,COMPS <PP[*to*]>]
(40) A[SUBJ <NP$_{it}$>,COMPS <PP[*to*],S>]

This suggests that V should replaced by X in the HPSG extraposition lexical rule.

We now turn briefly to some other valency alternations. We look first at impersonal passives. These are found in a variety of languages, and resemble ordinary passives in various ways, but do not involve the promotion of a complement to subject. Consider, for example, Ukrainian, discussed in Sobin (1985), where we have the following data:

(41) Zbudovali cerkvu   v 1640 roc'i
      built-3PL church-ACC in 1640 year
      'They built the church in 1640.'

(42) Cerkva   bula zbudovana v 1640 roc'i
      church-NOM was built   in 1640 year
      'The church was built in 1640.'

(43) Cerkvu   bulo zbudovano v 1640 roc'i
      church-ACC was built   in 1640 year
      'The church was built in 1640.'

(41) is an active sentence, (42) is an ordinary passive, and (43) is an impersonal passive. (43) involves the same auxiliary and participle as (42), although it has a different form, neuter singular rather than feminine singular. The central feature of (43) is that it contains an accusative NP just like the related active. It appears in a pre-verbal position but Sobin shows that it is not a subject. A natural assumption is that it has an empty expletive subject. Sobin notes that passives can contain an instrumental NP with the same interpretation as the active subject. Within HPSG, this suggests that the verbs in (41)–(43) involve the following categories:

(44) V[SUBJ <NP[NOM]>,COMPS <NP[ACC]>]
(45) V[*pass*,SUBJ <NP[NOM]>,COMPS <(NP[INST])>]
(46) V[*pass*,SUBJ <NP$_{it}$>,COMPS <NP[ACC],(NP[INST])>]

We could derive (45) from (44) with a revised version of the lexical rule in (22), and we could derive (46) from (44) with the following lexical rule:

(47) IMPERSONAL PASSIVE LEXICAL RULE (Ukrainian)
V[SUBJ <NP$_{[1]}$>,COMPS < ... >] $\Longrightarrow$
V[*pass*,SUBJ <NP$_{it}$>,COMPS < ... (NP[INST]$_{[1]}$)>]

Other languages have rather different impersonal passives. In German, for example, impersonal passives only occur with verbs that do not take an accusative NP complement. Such verbs do not appear in ordinary passives. Verbs that take an accusative NP complement appear in ordinary passives but not in impersonal passives. Obviously, then, somewhat different lexical rules would be necessary here. For some discussion within a version of GPSG, see Nerbonne (1986b).

Another valency alternation in English is the dative alternation, exemplified by the following:

(48) a. John gave a book to Mary.
      b. John gave Mary a book.

The English dative alternation affects a limited number of verbs and does not involve any distinctive morphology. Other languages have more productive alternations, which do involve distinctive morphology. An example is Chichewa, where we have pairs of sentences like the following (from Spencer 1991: 287):

(49) a. Mbidzi zi-na-perek-a   msampha kwa nkhandwe.
          zebras SUBJ-PAST-hand-ASP trap   to   fox
          'The zebras handed the trap to the fox.'

      b. Mbidzi zi-na-perek-er-a   nkhandwe msampha.
          zebras SUBJ-PAST-hand-APPL-ASP fox   trap
          'The zebras handed the fox the trap.'

(49b) contains a so-called applicative verb. Within HPSG, the verbs in these examples will have something like the following categories:

(50) a. V[SUBJ <NP>,COMPS <NP$_{[1]}$,PP[*kwa*]$_{[2]}$>]
      b. V[APPL +,SUBJ <NP>,COMPS <NP$_{[2]}$,NP$_{[1]}$>]

We can derive (50b) from (50a) with the following lexical rule:

(51) APPLICATIVE LEXICAL RULE (Chichewa)
V[COMPS <NP$_{[1]}$,PP$_{[2]}$>] $\Longrightarrow$
V[APPL +,COMPS <NP$_{[2]}$,NP$_{[1]}$>]

We now look briefly at sentences with an expletive *there* subject. Here, corresponding to the examples in (52), we have the examples in (53).

(52) a. A fly was in the soup.
      b. A chimpanzee was hanging from the branches.
      c. A shelf was fixed to the wall.

(53) a. There was a fly in the soup.
      b. There was a chimpanzee hanging from the branches.
      c. There was a shelf fixed to the wall.

Within HPSG, *was* in (52) will have the following category (see 8.5):

(54) V[SUBJ <[1]>,COMPS <XP[PRD +,SUBJ <[1]>]>]

For *was* in (53), we can propose the following category:

(55) V[SUBJ <NP$_{there}$>,COMPS <[1]NP,XP[PRD +,SUBJ <[1]>]>]

This ignores the fact that *there* and the notional subject must have the same number, but otherwise it seems adequate. We can derive (55) from (54) with the following lexical rule:

(56) *THERE*-INSERTION LEXICAL RULE
      [SUBJ <[1]>,COMPS <...>] $\implies$
      [SUBJ <NP$_{there}$>,COMPS <[1], ...>]

Other verbs that appear in sentences like those in (52) and those in (53) are *exist* and *remain*. The following illustrate:

(57) a. Lions exist in Africa.
      b. Three problems remain.

(58) a. There exist lions in Africa.
      b. There remain three problems.

Exist and *remain* in (57) will have the following categories:

(59) a. V[SUBJ <NP[*plur*]>,COMPS <PP[LOC]>]
      b. V[SUBJ <NP[*plur*]>,COMPS <>]

Exist and *remain* in (58) will have the following categories:

(60) a. V[SUBJ <NP$_{there}$>,COMPS <NP[*plur*],PP[LOC]>]
     b. V[SUBJ <NP$_{there}$>,COMPS <NP[*plur*]>]

We can derive the categories in (60) from those in (59) with the lexical rule in (56).

Be, *exist*, and *remain* are not the only verbs that take an expletive *there* subject. Others, however, appear in what seems to be a rather different type of sentence, called by Aissen (1975) a 'presentational *there*-insertion' sentence. Corresponding to the examples in (61), we have those in (62).

(61) a. A picture of Victor Trumper hangs on the wall.
     b. A large green monster emerged from the lake.

(62) a. There hangs on the wall a picture of Victor Trumper.
     b. There emerged from the lake a large green monster.

In the examples in (62), the notional subject appears at the end of the VP whereas in the earlier examples it immediately follows the verb. *Hangs* in (61a) will have the category in (63), while *hangs* in (62a) will apparently have the category in (64).

(63) V[SUBJ <NP>,COMPS <PP[LOC]>]
(64) V[SUBJ <NP$_{there}$>,COMPS <PP[LOC],NP>]

We cannot derive (64) from (63) with the lexical rule in (56). On the face of it, then, we need a second lexical rule here. Given the similarity between the two sentence types, this seems rather unsatisfactory. It would be preferable to have a single lexical rule. It is not at all clear, however, what could be proposed.

11.4   Other approaches to passives

In section 11.2 we looked at what we can call the standard GPSG and HPSG approaches to passives. In this section, we look at a number of alternative approaches that have been proposed.

We noted earlier that there is an approach to passives within a version of GPSG, which does not involve the assumption that passive subjects always correspond to active objects. This is the approach developed in Zwicky (1987).[3] Zwicky cites pseudo-passives like the following as evidence against standard Modern PSG approaches:

(65)   These matters are attended to by Robin.
(66)   This ocean has been sailed across by numerous explorers.

These have the following active counterparts:

(67)   Robin attended to these matters.
(68)   Numerous explorers have sailed across this ocean.

On the face of it, we have passive subjects corresponding not to active verbal objects but to active prepositional objects. The obvious way to bring pseudo-passives within the scope of standard GPSG and HPSG approaches is to assume that they and their active counterparts involve complex verbs. However, as Zwicky points out, there is important evidence in Postal (1986: ch. 6.1) against this assumption. Examples like the following show that the verbs in (67) and (68) can take a PP complement:

(69)   To which matters does Robin attend?
(70)   Across this ocean numerous explorers have sailed.

One might suppose that they can also combine with the following preposition to form a complex verb with an NP object. Postal points out, however, that heavy-NP-shift provides evidence against this possibility. Heavy-NP-shift can move a verbal object but not a prepositional object. If the NPs following the preposition in the active counterparts of pseudo-passives could be verbal objects, it would be possible for them to undergo heavy-NP-shift. The following show that this is not possible:

(71)   *Robin attended to last week all of the problems that had arisen since Christmas.

(72)   *Numerous explorers have sailed across for many years the ocean that once struck fear into every heart.

Thus, passives like (65) and (66) suggest rather strongly that passive subjects do not always correspond to active objects.

Zwicky proposes that passive *be* takes a VP from which some constituent is missing. The fact that a constituent is missing is encoded by a category-valued feature BSLASH (back slash). On his analysis, (2a) and (65) have the following structures:

(73)

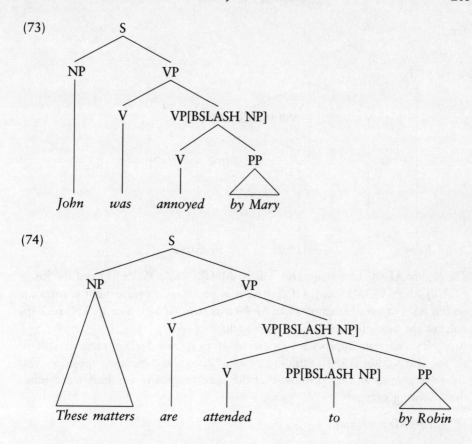

(74)

A notable feature of this analysis is that it does not require the post-verbal NPs in the examples in (25) to be an object and not a subject. Thus, it is compatible with the assumption that (25a) has the structure in (75) and (26a) that in (76).

(75)

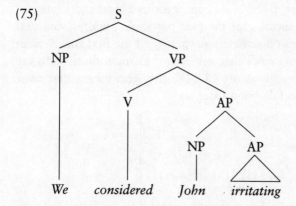

(76)

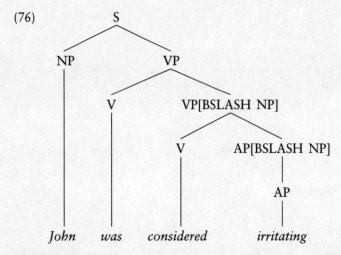

The higher AP in these structures will be A[SUBJ <>,COMPS <>] and the lower
A[SUBJ <NP>,COMPS <>]. Of course, it is necessary to place tight constraints
on BSLASH to avoid examples like *John was painted a picture of*. This perhaps
reduces the attractiveness of the approach.[4]

A very different approach to passives is proposed for German in Pollard
(1994) and Kathol (1994). Building on ideas about 'argument composition' discussed in chapter 6, they propose that the German passive auxiliary *werden* has
the following category:

(77)
$$
\begin{bmatrix}
\text{HEAD } verb[bse] \\
\text{SUBJ } [1]\text{<NP>} \\
\text{COMPS } [2] \ \& \ <\begin{bmatrix} \text{HEAD } verb[part] \\ \text{SUBJ <NP>} \\ \text{COMPS } [1] \ \& \ [2] \end{bmatrix}>
\end{bmatrix}
$$

This makes it clear that *werden* takes as its complements a past participle and
all but the first of the complements that the past participle requires, and that
its subject has all the syntactic and semantic properties of the first complement
of the past participle. Pollard assumes that subjects of German finite verbs are
the realization of an extra element on the COMPS list. This means that finite
forms of *werden* will have the following category:

(78)
$$
\begin{bmatrix}
\text{HEAD } verb[fin] \\
\text{SUBJ } <> \\
\text{COMPS } [1]\text{<NP>} \ \& \ [2] \ \& \ <\begin{bmatrix} \text{HEAD } verb[part] \\ \text{SUBJ <NP>} \\ \text{COMPS } [1] \ \& \ [2] \end{bmatrix}>
\end{bmatrix}
$$

Given this category the passive clause in (79) will have the structure in (80).

(79)   dass ein Klavier seinem Neffen   geschenkt wird
       that a   piano   his   nephew presented is-being
       'that a piano is being presented to his nephew'

(80)

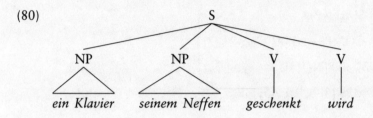

Pollard goes on to extend this analysis to impersonal passives. An analysis of this kind may be appropriate for German, but it seems untenable for English. English has passive VPs with no associated auxiliary, such as the bracketed string in the following:

(81)   the man [given the book]

This string must be a VP and not an AP because adjectives, including passive adjectives, cannot take an NP complement. Thus, the English passive alternation cannot be tied to an auxiliary. Notice also that this analysis involves the assumption that passive subjects always correspond to active objects. This may well be a further weakness where English is concerned.

Another alternative to a lexical rule approach to passives is suggested in Kathol (1994). Kathol points out that instead of deriving one lexical sort from another lexical sort, one could derive both from a proto-sort. He suggests that this is a plausible way of handling the relation between predicative and attributive adjectives, and that it is also a possible approach to the active–passive alternation. To handle the active–passive alternation, we need a proto-sort with a number of proto-features. We can call the proto-sort *proto-verb* and the proto-features PROTO-SUBJ and PROTO-COMPS. Thus, we can propose the following:

(82)
$$\textit{proto–verb}\begin{bmatrix} \text{PR-SUBJ} \\ \text{PR-COMPS} \end{bmatrix}$$

Assuming this proto-sort, we can propose the following sorts for *verb* and *passive-participle*:

(83)

$$\begin{bmatrix} \text{PR-SUBJ [1]} \\ \text{PR-COMPS [2]} \\ \text{SUBJ [1]} \\ _{verb}\text{COMPS [2]} \end{bmatrix}$$

(84)

$$\begin{bmatrix} \text{PR-SUBJ NP}_{[1]} \\ \text{PR-COMPS <NP[ACC]}_{[2]}\text{> \& [3]} \\ \text{SUBJ <NP[NOM]}_{[2]}\text{>} \\ _{pass\text{-}part}\text{COMPS [3] \& <(PP[}by]_{[1]})\text{>} \end{bmatrix}$$

In (83) the value of SUBJ is equated with the value of PROTO-SUBJ and the value of COMPS with the value of PROTO-COMPS. In (84), things are more complex. The value of SUBJ is a nominative NP with the same index as the accusative NP that is the first member of the PROTO-COMPS list. The value of COMPS is the remainder of the PROTO-COMPS list and a PP[*by*] with the same index as the value of PROTO-SUBJ. One important point to note is that the analysis involves the assumption that passive subjects correspond to active objects. As we have seen, this may well be a weakness.

How far proto-sorts offer an alternative is something that has not been fully explored. Kathol (1994: 263) suggests that it is possible to simulate the effect of one lexical rule feeding another, that is, giving rise to lexical entries to which another lexical rule applies. He notes, however, that it is difficult to replace lexical rules by proto-sorts where two lexical rules feed each other.

A related approach to passives is developed in Wechsler (forthcoming). Wechsler assumes a list-valued ROLES feature, which might be seen as encoding under-lying grammatical functions. The order of the list is determined by certain general principles, and general linking principles map the ROLES list onto the SUBJ and COMPS lists. An active verb and the related passive participle have essentially the same ROLES list but the first item on the ROLES list of a passive is a PP[*by*] and not an NP. In an active verb, the first item on the ROLES list is the single item on the SUBJ list. In a passive verb, the first item on the ROLES list is the final item on the COMPS list and the second item on the ROLES list is the single item on the SUBJ list. Thus, if an active verb involves the schematic sign in (85), the related passive participle will involve the schematic sign in (86).

(85)

$$\begin{bmatrix} \text{SUBJ <[1]>} \\ \text{COMPS <[2]>} \\ \text{ROLES <[1]NP,[2]NP>} \end{bmatrix}$$

(86) $\begin{bmatrix} \text{SUBJ} <[2]> \\ \text{COMPS} <[1]> \\ \text{ROLES} <[1]\text{PP}[by],[2]\text{NP}> \end{bmatrix}$

Wechsler argues that the ROLES feature is independently motivated, unlike Kathol's PROTO-SUBJ and PROTO-COMPS features. If so, this would be a reason for preferring his approach. Like Kathol's, this approach assumes that passive subjects correspond to active objects, which may be a weakness.

All of the approaches that we have considered in this section handle passives without a lexical rule. One might wonder if there is any general motivation for trying to accommodate valency alternations without lexical rules. In other words, one might wonder if there are any general objections to such rules. Fodor (1992b) argues that learnability considerations provide an objection to 'productive lexical rules', lexical rules which apply to all lexical signs with specific syntactic and semantic properties except for certain listed exceptions. She observes that all proposed lexical rules have exceptions. She suggests, for example, that *cost* and *resemble* will be exceptions to any passive lexical rule. She then points out that such exceptions are not learnable without negative data. Given standard assumptions about learning, this means that they cannot be learned. If they cannot be learned, they cannot exist, and if the exceptions cannot exist, nor can the rules. It seems, then, that there is an important objection to productive lexical rules. One response to this objection would be to assume non-productive lexical rules, which only apply to lexical signs with a certain feature which a sign will only have if the result of applying the lexical rule to it has been observed. Perhaps, however, a better response is to seek other methods of capturing lexical generalizations such as Kathol's proto-sorts or Wechsler's ROLES feature.

11.5 Summary

In this chapter, we have looked at the active–passive alternation and a number of other valency alternations. We have outlined the standard GPSG approach to such alternations, which involves both a metarule and a lexical rule, and the standard HPSG approach, which involves just a lexical rule. HPSG seems preferable to GPSG here. We have seen, however, that there are alternative approaches to passives, which do not involve a lexical rule. We have also seen that there is an important objection to productive lexical rules. Thus, alternative approaches both to the active–passive alternation and to other alternations deserve to be investigated fully. It is likely that this will be an important area of research in the coming years.

Notes

1   Some passive sentences do not have active counterparts, as the following illustrate:

(i)   a.   Kim is said to be a genius.
       b.   Kim was alleged to be a spy.

(ii)   a.   *They say Kim to be a genius.
       b.   *They alleged Kim to be a spy.

This means in GPSG that there must be some passive ID rules which are not derived from active ID rules, and in HPSG that there must be some passive lexical signs which are not derived from active lexical signs.

2   Borsley (1990b) provides an HPSG analysis using a lexical rule of Welsh passives such as the following, in which the non-finite verb is preceded by a clitic agreeing with the subject:

(i)   Cafodd Gwyn ei   weld gan Megan.
       got   Gwyn 3SGM seen by   Megan
       'Gwyn was seen by Megan.'

3   An analysis of passives quite like Zwicky's is developed in Pulman (1987).
4   Grover (1994) provides an HPSG analysis of pseudo-passives using a lexical rule.

Exercises

1   The following sentences show that there are some verbs that take a 'bare' VP in the active but a VP containing *to* in the passive. Discuss how such data could be handled in either GPSG or HPSG.

(1)   a.   Kim made Sandy (*to) read the book.
      b.   Kim saw Sandy (*to) kick the dog.

(2)   a.   Sandy was made *(to) read the book.
      b.   Sandy was seen *(to) kick the dog.

2   Provide HPSG lexical signs for the active and passive verbs in bold in the following items. Use the SUBJ and COMPS and SUBCAT features. Assume that *as* in (1b) and (2b) is a marker.

(1) a. Kim **expected** Sandy to be on time.
  b. Kim **regarded** Sandy as a genius.
  c. Kim **persuaded** Sandy that it was time to leave.

(2) a. Sandy was **expected** by Kim to be on time.
  b. Sandy was **regarded** by Kim as a genius.
  c. Sandy was **persuaded** by Kim that it was time to leave.

3 It is commonly assumed that there are passive NPs as well as passive clauses. For example, one might regard both (2) and (3) as passive counterparts of (1).

(1) the barbarians' destruction of the city
(2) the destruction of the city by the barbarians
(3) the city's destruction by the barbarians

Provide HPSG lexical signs for *destruction* in these examples and provide lexical rules to derive the second and third signs from the first.

4 Provide a Kathol-style analysis of the Ukrainian impersonal passives discussed in 11.3.

5 Provide a Kathol-style analysis of the Chichewa applicatives discussed in 11.3.

12   Some Further Phenomena

12.1   Introduction

The preceding chapters have dealt with some of the central phenomena of syntax. However, they have been particularly concerned with English syntax. There are other important syntactic phenomena which either play a less prominent role in English than in other languages or do not occur at all in English. This chapter will look at some of these phenomena. We will look first at verb-initial sentences. Then we will consider certain features of German and Dutch. Next we will look at Romance clitics. Finally, we will consider free word order.

12.2   Verb-initial clauses

Verb-initial clauses are a relatively minor feature of English. Only auxiliaries can appear in pre-subject position and they only do so in certain sorts of clauses, notably root interrogatives. Verb-initial clauses are rather more important in German since all verbs can appear in pre-subject position in root interrogatives. They are obviously a central feature of VSO languages such as Welsh, in which the verb appears in pre-subject position in all sorts of clauses. Verb-initial clauses have had considerable attention within Modern PSG, and a variety of different approaches have been proposed.

The most obvious approach is one in which a verb combines simultaneously with its subject and its complement(s) and in which such clauses do not in any sense contain a VP. Within GPSG, this approach requires a number of additional rules, one for each different complement or set of complements that appears in verb-subject clauses. Consider firstly the bracketed VPs in the following:

(1) a. Mary [will know the answer]
     b. John [has seen the light]
     c. Mary [is reading a book]

Here, we need something like the following ID rules:

(2) a. VP ⟶ H°, VP[BASE]
     b. VP ⟶ H°, VP[EN]
     c. VP ⟶ H°, XP[PRED +]

Consider now the related verb-initial clauses:

(3) a. Will Mary know the answer?
     b. Has John seen the light?
     c. Is Mary reading a book?

Here, we need the following ID rules:

(4) a. S[INV +] ⟶ H°, NP, VP[BASE]
     b. S[INV +] ⟶ H°, NP, VP[EN]
     c. S[INV +] ⟶ H°, NP, XP[PRED +]

These rules can be derived from the rules in (2) with a metarule. Gazdar et al. (1985) propose the following:

(5) INVERSION METARULE
     VP ⟶ W
         ⇓
     S[INV +] ⟶ W, NP

To ensure that only finite auxiliaries can be the head of a verb-initial sentence, they propose the following feature co-occurrence restriction:

(6) FCR 1: [INV +] ⊃ [AUX +,FIN]

Within HPSG, a single additional rule is necessary, which we can call the head–subject–complement rule. We can formulate it as follows:

(7) HEAD–SUBJECT–COMPLEMENT RULE
     [COMPS <>,SUBJ <>] ⟶ [COMPS L,SUBJ <[ ]>], [ ],   [ ]*
                              HEAD   SUBJ COMPS

We can paraphrase this as follows:

(8) A sign with the feature specifications COMPS <> and SUBJ <> can have a head daughter with the feature specifications COMPS L and SUBJ <[ ]>, a subject daughter, and any number of complement daughters.

Interacting with the Valence Principle, this will give structures like the following:

(9)

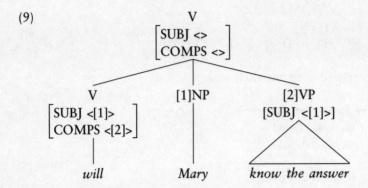

Various other approaches to verb-initial clauses have been advanced within Modern PSG. Borsley (1989a) provides evidence that the subjects of Welsh verb-initial clauses should be analysed as a realization not of the SUBJ feature but of an extra member of the COMPS list. On this approach, the verb in (10) will have the category in (11a) and not that in (11b).

(10)   Darllenodd Emrys y   llyfr.
       read   Emrys the book
       'Emrys read the book.'

(11)   a.   V[SUBJ <>,COMPS <NP[PRO –],NP>]
       b.   V[SUBJ <NP[PRO –]>,COMPS <NP>]

The category in (11a) will interact with the Head–Complement Rule, the Head Feature Principle and the Valence Principle to give the following structure for (10):

(12)

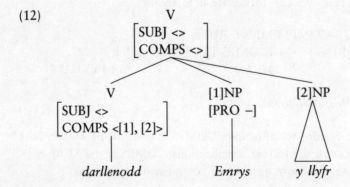

The main motivation for this analysis comes from clitics. In Welsh, a clitic appears instead of or in addition to a pronominal object of a non-finite verb. Thus, corresponding to (13), we have (14).

(13) Dymunai Gwyn i   Megan weld Emrys.
     wanted   Gwyn to Megan see   Emrys
     'Gwyn wanted Megan to see Emrys.'

(14) Dymunai Gwyn i   Megan ei   weld (ef).
     wanted   Gwyn to Megan 3SGM see   he
     'Gwyn expected Megan to see him.'

If we assume that clitics are the realization of an additional valence feature CL, we will have the category in (15) for *weld* in (13) and the category in (16) for *weld* in (14).

(15)   V[SUBJ <NP>,COMPS <NP[PRO –]>,CL <>]
(16)   V[SUBJ <NP>,COMPS <[1]NP[PRO +]>,CL <[1]>]

We can derive the latter from the former with the following lexical rule:

(17)   CLITIC LEXICAL RULE (Welsh)
       V[SUBJ <[2]>,COMPS <NP[PRO –], . . . >,CL <>] $\Longrightarrow$
       V[SUBJ <[2]>,COMPS <[1]NP[PRO +], . . . >,CL <[1]>]

The non-finite clauses in (13) and (14) show subject-initial order. Welsh also has verb-initial non-finite clauses with *bod* 'be'. Here, we have a clitic instead of or in addition to a pronominal subject. Thus, corresponding to (18), we have (19).

(18) Dywedodd Gwyn [fod Megan yn ddiog]
     said   Gwyn be   Megan in lazy
     'Megan said Megan was lazy.'

(19) Dywedodd Gwyn [ei   bod (hi) yn ddiog]
     said   Gwyn 3SGF be   she in lazy
     'Gwyn said she was lazy.'

If we assume that the subjects here are realizations of the SUBJ feature, we will have the following categories:

(20)   V[SUBJ <NP[PRO –]>,COMPS <AP>,CL <>]
(21)   V[SUBJ <[1]NP[PRO +]>,COMPS <AP>,CL <[1]>]

Notice that there is no possibility of deriving (21) from (20) with the lexical rule in (17). Consider in contrast the situation if we assume that the subjects of Welsh verb-initial clauses are the realization of an extra item on the COMPS list. This will give us the following categories:

(22)   V[SUBJ <>,COMPS <NP[PRO –],AP>,CL <>]
(23)   V[SUBJ <>,COMPS <[1]NP[PRO +],AP>,CL <[1]>]

We can derive (23) from (22) with the lexical rule in (17). Here, then, we have an important argument for this analysis.[1,2]

It is natural to ask whether this approach could be extended to English auxiliary-initial clauses. As Pollard and Sag (1994: ch. 9) point out, examples like the following seem to provide an objection to extending it to English:

(24)   Who will do it?

Given the basic HPSG approach to unbounded dependencies outlined in chapter 9, this approach will give an extra analysis for such an example, in which it has a trace in post-verbal position. This analysis is not available on the standard HPSG approach to auxiliary-initial clauses given the assumption that traces can only be complements. We have seen, however, that this assumption is problematic. We have also seen that a traceless approach to unbounded dependencies is advocated in Pollard and Sag (1994: ch. 9) and Sag and Fodor (1994). Warner (1993b) argues that the extra analysis can be avoided within a traceless approach. It may be, then, that the Welsh approach should be extended to English.

On all the analyses that we have been looking at, verb-initial clauses do not in any sense involve a VP. There are, however, a number of approaches in which such clauses do in some sense involve a VP. As Zwicky (1986a) and Borsley (1988) point out, such an approach seems necessary within the standard version of GPSG because the account of subject-selection presupposes a VP. Both outline approaches to verb-initial clauses which in a sense involve a VP. Both propose that ID rules should be allowed to specify that a category includes among its daughters any multiset of categories that can be the daughters of some other category. For Zwicky, an ID rule is an ordered triple <M,C,L>, where M is a category and C and L are multisets of categories. M is a mother, the members of C are daughters of M, and the members of L are categories whose daughters can be daughters of M. He proposes the following rule for verb-initial clauses:

(25) [S,[NP],[VP]]

This says that an S can immediately dominate an NP and any multiset of categories that can be the daughters of VP. Borsley (1988), drawing on an idea of Gazdar et al. (1985), uses a daughters operator 'D' to achieve the same result. D(α) stands for any multiset of categories that can be the daughters of α. He proposes the following ID rule for verb-initial clauses:

(26) S $\longrightarrow$ NP, D(VP)

This has exactly the same interpretation as Zwicky's rule.

A rather different approach that involves a VP is proposed within a version of GPSG in Ojeda (1988). This involves discontinuous VPs.[3] In other words, it involves structures like the following:

(27)

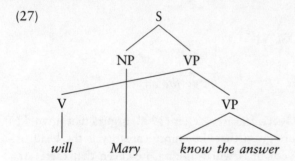

Ojeda's analysis makes crucial use of partial LP rules, LP rules which can order proper parts of sister constituents. He proposes the following rule for English:

(28) H(VP[INV +]) << NP

This requires the head of a VP[INV +] to immediately precede an NP sister of the VP. Ojeda assumes, following a long tradition, that more specific rules take precedence over more general rules. Thus, this rule takes precedence over the following ID rule:

(29) NP < VP

One point to stress about this approach is that it has a VP in the structure that is assigned to verb-initial sentences, whereas Zwicky's and Borsley's approaches only have a VP in the licensing rules.[4]

A final approach that involves a VP is sketched in Borsley (1989b). He shows that it is possible within HPSG to adopt what is essentially the P&P analysis of such clauses, in which pre-subject verbs are sisters of a clause containing an associated empty V. Following Jacobson (1987a), he proposes that pre-subject verbs involve a bounded dependency encoded in a DSL (double slash) feature. This involves structures like the following:

(30)

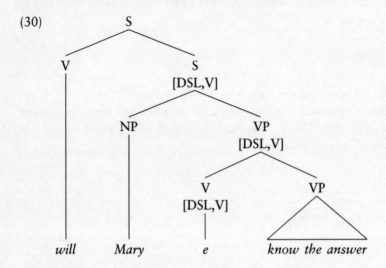

DSL, like SLASH, is a NON-LOCAL feature. Netter (1992) argues that it would be better to use a HEAD feature given that the empty category is the head of the complement of the initial verb. It is worth noting, however, that there are sentence-types in other languages that are plausibly analysed as involving an initial verb with an associated empty category which is not the head of its complement. Consider the following Breton sentence:

(31) Lennet en   deus Yann al levr.
      read   3SGM has   Yann the book
      'Yann has read the book.'

Here, we have an initial past participle, followed by an auxiliary, followed by the subject and object of the sentence. Similar sentences are found in a variety of languages, notably Bulgarian, Serbo-Croatian, Czech, Slovak, Old Spanish and European Portuguese before the twentieth century. They have been analysed within P&P as involving a process of 'long-head movement' which moves a head not to the first head up but to the next one. See, for example, Rivero (1991, 1994), Lema and Rivero (1989, 1991), Borsley, Rivero and Stephens (1996). Within Modern PSG, one might invoke the DSL feature and propose structures like the following:

(32)

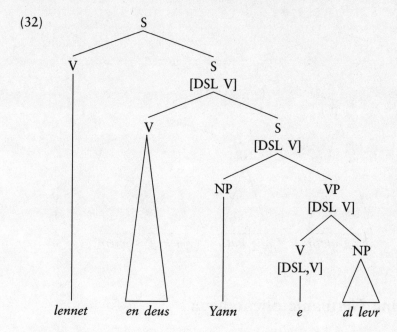

Here, the empty category is not the head of the complement of the initial verb. Hence, the case for an analysis involving a NON-LOCAL feature seems rather stronger than it is in the case of sentences with a finite verb in initial position.

There is one further approach to verb-initial clauses that we should note. This is proposed by Netter (1992) for German verb-initial clauses. Netter argues that such clauses should have a binary right-branching structure. To achieve this, he proposes an empty head which takes as its complements a finite V and the complements that the V takes in a binary branching structure. This gives the structure in (34) for the example in (33).

(33)   Gibt der Doktor   die Pille   dem Patientem?
        gives the doctor-NOM the pills-ACC the   patient-DAT
        'Does the doctor give the pills to the patient?'

(34)

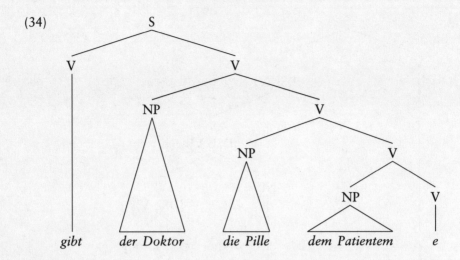

12.3 Some Germanic phenomena

We turn now to a number of features of the Germanic languages. We will look first at the verb-second phenomenon, then we will consider partial VPs, and finally we will look at cross-serial dependencies.

The verb-second phenomenon is a feature of all the Germanic languages except English. What it involves is the appearance of verbs in second position in root clauses.[5] One consequence is that the subject must follow the verb if some other constituent appears in initial position for some reason. Consider the following German examples:

(35) Der Doktor   gibt die Pille   dem Patienten.
      the doctor-NOM gives the pills-ACC the   patient-DAT
      'The doctor gives the pills to the patient.'

(36) Die Pille   gibt der Doktor   dem Patienten.
      the pills-ACC gives the doctor-NOM the   patient-DAT
      'The doctor gives the pills to the patient.'

In (35), the subject precedes the verb, but in (36) the object precedes and the subject follows. Another consequence is that root clauses contrast with subordinate clauses. This is particularly obvious in German and Dutch, where the verb is in final position in subordinate clauses. The following German example illustrates:

(37)   dass der Doktor   die Pille   dem Patienten   gibt.
       that the doctor-NOM the pills-ACC the patient-DAT gives
       'that the doctor gives the pills to the patient'

However, we also have a contrast in the Scandinavian languages, which have SVO subordinate clauses. In subordinate clauses, the verb may be preceded both by the subject and by an adverb and hence is not necessarily in second position. Thus, we have the following Danish examples from Vikner (1994):

(38)   Marie ryger   ofte disse cigarer
       Marie smokes often these cigars
       'Marie often smokes these cigars.'

(39)   at   Marie ofte   ryger   disse cigarer
       that Marie often smokes these cigars
       'that Marie often smokes these cigars'

Clearly this is an important phenomenon which any theory of syntax needs to be able to handle.

Rather similar analyses of the verb-second phenomenon are developed within GPSG in Uszkoreit (1984) and within HPSG in Pollard (forthcoming). Following earlier transformational work, both assume that verb-second clauses are essentially verb-initial clauses with a topicalized constituent. They assume, unlike Netter, that verb-initial clauses have a flat structure. Thus, they have structures like the following:

(40)

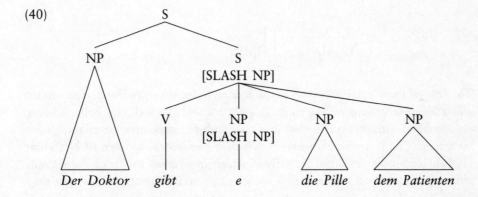

(41)

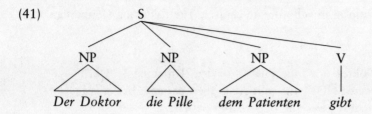

As they stand, these trees pose a problem for LP rules since the verb precedes all its sisters in (40), but follows all its sisters in (41). However, as we noted in chapter 4, there is no problem if main clauses and their head verbs are marked [INV +] and subordinate clauses and their head verbs are marked [INV −]. Then one simply has to say that [INV +] verbs precede all their sisters while [INV −] verbs follow all their sisters.

A second interesting feature of both German and Dutch is what have been called partial VPs, constituents consisting of a verb and some but not all of its complements. Consider the following German example:

(42)   [Ein Märchen erzählen] kann er ihr.
       a   story   tell   can he her
       'He can tell her a story.'

Here a verb and one of its complements appear in initial position while the other complement is in final position. Partial VPs are discussed in Nerbonne (1986a), Johnson (1986) and Pollard (forthcoming). All three note that there is no problem if a head can combine with its complements 'one at a time'. As we noted in 6.2, we can allow this with either of the following rules:

(43)   [LEX −] ⟶ [COMPS L], [ ]
                   HEAD   COMPS

(44)   [LEX −] ⟶ [COMPS L], [ ]*
                   HEAD   COMPS

The first of these rules will only allow binary branching structures. The second will allow flat structures like those in (40) and (41) as well. As Pollard notes, one problem with this rule is that it allows multiple structures for unambiguous sentences. This is a serious problem, which is the central concern of Nerbonne (1994). Nerbonne develops an analysis which overcomes this problem by only allowing a verb to combine with a subset of its complements in topic position.

We turn finally to cross-serial dependencies. As we noted in chapter 2, these occur in Swiss German. They are also a feature of Dutch, where we have examples like the following:

(45) dat Jan Piet een boek op de tafel zag neerleggen
      that Jan Piet a   book on the table saw put-down
      'that Jan saw Piet put a book down on the table'

Here, *Piet* is the object of *zag* and *een boek* is the object of *neerleggen*. As we noted in chapter 2, such dependencies are beyond the capacity of CFGs. They are no problem, however, for a number of versions of Modern PSG.

We will look first at the analysis offered by Ojeda (1988). As we noted above, Ojeda assumes a version of GPSG which allows discontinuous constituents. Within his analysis, (45) will have the following structure:

(46)

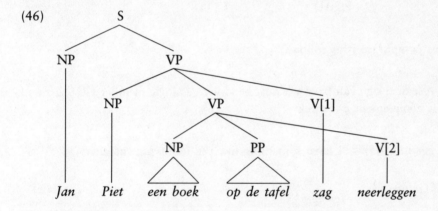

To provide for this structure, we need the following partial LP rule:

(47) V[1] << H(VP)

This requires a V[1] to immediately precede the head of a VP sister. It is this that gives rise to the discontinuity in (46).

We turn now to Rentier's (1994a) HPSG analysis. As we noted in chapter 6, Rentier assumes that German and Dutch auxiliaries combine with a lexical verb to form a verbal cluster, which then combines with whatever complements the lexical verb takes. As we also noted, he provides for verbal clusters with an extra valence feature GOV selecting lexical complements. He proposes that a verb like *zag* also combines with another verb to form a verbal cluster. It will have the following category:

(48)
$$\begin{bmatrix} \text{HEAD } verb \\ \text{SUBJ <NP[NOM]>} \\ \text{COMPS <[2]NP[ACC]> \& [3]} \\ \text{GOV <V[SUBJ <[2]>, COMPS [3]]>} \end{bmatrix}$$

This makes it clear that what complements *zag* takes is determined by the verb that it combines with. It takes an accusative NP complement, which has all the syntactic properties of whatever subject the verb requires, and it also takes as complements whatever complements the verb requires. The following rule combines heads with a non-empty GOV feature with the lexical complement that they require:

(49)   [LEX +] $\longrightarrow$ [LEX +,GOV <[ ]>], [ ]
                         HEAD   COMPS

We can paraphrase it as follows:

(50)   A lexical sign can have a lexical head with a single member GOV list and a complement daughter.

Neerleggen in (45) will have something like the following category:

(51)
$$\begin{bmatrix} \text{HEAD } verb \\ \text{SUBJ NP} \\ \text{COMPS <NP[ACC],PP>} \\ \text{GOV <>} \end{bmatrix}$$

When *zag* combines with *neerleggen*, the category in (48) will acquire the following form:

(52)
$$\begin{bmatrix} \text{HEAD } verb \\ \text{SUBJ [1]NP[NOM]} \\ \text{COMPS <[2]NP[ACC]> \& [3]<NP[ACC],PP>} \\ \text{GOV <V[SUBJ <[2]>,COMPS [3]]>} \end{bmatrix}$$

The resulting verbal cluster will have the same COMPS list and hence will combine with two accusative NPs and a PP. As a result we will have a tree like the following for (45).

(53)

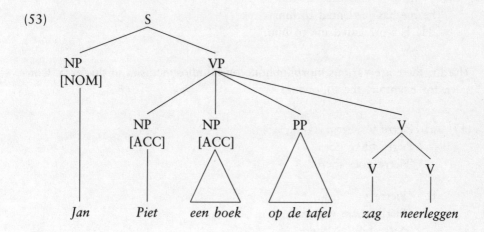

S
NP [NOM] — *Jan*
VP
NP [ACC] — *Piet*
NP [ACC] — *een boek*
PP — *op de tafel*
V
V — *zag*
V — *neerleggen*

12.4 Romance clitics

We referred in 12.2 to Welsh clitics. Much better known and much more fully studied are Romance clitics. They have not been as fully studied in Modern PSG as they have in P&P, but they have had considerable attention in recent HPSG work.

A major Modern PSG work on Romance clitics is Miller (1992), which assumes a framework intermediate between GPSG and HPSG. Miller argues that French clitics are in fact inflections. He presents various kinds of evidence for this position. Firstly, they are always attached to verbs and not to other VP-initial elements. Secondly, there are various arbitrary gaps in the set of combinations. Consider the following contrast:

(54) Il la lui a présenté.
      he her to-him has presented
      'He has presented her to him.'

(55) *Il me lui a présenté.
      he me to-him has presented
      'He has presented me to him.'

While *la lui* is fine, *me lui* is impossible, and it is necessary to say something like the following:

(56) Il m' a présenté à lui.
      he me has presented to him
      'He has presented me to him.'

Thirdly, there are various morphophonological idiosyncrasies in this area. Consider, for example, the following:

(57) a. Pierre y va.
          Pierre there goes
          'Pierre goes there.'

      b. *Pierre y ira.
          Pierre there will-go
          'Pierre will go there.'

      c. Pierre ira.
          Pierre will-go
          'Pierre will go there.'

These show that the locative clitic *y* has a null realization before the future form *ira*. Fourthly, they show a rigid and idiosyncratic ordering, something which has been an important concern for syntactic theory since at least Perlmutter (1970). Fifthly, they undergo lexical phonological rules.

Miller proposes an OC (object clitic) feature with three slots to allow three clitics. Miller and Sag (1993) and Sag and Godard (1994) propose a set-valued CLTS feature. Within this approach *aime* in (58) will have the category in (59) and *aime* in (60) will have that in (61).

(58) Mimi aime le chien.
      Mimi likes the dog
      'Mimi likes the dog.'

(59) $\begin{bmatrix} \text{HEAD V} \\ \text{SUBJ <NP[nom]>} \\ \text{COMPS <NP[acc]>} \\ \text{SLASH \{ \}} \end{bmatrix}$

(60) Mimi l'   aime.
Mimi 3SGM likes
'Mimi likes him.'

(61) ⎡ HEAD V[CLTS {NP[acc]}] ⎤
      ⎢ SUBJ <NP[nom]>   ⎥
      ⎢ COMPS <>   ⎥
      ⎣ SLASH { }   ⎦

On the face of it, a problem arises with the following data, which show that the clitic appears on the auxiliary and not on the participle in the perfect tense.

(62) a. Marie l'   a   vu.
         Marie 3SGM has seen
         'Marie saw him.'

     b. *Marie a   le   vu.
          Marie has 3SGM seen

Recall, however, the proposal mentioned in chapter 6 that the auxiliary *avoir* 'have' involves 'argument composition', i.e. that it takes as its complements a participle and whatever complements the participle requires. This proposal is embodied in the following category:

(63) ⎡ HEAD *verb*   ⎤
      ⎢ SUBJ <[1]>   ⎥
      ⎢ COMPS <⎡ HEAD *verb*[*part*]> & [2] ⎤ ⎥
      ⎢   ⎢ SUBJ <[1]>   ⎥ ⎥
      ⎣   ⎣ COMPS [2]   ⎦ ⎦

Given this category, (64) has the structure in (65).

(64) Jean a   mangé à midi.
     Jean has eaten at 12
     'Jean has eaten at 12.'

(65)

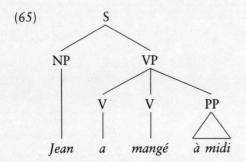

Miller and Sag (1993) argue that this allows a clitic to appear on the auxiliary. Thus, examples like (62a) are no problem. Some additional mechanism is necessary to rule out examples like (62b). It seems, however, that there is no real problem here.

Miller and Sag propose that categories like (61) are the product of a Complement Clitic Lexical Rule. They propose that this rule applies to the output of the Complement Extraction Lexical Rule, which we introduced in chapter 9. This takes the following form:

(66)   COMPLEMENT EXTRACTION LEXICAL RULE
       X[COMPS <...,[LOCAL [1]],...>] $\Longrightarrow$
       X[COMPS <... ...>,SLASH {[1]}]

Simplifying somewhat, we can formulate the Complement Clitic Lexical Rule as follows:

(67)   COMPLEMENT CLITIC LEXICAL RULE (French)
       V[CLTS [1], SLASH {[2]} ∪ [3]] $\Longrightarrow$
       V[CLTS [1] ∪ {[2]}, SLASH [3]]

This transfers an item from the SLASH set to the CLTS set. (66) will apply to (59) to give the following category:

(68) $\begin{bmatrix} \text{HEAD V} \\ \text{SUBJ <NP[nom]>} \\ \text{COMPS <>} \\ \text{SLASH \{NP[acc]\}} \end{bmatrix}$

(67) will apply to this to give (61). As evidence for this approach, Miller and Sag point *inter alia* to the fact that past participles show agreement with a cliticized and a *wh*-extracted direct object but not with an ordinary direct object. The following illustrate:

(69) Marie l'   a   *écrit/ écrite
      Marie 3SGF has written written-3SGF
      'Marie has written it.'

(70) Quelle lettre as- tu   *écrit/ écrite?
      which letter have you   written written-3SGF
      'Which letter have you written?'

(71) *Marie a   écrite   la lettre.
       Marie has written-3SGF the letter
      'Marie has written the letter.'

Miller and Sag do not provide a full account of French clitics but they do provide a promising basis for such an account and a promising basis for an account of clitics in other Romance languages. In the latter context, we should note that important work has been done on Italian clitics in Monachesi (1993, 1994).

12.5 Free word order

We have already referred to free word order in chapter 4, where we noted that languages with free word order require either few or many LP rules depending on whether LP rules identify necessary or possible orders. There is, however, much more to be said about this topic.

We begin by considering a language with the same constituent structure as English but with no ordering restrictions. In addition to the SVO order of English, such a language will allow SOV, VOS and OVS orders. It will not allow either VSO or OSV because neither is compatible with a conventional VP constituent, i.e. one whose constituents form a continuous string. It is clear that there are languages in which all six orders of S, V and O are possible. One is Polish, where we have data like the following:

(72) a. Piotr   kocha Marię.   (SVO)
          Piotr-NOM loves Maria-ACC
          'Piotr loves Maria.'

      b. Piotr Marię kocha.   (SOV)
      c. kocha Marię Piotr.   (VOS)
      d. Marię kocha Piotr.   (OVS)
      e. kocha Piotr Marię.   (VSO)
      f. Marię Piotr kocha.   (OSV)

If all these sentences have the same structure, they cannot have a conventional VP constituent. Generalizing, we might suggest that the greater word order freedom a language allows, the fewer conventional constituents it can have. In 12.2, we considered various ways of avoiding a conventional VP constituent and hence allowing VSO order. In this section, we will consider various other ways of avoiding conventional constituents and hence allowing greater freedom of word order.[6]

One, rather minor, way of avoiding conventional constituents is 'argument composition', which we have referred to in chapters 6 and 11. This allows a head to take as complements elements that one might expect to be the constituents of a single complement. It does not offer any way of accommodating cases where elements which one might expect to form a phrasal head do not form a conventional constituent. For such cases, other mechanisms are necessary.

We have in fact already considered some mechanisms that allow the elements that one might expect to form a phrasal head to be discontinuous. The mechanisms proposed in Zwicky (1986a), Borsley (1988) and Ojeda (1988), which were discussed in 12.2, all allow this possibility. At least the first two will allow verb–adjunct–complement structures such as the bracketed string in (73).

(73)   Mary [said last week that she would be here]

Within these approaches, one could allow this string with the following rules:

(74)   [V',[AdvP],[V']]
(75)   V' ⟶ D(V'), AdvP

It is less easy to exploit Ojeda's approach here. As we have seen, it allows a category to be positioned adjacent to the head of a sister. It is arguable that this is what we have in (73). However, it is also necessary to allow the following:

(76)   Mary [said that she would be here last week]

If an AdvP is required to be positioned immediately after the head of its V' sister, this will be excluded.

Pollard and Sag (1987: 189) sketch a very general approach to free word order within HPSG. As we noted in chapter 4, they assume that LP rules order not signs but only their PHONOLOGY attributes. Normally, the PHONOLOGY attribute of a sign is formed by concatenating the PHONOLOGY attributes of its daughters. Pollard and Sag suggest that some languages may allow 'the pieces of the PHONOLOGY strings of daughter signs to be interleaved with those of other daughters in the construction of larger signs'. The idea here is that free word order languages might allow signs of the following form:

(77)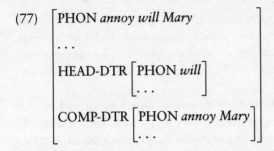

$$\begin{bmatrix} \text{PHON } annoy \ will \ Mary \\ \ldots \\ \text{HEAD-DTR} \begin{bmatrix} \text{PHON } will \\ \ldots \end{bmatrix} \\ \text{COMP-DTR} \begin{bmatrix} \text{PHON } annoy \ Mary \\ \ldots \end{bmatrix} \end{bmatrix}$$

Pollard and Sag only offer the sketch of an approach to free word order phenomena. A related approach is developed in some detail in Reape (forthcoming, 1994). Reape proposes that LP rules apply to word order domains, which are the value of a DOMAIN attribute. The members of the domain of a phrase may not be identical to the daughters of a phrase. Reape in fact proposes that the domain of a phrase consists of its head and either its non-head daughters or their domains. He also proposes that any pair of elements must have the same order in all the domains in which they appear, i.e that there is no 'reordering'. Within this framework, we might have a sign like the following:

(78) $$\begin{bmatrix} \text{DOM } <annoy, \ will, \ Mary> \\ \ldots \\ \text{HEAD-DTR} \begin{bmatrix} \text{DOM } <will> \\ \ldots \end{bmatrix} \\ \text{COMP-DTR} \begin{bmatrix} \text{DOM } <annoy, \ Mary> \\ \ldots \end{bmatrix} \end{bmatrix}$$

Reape notes that a sign like (78) can be seen as embodying two different trees: a syntax tree based on the DAUGHTERS attribute, and a domain tree based on the DOMAIN attribute. In the case of (78), these take the following form:

(79)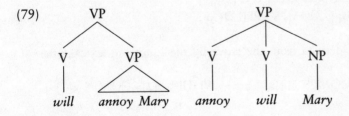

Reape shows how this framework can provide an interesting account of a variety of German word order phenomena.

An approach quite like Reape's is developed within a version of Categorial

Grammar in Dowty (forthcoming). Dowty explicitly distinguishes two different structures, a tectogrammatical structure, which corresponds to Reape's syntax tree, and a phenogrammatical structure, which corresponds to his domain tree. Dowty offers analyses of a variety of phenomena in a variety of languages within this framework.

The Reape–Dowty approach allows both structures where elements that one might expect to form a complement do not form a conventional constituent, and structures where elements which one might expect to form a phrasal head do not form a conventional constituent. Thus, as Kasper (1994) notes, it permits a simple account of verb–adjunct–complement structures such as the bracketed string in (73).

Kathol and Levine (1993) provide an interesting account within this approach of sentences involving what is sometimes known as focus inversion.[7] They are concerned *inter alia* with sentences like the following:

(80)   In the garden stands a fountain.
(81)   In the hallway hangs a large picture of Hobbs.
(82)   Into the woods went the hunter.

These are obviously related to the following:

(83)   A fountain stands in the garden.
(84)   A large picture of Hobbs hangs in the hallway.
(85)   The hunter went into the woods.

Gazdar et al. (1982) propose that the initial constituent in examples like (80)–(82) is a realization of the SLASH feature. Levine (1989a) presents evidence against this. An obvious alternative is that it is a realization of SUBJ. Pursuing this idea, one might propose the category in (86) for *stands* in (80) and the category in (87) for *stands* in (83).

(86)   V[SUBJ <PP[LOC]>,COMPS <NP[3sg]>]
(87)   V[SUBJ <NP[3sg]>,COMPS <PP[LOC]>]

The former could be derived from the latter by the following lexical rule:

(88)   V[SUBJ <[1]>,COMPS <[2]>] $\implies$ V[SUBJ <[2]>,COMPS <[1]>]

Levine (1989a) in fact proposes an analysis rather like this within a framework intermediate between GPSG and HPSG. There is evidence, however, that the initial constituent in sentences like (80)–(82) is not a subject. The most important point is that it cannot appear as a subject in an auxiliary-initial sentence.

(89) *Does in the garden stand a fountain?
(90) *Does in the hallway hang a large poster of Hobbs?
(91) *Did into the woods ride the hunter?

It seems, then, that the initial constituent in (80)–(82) cannot be a realization of SUBJ.

Kathol and Levine propose that the domain of the VP in a simple clause is merged into the domain of its mother. This means that the clausal domain in (80)–(82) and (83)–(85) will contain the subject, the finite verb and the PP complement. They then propose that certain complements can appear before a finite verb. Within this approach, (80) has the syntax tree in (92) and the domain tree in (93).

(92)

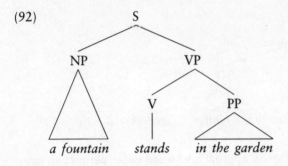

(93)

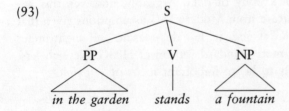

Kathol and Levine go on to show how their approach allows an interesting account of examples like the following:

(94) Into the woods went the hunter and shot a hare.

Here, the example in (82) is conjoined with a VP. (94) is related to the following:

(95) The hunter went into the woods and shot a hare.

In both examples, *the hunter* is understood as the subject of the second VP. Kathol and Levine propose that the domain of the first conjunct in a coordinate structure is merged into the domain of the coordinate structure. This is all they need to allow an example like (94). It will have the syntax tree in (96) and the domain tree in (97).

(96)

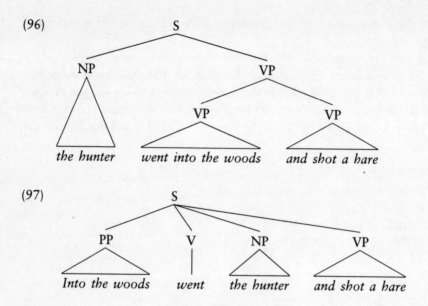

It seems, then, that the Reape–Dowty approach to word order permits an interesting account of a very complex body of data. Arguably, however, this approach represents a major departure from Modern PSG assumptions given that it in a sense involves two separate structures. For this reason, one might prefer to look for a solution within a more standard version of HPSG. Nevertheless, this is an approach that is likely to be an important focus of research.[8]

12.6 Summary

In this chapter we have looked at a range of phenomena which either do not occur in English or are less important in English than they are in many other languages. We looked first at verb-initial sentences and considered the variety of approaches that have been proposed within Modern PSG. Then, we considered certain features of German and Dutch, specifically the verb-second phenomenon, partial VPs and cross-serial dependencies. Next we looked at Romance clitics. Finally, we considered various approaches to free word order. More precisely, we considered various ways of avoiding conventional constituents. Among other things, we looked at the Reape–Dowty approach to word order and the way that it is applied by Kathol and Levine to English focus-inversion sentences.

Notes

1 Many VSO languages have NPs in which a possessor NP, which is sometimes seen as a subject, follows the noun and precedes any complements. An example is Welsh, where we have NPs like the following:

(i)   darlun Emrys o 'r   ddraig
      picture Emrys of the dragon
      'Emrys's picture of the dragon'

(ii) disgrifiad Megan o 'r   dref
      description Megan of the town
      'Megan's description of the town'

Borsley (1989a) argues that the possessor in such NPs should be analysed as the realization of an extra member of the COMPS list. Borsley (1995) argues that the same analysis is appropriate for similar NPs in Syrian Arabic.

2 Borsley (1995) argues that while subjects of Welsh VSO clauses should be analysed as the realization of an extra item on the COMPS list, subjects of Syrian Arabic VSO clauses should be analysed as the realization of the SUBJ feature.

3 An approach rather like Ojeda's is developed in Bunt (1991). Blevins (1994) develops an approach to unbounded dependencies within a version of GPSG in which they involve discontinuous constituents.

4 Hoeksema (1991: 668) points out that rules of the kind proposed by Zwicky (1986a) allow the generation of the non-context-free language $a^n b^n c^n$. The two ID rules in (ia) and (ib) and the LP rule in (ic) will generate this language.

(i)   a.   S $\longrightarrow$ [S], a, b, c
      b.   S $\longrightarrow$ a, b, c
      c.   a < b < c

5 Two Germanic languages, Icelandic and Yiddish, have verbs in second position not only in root clauses but also in subordinate clauses.

6 An early GPSG way of avoiding conventional constituents involves so-called liberation metarules, metarules which replace a category in the right-hand side of a rule by any multiset of categories which can be its daughters. See Pullum (1982b), Zwicky (1986b), Hukari and Levine (1988).

7 Focus inversion and other kinds of inversion are discussed within GPSG in Green (1985).

8 German counterparts of (94), *Into the woods went the hunter and shot a hare*, are discussed in Kathol (1993). Reape and Dowty's ideas are refined and applied to other aspects of German in Kathol (1995a) and Kathol and Pollard (1995). See also Kathol (1995b).

Exercises

1　Discuss the implications for the analysis of adjuncts discussed in 7.3 of the various analyses of verb-initial sentences discussed in 12.2. Focus on examples like the following ((2) is Welsh).

(1)　Was Kim drunk last night?

(2)　Aeth Emrys i　Fangor ddoe.
　　　went Emrys to Bangor yesterday
　　　'Emrys went to Bangor yesterday.'

2　Explain why the examples in (1) and (2) might be seen as evidence for analyses of English auxiliary-initial sentences like that in (30) in which the subject and the following material form a constituent. Discuss whether they really provide any support for such an analysis. Also discuss the implications of examples like (3) for such an analysis.

(1)　Will Kim sing and Lee dance?
(2)　Never should and never will such mistakes be tolerated.
(3)　*Will probably Lee sing?

3　Provide a representation of the kind given in (78) that corresponds to the discontinuous tree in (27).

4　A plausible alternative to the analysis in (32) for the Breton sentence in (31) is a Reape–Dowty analysis. Outline such an analysis using both a representation of the kind in (78) and separate syntax and domain trees.

5　Provide a Reape–Dowty analysis of the following example using both a representation of the kind in (78) and separate syntax and domain trees.

(1)　In the garden appeared to be a unicorn.

Show how such examples pose a problem for Ojeda's conception of discontinuous constituents.

13 Modern PSG and Other Frameworks

13.1 Introduction

In this final chapter, I want to say something about the relation between Modern PSG and other frameworks. I will concentrate on two other approaches: the Principles and Parameters framework (P&P) and Categorial Grammar. P&P has been the dominant syntactic theory since 1980, and hence it is one with which any other syntactic theory should be compared.[1] Categorial Grammar is a framework that can be traced back to the 1930s, but it has developed as an important theoretical framework over much the same period as Modern PSG has developed. As we will see, it is similar in some important respects but different in others.

13.2 Principles and Parameters theory

We noted in chapter 1 that proponents of Modern PSG and P&P sometimes suggest that they are fundamentally different enterprises. I suggested that this is not the case and that they in fact have broadly similar aims. There are, however, some important differences between them. In particular, they have rather different conceptions of syntactic structure and syntactic rules and different attitudes towards formalization. In this section, we will look at these differences.

We noted in chapter 2 that Modern PSG, like Classical PSG, is a monostratal framework, in which the syntactic structure of a sentence is a single tree. We also noted that for standard versions of Modern PSG, as for context-free versions of Classical PSG, grammatical statements are strictly local, never referring to anything larger than a local tree. This entails that a tree is well-formed if and only if every local tree that it contains is well-formed. In contrast, P&P, like earlier forms of TG, is a multistratal framework, in which the structure of a sentence is a number of trees. It is also a framework in which grammatical statements can refer to structures larger than a local tree. This means that a tree can be ill-formed even if every local tree is well-formed. Here, then, we have two important differences between the frameworks.

Another important difference between the frameworks concerns the type of trees that they assume. Put simply, those assumed in P&P are much more complex than those assumed in Modern PSG. For Chomsky (1993), a simple active sentence has the following structure:

(1)

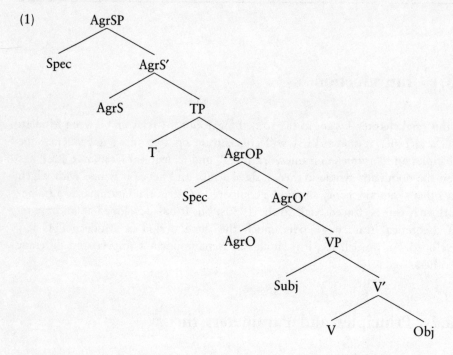

Here, the basic core of the sentence is the VP. This is embedded below a number of so-called functional categories. The subject must move to the specifier position of AgrSP and the object to the specifier position of AgrOP for the licensing or 'checking' of case features. Languages differ in whether these movements take place overtly or in Logical Form (LF). In English, the former is overt while the latter takes place in LF. In addition, the V must move via AgrO and T to AgrS. Again, this movement may take place overtly or in LF. In English it takes place in LF. It is not possible here to go into the motivation for these assumptions. All I want to stress is that they give a much more complex tree than we would have in any version of Modern PSG.[2]

The structure in (1) reflects relatively recent developments within P&P. Early work in the framework assumes simpler structures. However, P&P has always assumed more complex structures than Modern PSG. In particular, it has always assumed empty subjects in raising and control sentences and empty objects in typical passive sentences. It also assumes empty categories in clause-initial position in complex unbounded dependency sentences. Thus, the following examples have the empty categories indicated:

(2) Kim seems *e* to know the answer.
(3) Kim tried *e* to get up.
(4) Sandy was wanted *e* for murder.
(5) What do you think *e* Sandy did *e*?

Of these empty categories, only the second one in (5) is assumed in Modern PSG and, as noted in chapter 9, even that is not assumed in some recent work.

A proponent of P&P might respond to these observations by arguing that while Modern PSG has simpler trees than P&P, it has more complex categories. This is probably true, but it must be said that the nature of P&P categories is quite obscure. What sort of categories are necessitated by P&P analyses has never really been investigated. This is an important weakness, especially given the centrality in recent work of the idea that movement is required for the checking of features.

The complexity of the structures assumed within P&P is arguably more important than the number of structures that are assumed. This is because monostratal versions of P&P have sometimes been proposed. The most notable example is Koster (1986), who argues at some length that neither D-structure nor LF are necessary. We also noted in chapter 1 that computational grammars based on P&P have often assumed just a single-level structure. We should also note that the recent 'minimalist' version of P&P, sketched in Chomsky (1993), abandons the level of D-structure.

It is also worth noting that non-local conditions on trees play less of a role in P&P now than they once did. In pre-minimalist P&P, the notion of government plays a central role, hence the alternative title Government–Binding theory (GB). A head governs its complements, but it can also govern an immediate constituent of its complement. An example like the following, which for P&P has the structure indicated, is relevant here:

(6) Kim considered [$_S$ Sandy to be intelligent]

In pre-minimalist P&P, it is assumed that a verb like *consider* assigns Case to the following NP and that it can do so because it governs it. In minimalist P&P, government is abandoned, and hence a different account of Case in examples like (6) is necessary. It is proposed that the NP moves just like an object to the specifier position of AgrOP in LF and has its case checked in this position. Thus, Case-checking involves the strictly local specifier–head relation.

A further difference between P&P and Modern PSG relates to semantics. As we have emphasized, syntactic analyses in Modern PSG are generally allied to explicit semantic analyses drawing on well worked out conceptions of semantics. Various elements of P&P, notably Theta-Theory and Binding Theory, provide a basis for an account of various semantic facts, but proponents of P&P have generally not been concerned to develop explicit semantic analyses in the way that proponents of PSG have. Some would see this as a major weakness of P&P.[3]

Although there are a number of important differences between P&P and Modern PSG, there are also some important similarities. As we have noted, both are modular theories, in which whether or not an expression is well-formed is determined by the interaction of a number of different rules and principles. More specifically, both assume separate immediate dominance and linear precedence statements. P&P and HPSG are also similar in assuming a small number of category-neutral immediate dominance rules, and the Projection Principle of P&P and the Valence Principle of HPSG are very similar. There is also a considerable measure of agreement about what the most important syntactic phenomena are and how they are like and unlike each other.

We turn now to the different attitudes towards formalization that characterize the two frameworks. Put simply, formalization is seen as much more important in Modern PSG than it is in P&P. In GPSG, it is suggested that P&P is not an example of generative grammar because of its lack of formalization. Gazdar et al. (1985: 6) suggest that ' "generative grammar" . . . includes little of the research done under the rubric of the "Government–Binding" framework, since there are few signs of any commitment to the explicit specification of grammars or theoretical principles in this genre of linguistics'. The HPSG literature takes a more positive view of P&P, but the importance of formalization is stressed. Pollard and Sag (1994: 7, 8) remark that 'we emphatically reject the currently widespread view which holds that linguistic theory need not be formalized' and that 'linguistic theory has become sufficiently modular, complex and deductive that a need for formalization has become apparent, especially to researchers concerned with the computational implementation of current theories'.

The view of formalization in Modern PSG is essentially that espoused by Chomsky in *Syntactic Structures*, where he writes (1957: 5):

> Precisely constructed models of linguistic structure can play an important role, both negative and positive, in the process of discovery itself. By pushing a precise but inadequate formulation to an unacceptable conclusion, we can often expose the exact source of this inadequacy and, consequently, gain a deeper understanding of the linguistic data. More positively, a formalized theory may automatically provide solutions for many problems other than those for which it was explicitly designed. Obscure and intuition-bound notions can neither lead to absurd

conclusions nor provide new and correct ones, and hence they fail to be useful in two important respects.

In contrast to this, the dominant view within P&P has been that formalization is not an important matter. Interestingly, Chomsky (1981: 335–6) remarks:

> It is an open question whether full scale formalization is a worthwhile endeavour at the moment as compared with the task of considering a broader class of phenomena or attempting to resolve problems within this framework ... My personal feeling is that the point has been reached where these further steps should be undertaken, that there is sufficient depth and complexity of argument so that formalization will not merely be a pointless technical exercise but may bring to light errors or gaps and hidden assumptions, and may yield new theoretical insights and suggest new empirical problems for investigation.

However, a few years later Chomsky (1986b: fn. 3) writes in connection with X-bar systems that 'further formalization is pointless, since there are no theorems of any interest to be proved or hidden assumptions to be teased out in these systems'. We also find Barton, Berwick and Ristad (1987) in their discussion of the formal properties of various types of grammars remarking that 'we lack a complete, faithful formalization of GB theory'. In a review, Pulman (1988) observes that: 'It surely isn't a good advertisement for a theory if the only reason it escapes unwelcome discoveries like those presented here for GPSG and Lexical Functional Grammar is the fact that no-one knows exactly what that theory is saying – for that is what their quotation amounts to.'

A defence of the low priority assigned to formalization in P&P is offered by Ludlow (1992). He argues that there is no need for 'mechanical procedures' to determine the predictions of current theories given that counterexamples to current theories are obvious (p. 338). This seems a rather poor response. We are presumably interested not just in whether there are counterexamples to a particular theory but in what the precise nature and extent of the counterexamples is, and also whether it has any unsuspected desirable consequences. Ludlow also notes (p. 341) that other activities may have a higher priority than formalization and that formalization is sometimes pointless. Both these points are reasonable, but it is not clear that they justify the general lack of concern with formal matters that characterizes P&P.

Ludlow is no doubt right that it is possible to overstate the importance of formalization. Precise descriptions that embody no real insight are of limited value. The same is true, however, of apparently deep analyses in which crucial features are fundamentally vague. Many P&P analyses seem to outsiders to have just this character.

One further point that should be stressed here is that P&P appears at present to be in a state of flux. Works such as Chomsky (1995) and Kayne (1994) propose important and potentially far-reaching changes. It is likely, then, that P&P will look very different in a few years' time. It is far from clear, however, whether it will look more or less like Modern PSG.

13.3   Categorial Grammar

We now turn to Categorial Grammar, an approach that we referred to briefly in chapter 3 and chapter 6. As we noted in chapter 3, Categorial Grammar was originally developed between the wars by the Polish logician Ajdukiewicz and it demonstrated the potential of complex categories well before it was recognized within mainstream syntactic theorizing. From the late 1970s onwards, it was developed as a theory of syntax by Bach, Dowty, Steedman and others, and, as we noted in chapter 6, it was an important influence on HPSG.[4]

Categorial Grammar standardly assumes a small number of basic categories, in terms of which all others are defined. For example, we might have just S, NP and N as our basic categories, and we might have complex categories of the form X/Y or X\Y, where X and Y are categories. An X/Y will be an expression which combines with a following Y to form an X, and an X\Y will be an expression which combines with a preceding Y to form an X. Within this version of Categorial Grammar, we might have the following complex categories:

(7)   S\NP   Intransitive V, e.g. *sleep*
       (S\NP)/NP   Transitive V, e.g. *hit*
       ((S\NP)/NP)/NP   Ditransitive V, e.g. *give*
       NP/N   Determiner, e.g. *this*
       (S\NP)/(S\NP)   Auxiliary verb, e.g. *must*
       (S\NP)\(S\NP)   Adverb, e.g. *slowly*

These are too simple in a number of respects. For example, nothing makes it clear that *this* only combines with a singular N, and nothing ensures that *must* combines with a base VP and not, for example, a past participle VP. It is convenient, however, to ignore such matters here.

One might represent the fact that an X/Y combines with a following Y to form an X and an X\Y with a preceding Y to form an X as follows:

(8)   X ⟶ X/Y Y
(9)   X ⟶ Y X\Y

However, the standard Categorial Grammar notation is as follows:

(10) X/Y Y $\implies$ X
(11) Y X\Y $\implies$ X

These two rules are referred to as forwards and backwards functional application, respectively. Assuming just these rules, we might have trees like (12).

(12)

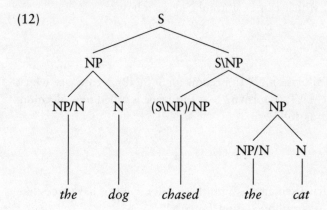

In fact, the following notation is preferred in Categorial Grammar:

(13)
The	*dog*	*chased*	*the*	*cat*
NP/N	N	(S\NP)/NP	NP/N	N

$$\begin{array}{ccccc}
\underline{\hspace{2cm}} & & & \underline{\hspace{2cm}} & \\
\text{NP} & & & \text{NP} & \\
\end{array}$$

$$\underline{\hspace{5cm}}$$
S\NP

$$\underline{\hspace{6cm}}$$
S

However, in the interests of clarity I will use ordinary trees here.

Categorial Grammar assumes a model-theoretic semantics of the kind assumed in GPSG. Semantically, X/Y denotes a function from X-type meanings to Y-type meanings. The same is true of an X\Y. To make this explicit, we might expand the rules in (10) and (11) as follows:

(14) X/Y:F Y:y $\implies$ X:Fy
(15) Y:y X\Y:F $\implies$ X:Fy

It is in fact one of the central features of Categorial Grammar that syntax and semantics go hand in hand in this way.

A major development in Categorial Grammar in the 1980s was the emergence, beginning in Ades and Steedman (1982), of an approach to unbounded dependencies. This involves a number of additional rules. One is forwards functional composition, which we can formulate as follows:

(16)   X/Z Z/Y $\Longrightarrow$ X/Y

A second is type-raising, which can be formulated as follows:

(17)   X $\Longrightarrow$ Y/(Y\X)

Among other things, this allows an NP to become an S/(S\NP), a category which combines with an S\NP, i.e. a VP, to form an S. A third rule is called topicalization, and it can be formulated as follows:

(18)   X $\Longrightarrow$ S$_t$/(S/X)

S$_t$ here stands for 'topicalized sentence'. With these rules, we can have trees like the following ('VP' here is an abbreviation for S\NP):

(19)

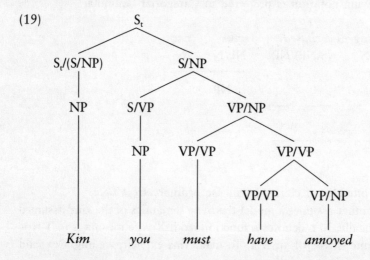

The important point to note here is the way functional composition does the work that is done by the SLASH feature and the Foot Feature Principle or the Non-Local Feature Principle in Modern PSG.

An important consequence of including functional composition and type-raising in a grammar is that sentences receive a variety of unconventional analyses. For example, as well as the rather conventional analysis in (20) using just functional application, we will have the very unconventional analysis in (21) using functional composition and type-raising:

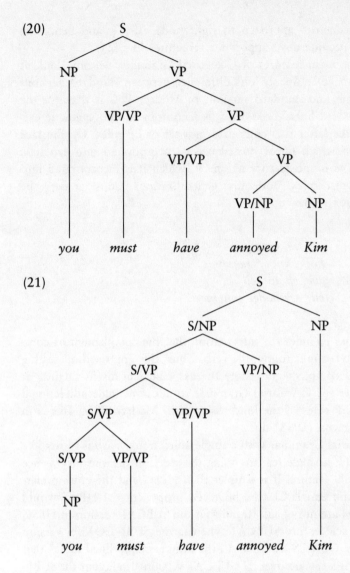

(20)

(21)

Proponents of Categorial Grammar have suggested that non-standard structures like (21) are motivated by the phenomenon of right node raising. Given such structures, a right node raising example like (22) will be a simple case of constituent coordination:

(22) You must have annoyed but we must have impressed Kim.

This approach assimilates right node raising to ordinary unbounded dependencies. However, as we saw in chapter 9, right node raising differs from ordinary unbounded dependencies in not obeying certain island constraints. Thus, this does not seem a satisfactory approach to right node raising, and hence the phenomenon cannot provide any support for structures like (21).[5]

Having outlined the main features of Categorial Grammar, we now look at its relation to Modern PSG. An obvious difference between standard versions of Categorial Grammar and standard versions of Modern PSG is that, for the former, information about linear precedence is incorporated into syntactic categories, whereas for the latter it is embodied in a set of LP rules. On the face of it, a framework in which linear precedence is incorporated into syntactic categories seems just as unsatisfactory as one in which it is incorporated into a set of phrase structure rules. Both miss generalizations. Consider here the following categories for verbs:

(23)   (S\NP)/NP   *hit, see, read*
       (S\NP)/S   *think, know, regret*
       ((S\NP)/NP)/NP   *give, show, tell*
       ((S\NP)/NP)/S   *tell, persuade, convince*

Each of these categories includes the information that the complement or complements that the verb requires follow the verb. Thus, this approach misses the generalization that all complements follow the associated heads in English. It would clearly be better for Categorial Grammar to adopt a single adirectional slash and to assume LP rules of the kind assumed in Modern PSG. This is in fact essentially what Flynn (1983) does.

A version of Categorial Grammar with a single adirectional slash is rather like a version of HPSG with a single feature doing the work of the various valence features and the SLASH feature. It is simpler than HPSG and therefore preferable, other things being equal. Clearly, however, proponents of HPSG would argue that other things are not equal. Recall that the SUBCAT version of HPSG assumes a single valence feature SUBCAT whereas the SUBJ–COMPS version has separate SUBJ and COMPS features. All the arguments outlined in 6.3 that favour the SUBJ–COMPS version over the SUBCAT version also favour the SUBJ–COMPS version over Categorial Grammar.

A version of Categorial Grammar with a single adirectional slash is a framework in which a single notational device encodes both valency information and unbounded dependency information. As we have seen, such a framework requires functional composition and type-raising, which give rise to a variety of dubious structures. Proponents of Categorial Grammar have sought to make a virtue out of such structures, but it is not clear that they have been successful. There is also a problem about complement selection. Consider a verb like *seems* that takes a VP complement. In a version of Categorial Grammar with an adirectional slash,

VP will be S|NP. So, however, will a clause with a missing NP. Thus, it is not clear how to allow (24) without also allowing (25).

(24)   John seems to like Mary.
(25)   *John seems Bill to like.

On the face of it, this is an important objection to encoding valency information and unbounded dependency information in the same way.

It seems, then, that Categorial Grammar is less satisfactory in a number of respects than HPSG. From the standpoint of HPSG, Categorial Grammar is rather like a simplified version of HPSG. The evidence suggests that it is too simple. It is likely, however, that Categorial Grammar will be an influence on Modern PSG in the future as it has been in the past.

13.4   Summary

In this chapter, we have compared Modern PSG, and especially HPSG, with two other frameworks, P&P and Categorial Grammar.[6] Comparison is not an easy matter, but it is possible to identify some important differences, and some respects in which Modern PSG, especially HPSG, may be preferable. This does not mean, however, that Modern PSG has nothing to learn from these frameworks. As we have seen, HPSG has borrowed ideas from both P&P and Categorial Grammar, and it may well borrow further ideas from these frameworks. Equally, the other frameworks may borrow ideas from HPSG. In the long run, it is to be hoped that there will be greater agreement among syntacticians and less division of the field into competing approaches. However, it seems clear that competing approaches will be a feature of the field for some time to come. Modern PSG is likely to be one of the most prominent.

Notes

1   For textbook discussion of P&P, see Haegeman (1994). For an introduction to the minimalist version of P&P, see Marantz (1995).
2   A further complexity in P&P arises from the fact that it is widely assumed, following Larson (1988a), that an example like (i) involves a VP of the form in (ii) and movement of the lower V to the higher V.

(i)   Kim gave a book to Sandy.

(ii)

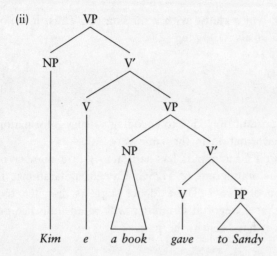

Kayne (1994) proposes that all languages have specifier–head–complement order in D-structure. One consequence of this is longer derivations and more complex structures than in earlier P&P work. Thus, it takes P&P further away from PSG.

3 Although P&P syntactic analyses have generally not been allied to precise semantic analyses, Larson (1988b) combines P&P assumptions with Montague semantics and Larson (1988c) combines P&P assumptions with situation semantics.

4 For textbook discussion of Categorial Grammar, see McGee Wood (1993).

5 Proponents of Categorial Grammar have argued that parsing considerations (Ades and Steedman 1982) and intonation (Steedman 1991) provide further support for unconventional structures like (21). The large number of structures that a typical sentence has within this approach is a potential problem for a parsing system. For some discussion, see McGee Wood (1993: 143–7). The argument from intonation is criticized in Vallduvi and Engdahl (1995).

6 Another approach which it is interesting to compare with the various versions of Modern PSG is the Tree Adjoining Grammar framework developed by Aravind Joshi and others. For a brief introduction to the framework, see Joshi (1987), and for some discussion of its relation to HPSG, see Kasper et al. (1995).

Exercises

1 Compare and contrast the HPSG approach to either passives or *wh-* questions with the P&P approach, drawing if necessary on an introduction to P&P such as Haegeman (1994).

2 Compare and contrast the HPSG binding theory and that of P&P. Draw on the discussion in Pollard and Sag (1994: ch. 6) and relevant P&P literature.

3 Whereas only auxiliaries appear before the subject in English interrogatives, all verbs appear before the subject in French interrogatives. The following illustrate:

(1) Has John read the book?

(2) *Read John the book?

(3) A-t-il   compris?
has he understood
'Has he understood?'

(4) Aime-t-il   Marie?
likes he Marie
'Does he like Marie?'

Within P&P this is seen as a consequence of the fact that only auxiliaries appear in a functional head position outside VP in English while all verbs appear in such a position in French. In support of this idea it is pointed out that whereas only auxiliaries appear before the negative particle and adverbs in English, all verbs appear before the negative particle (*pas*) and adverbs in French. The following illustrate:

(5) John has not read the book.

(6) *John read not the book.

(7) John has often read the book.

(8) *John reads often the book.

(9) Il (n') a   pas compris.
he NEG has NEG understood
'He hasn't understood.'

(10) Jean (n')   aime pas Marie.
Jean NEG like NEG Marie
'Jean doesn't like Marie.'

(11) Jean embrasse souvent Marie.
Jean kisses   often   Marie
'Jean often kisses Marie.'

(12) Il est rarement satisfait.
he is   seldom   satisfied
'He is seldom satisfied.'

Discuss how these facts should be accommodated within HPSG.

4 Show how a version of Categorial Grammar which includes functional composition and type-raising allows all of the following structures for the sentence *You must have annoyed Kim*.

(1) [[[you [must have]] annoyed] Kim]
(2) [[you [[must have] annoyed]] Kim]
(3) [you [[[must have] annoyed] Kim]]
(4) [you [[must [have annoyed]] Kim]]

5 Within Categorial Grammar, it is natural to assume that a sentence like (1) has the structure in (2).

(1) John showed Mary the picture.

(2)

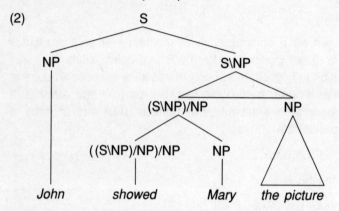

Show how it is difficult, given such an analysis, to account for the following data either with a condition referring to trees or with a condition referring to categories.

(3) John showed Mary himself.
(4) John showed Mary herself.
(5) *John showed herself Mary.

References

The following abbreviations are used throughout:

CLS n = *Proceedings of the nth Regional Meeting of the Chicago Linguistics Society*
BLS n = *Proceedings of the nth Annual Meeting of the Berkeley Linguistics Society*
NELS n = *Proceedings of the nth Annual Meeting of the North Eastern Linguistics Society*
WCCFL n = *Proceedings of the nth West Coast Conference on Formal Linguistics*

Abeillé, A. and D. Godard (1994), 'The complementation of tensed auxiliaries in French', *WCCFL*.

Abeillé, A., D. Godard, P. Miller and I. Sag (in progress), *The Major Syntactic Structures of French*.

Abney, S. P. (1987), 'The English Noun Phrase in Its Sentential Aspect', PhD dissertation, MIT.

Ades, A. and M. Steedman (1982), 'On the order of words', *Linguistics and Philosophy* 4, 517–58.

Aho, A. V. and J. D. Ullman (1972), *The Theory of Parsing, Translation and Compiling*, Prentice-Hall, Englewood Cliffs, NJ.

Aissen, J. (1975), 'Presentation *there*-insertion: a cyclic root transformation', *CLS* 11.

Akmajian, A. and F. Heny (1975), *An Introduction to the Principles of Transformational Syntax*, MIT Press, Cambridge, MA.

Alshawi, H. (1992), *The Core Language Engine*, MIT Press, Cambridge, MA.

Andrews, A. (1975), 'Studies in the Syntax and Semantics of Relative and Comparative Clause', PhD dissertation, MIT.

Arnold, D. and L. Sadler (1992), 'Noun modifying adjectives in HPSG', *Working Papers in Language Processing* 35, University of Essex.

Bach, E. (1973), *Syntactic Theory*, Holt, Rinehart and Winston, New York.

Baker, C. L. (1978), *Introduction to Generative-Transformational Syntax*, Prentice-Hall, Englewood Cliffs, NJ.

Baker, C. L. (1991), 'The syntax of English *not*: the limits of core grammar', *Linguistic Inquiry* 22, 387–429.

Barton, G. E., R. C. Berwick and E. S. Ristad (1987), *Computational Complexity and Natural Language*, MIT Press, Cambridge, MA.

Barwise, J. and J. Perry (1983), *Situations and Attitudes*, MIT Press, Cambridge, MA.

Bear, J. (1981), 'Gaps as Syntactic Features', MA dissertation, University of Texas.

Bennett, P. (1995), *A Course in Generalized Phrase Structure Grammar*, UCL Press, London.

Berwick, R. C., S. P. Abney and C. Tenny (eds) (1991), *Principle-Based Parsing: Computation and Psycholinguistics*, Kluwer, Dordrecht.

Berwick, R. C. and A. Weinberg (1982), 'Parsing efficiency, computational complexity and the evaluation of grammatical theories', *Linguistic Inquiry* 13, 165–91.

Bird, S. (1991), 'Constraint-Based Phonology', PhD dissertation, University of Edinburgh.

Bird, S. and E. Klein (1993), 'Enriching HPSG Phonology', Research Paper EUCCS/RP-56, Centre for Cognitive Science, University of Edinburgh.

Blevins, J. P. (1994), 'Derived constituent structure in unbounded dependency constructions', *Journal of Linguistics* 30, 349–409.

Bloch, B. (1946), 'Studies in colloquial Japanese II: syntax', *Language* 22, 200–48.

Bloomfield, L. (1933), *Language*, Holt, Rinehart and Winston, New York.

Bolinger, D. (1973), 'Ambient *it* is meaningful too', *Journal of Linguistics* 9, 261–70.

Börjars, K. E. (1994), 'Feature Distribution in Swedish Noun Phrases', PhD dissertation, University of Manchester.

Borsley, R. D. (1983), 'A Welsh agreement process and the status of VP and S', in G. Gazdar, E. Klein and G. K. Pullum (eds), 57–74.

Borsley, R. D. (1984), 'On the nonexistence of VP's', in Y. Putseys and W. de Geest (eds), *Sentential Complementation*, Foris, Dordrecht, 55–65.

Borsley, R. D. (1987), 'Subjects and complements in HPSG', CSLI Report 107, Stanford University.

Borsley, R. D. (1988), 'GPSG and Welsh clause structure', *Linguistics* 26, 365–82.

Borsley, R. D. (1989a), 'An HPSG approach to Welsh', *Journal of Linguistics* 25, 333–54.

Borsley, R. D. (1989b), 'Phrase structure grammar and the Barriers conception of clause structure', *Linguistics* 27, 843–63.

Borsley, R. D. (1990a), 'A GPSG approach to Breton word order', in R. Hendrick (ed.), *Syntax and Semantics* vol. 23: *The Syntax of the Modern Celtic Languages*, Academic Press, New York, 81–95.

Borsley, R. D. (1990b), 'Welsh passives', in M. J. Ball, J. Fife, E. Poppe and J. Rowland (eds), *Celtic Linguistics: Readings in the Brythonic Languages: Festschrift for T. Arwyn Watkins*, John Benjamins, Amsterdam, 89–107.

Borsley, R. D. (1991), *Syntactic Theory: A Unified Approach*, Edward Arnold, London.

Borsley, R. D. (1993), 'Heads in HPSG', in G. Corbett, N. Fraser and S. McGlashan (eds), *Heads in Grammatical Theory*, Cambridge University Press, Cambridge, 186–203.

Borsley, R. D. (1994), 'In defence of coordinate structures', *Linguistic Analysis* 24, 218–46.

Borsley, R. D. (1995), 'On some similarities and differences between Welsh and Syrian Arabic', *Linguistics* 33, 99–122.

Borsley, R. D. (forthcoming), 'Subjects, complements and specifiers in HPSG', to appear in R. D. Levine and G. Green (eds).

Borsley, R. D., M-L. Rivero and J. Stephens (1996), 'Long head movement in Breton', in R. D. Borsley and I. G. Roberts (eds), *The Syntax of the Celtic Languages*, Cambridge University Press, Cambridge.

Bouchard, D. (1984), *On the Content of Empty Categories*, Foris, Dordrecht.

Brame, M. K. (1975), 'On the abstractness of syntactic structure: the VP controversy', *Linguistic Analysis* 1, 191–203.

Brame, M. K. (1976), *Conjectures and Refutations in Syntax*, Elsevier North-Holland, New York.

Brame, M. (1977), 'Alternatives to the tensed-S and specified subject conditions', *Linguistics and Philosophy* 1, 381–411.

Bresnan, J. (1976), 'Transformations and categories in syntax', in R. F. Butts and J. Hintikka (eds), *Basic Problems in Methodology and Linguistics*, D. Reidel, Dordrecht, 261–82.

Bresnan, J. (1978), 'A realistic transformational grammar', in M. Halle, J. Bresnan and G. Miller (eds), *Linguistic Theory and Psychological Reality*, MIT Press, Cambridge, MA, 1–59.

Bresnan, J. (1982a), 'The passive in lexical theory', in J. Bresnan (ed.) (1982b), 3–86.

Bresnan, J. (ed.) (1982b), *The Mental Representation of Grammatical Relations*, MIT Press, Cambridge, MA.

Briscoe, T., V. de Paiva and A. Copestake (eds) (1993), *Inheritance, Defaults and the Lexicon*, Cambridge University Press, Cambridge.

Bunt, H. (1991), 'Parsing with discontinuous phrase structure grammar', in M. Tomita (ed.), 49–63.

Calder, J. (1994), 'Feature value logics: some limits on the role of defaults', in R. Johnson, M. Rosner and C. J. Rupp (eds), *Constraint Propagation, Linguistic Description and Computation*, Academic Press, New York, 205–22.

Cann, R. (1993), *Formal Semantics: An Introduction*, Cambridge University Press, Cambridge.

Carpenter, B. (1991), 'The generative power of categorial grammars and head-driven phrase structure grammars with lexical rules', *Computational Linguistics* 17, 301–14.

Carpenter, B. (1992), *The Logic of Typed Feature Structures*, Cambridge University Press, Cambridge.

Chomsky, N. A. (1957), *Syntactic Structures*, Mouton, The Hague.

Chomsky, N. A. (1962), 'A transformational approach to syntax', in A. A. Hill (ed.), *Proceedings of the Third Texas Conference on Problems of Linguistic Analysis*, University of Texas, Austin.

Chomsky, N. A. (1964), *Current Issues in Linguistics*, Mouton, The Hague.

Chomsky, N. A. (1965), *Aspects of the Theory of Syntax*, MIT Press, Cambridge, MA.

Chomsky, N. A. (1966), *Topics in the Theory of Generative Grammar*, Mouton, The Hague.

Chomsky, N. A. (1970), 'Remarks on nominalization', in R. Jacobs and P. S. Rosenbaum (eds), *Readings in English Transformational Grammar*, Ginn and Co., Waltham, MA, 184–221.

Chomsky, N. A. (1977a), *Essays on Form and Interpretation*, North-Holland, New York.

Chomsky, N. A. (1977b), 'On wh-movement', in P. Culicover, T. Wasow and A. Akmajian (eds), *Formal Syntax*, Academic Press, New York, 71–132. Reprinted in Chomsky (1977a).

Chomsky, N. A. (1981), *Lectures on Government and Binding*, Foris, Dordrecht.

Chomsky, N. A. (1982), *Some Concepts and Consequences of the Theory of Government and Binding*, MIT Press, Cambridge, MA.

Chomsky, N. A. (1986a), *Knowledge of Language*, Praeger, New York.

Chomsky, N. A. (1986b), *Barriers*, MIT Press, Cambridge, MA.

Chomsky, N. (1993), 'A minimalist program for linguistic theory', in K. Hale and S. J. Keyser (eds), *The View from Building 20*, MIT Press, Cambridge, MA, 1–52.

Chomsky, N. A. (1995), 'Bare phrase structure', in G. Webelhuth (ed.), 381–439.

Chomsky, N. A., R. Huybregts and H. van Riemsdijk (1982), *The Generative Enterprise*, Foris, Dordrecht.

Chomsky, N. and H. Lasnik (1993), 'Principles and parameters theory', in J. Jacobs, A. von Stechow, W. Sternefeld and T. Venneman (eds), *Syntax: An International Handbook of Contemporary Research*, Walter de Gruyter, Berlin, 506–69.

Chung, S. and J. McCloskey (1983), 'On the interpretation of certain island facts in GPSG', *Linguistic Inquiry* 14, 704–13.

Clements, G. N. (1985), 'The geometry of phonological features', *Phonology Yearbook* 2, 225–52.

Cooper, R. (1975), 'Montague's semantic theory and transformational syntax', PhD thesis, University of Massachusetts at Amherst.

Cooper, R. (1983), *Quantification and Syntactic Theory*, D. Reidel, Dordrecht.

Cooper, R. P. (1990), 'Classification-Based Phrase Structure Grammar: An Extended Revised Version of HPSG', PhD dissertation, Edinburgh University.

Culicover, P. (1993), 'Evidence against ECP accounts of the *that-t* effect', *Linguistic Inquiry* 24, 557–61.

Culy, C. (1985), 'The complexity of the vocabulary of Bambara', *Linguistics and Philosophy* 8, 345–51.

Daelemans, W., K. De Smedt and G. Gazdar (1992), 'Inheritance in natural language processing', *Computational Linguistics* 18, 205–18.

Davis, A. (forthcoming), 'Linking and the Hierarchical Lexicon', PhD dissertation, Stanford University.

Dowty, D. (1982), 'Grammatical relations in Montague grammar', in P. Jacobson and G. K. Pullum (eds).

Dowty, D. (1988), 'Type raising, functional composition, and non-constituent coordination', in R. Oehrle, E. Bach and D. Wheeler (eds), 153–97.

Dowty, D. (forthcoming), 'Towards a minimalist theory of syntactic structure', in W. Sijtsma and A. van Horck (eds).

Dowty, D., R. E. Wall and S. Peters (1981), *Introduction to Montague Semantics*, D. Reidel, Dordrecht.

Dyla, S. (1988), 'Quasi-comitative coordination in Polish', *Linguistics* 26, 383–414.

Ernst, T. (1992), 'The phrase structure of English negation', *Linguistic Review* 9, 109–44.

Flickinger, D. (1983), 'Lexical heads and phrasal gaps', *WCCFL* 2, 89–101.

Flickinger, D. (1987), 'Lexical Rules in the Hierarchical Lexicon', PhD dissertation, Stanford University.

Flickinger, D. and J. Nerbonne (1992), 'Inheritance and complementation: a case study of *easy* adjectives and related nouns', *Computational Linguistics* 18, 269–309.

Flickinger, D., C. Pollard and T. Wasow (1985), 'Structure sharing in lexical representation', *Proceedings of 23rd Meeting of the Association for Computational Linguistics*, Chicago, 262–7.

Flynn, M. (1983), 'A categorial theory of structure building', in G. Gazdar, E. Klein and G. K. Pullum (eds), 139–74.

Fodor, J. D. (1983), 'Phrase structure parsing and the island constraints', *Linguistics and Philosophy* 6, 163–223.

Fodor, J. D. (1989), 'Empty categories in sentence processing', *Language and Cognitive Processes* 4, 155–209.

Fodor, J. D. (1991), 'Sentence processing and the mental grammar', in P. Sells, S. Shieber and T. Wasow (eds), 83–113.

Fodor, J. D. (1992a), 'Learnability of phrase structure grammars', in R. D. Levine (ed.), *Formal Grammar: Theory and Implementation*, Oxford University Press, Oxford, 3–78.

Fodor, J. D. (1992b), 'Islands, learnability and the lexicon', in H. Goodluck and M. Rochemont (eds), *Island Constraints: Acquisition and Processing*, Kluwer, Dordrecht, 109–80.

Fodor, J. D. and S. Crain (1990), 'Phrase structure parameters', *Linguistics and Philosophy* 13, 619–59.

Freidin, R. (1975), 'The analysis of passives', *Language* 51, 384–405.

Gazdar, G. (1980), 'A phrase structure syntax for comparative clauses', in T. Hoekstra, H. van der Hulst and M. Moortgat (eds), *Lexical Grammar*, Foris, Dordrecht, 165–79.

Gazdar, G. (1981a), 'Unbounded dependencies and coordinate structure', *Linguistic Inquiry* 12, 155–84.

Gazdar, G. (1981b), 'On syntactic categories', *Philosophical Transactions (Series B) of the Royal Society* 295, 267–83.

Gazdar, G. (1982), 'Phrase structure grammar', in P. Jacobson and G. K. Pullum (eds), 131–86.

Gazdar, G. (1987), 'Linguistic applications of default inheritance mechanisms', in P. Whitelock, M. M. Wood, H. L. Somers and P. Bennett (eds), *Linguistic Theory and Computer Applications*, Academic Press, London, 37–67.

Gazdar, G. (1988), 'Applicability of indexed grammars to natural languages', in U. Reyle and C. Rohrer (eds), *Natural Language Parsing and Linguistic Theories*, D. Reidel, Dordrecht, 69–94.

Gazdar, G., E. Klein and G. K. Pullum (eds) (1983), *Order, Concord and Constituency*, Foris, Dordrecht.

Gazdar, G., E. Klein, G. Pullum and I. Sag (1985), *Generalized Phrase Structure Grammar*, Basil Blackwell, Oxford.

Gazdar, G. and C. Mellish (1989), *Natural Language Processing in PROLOG: An Introduction to Computational Linguistics*, Addison Wesley, New York.

Gazdar, G. and G. Pullum (1981), 'Subcategorization, constituent order and the notion "head"', in M. Moortgat, H. v. Hulst and T. Hoekstra (eds), *The Scope of Lexical Rules*, Foris, Dordrecht, 107–23.

Gazdar, G. and G. Pullum (1982), 'Generalized phrase structure grammar: a theoretical synopsis', Indiana University Linguistics Club, Bloomington, Indiana.

Gazdar, G. and G. Pullum (1985), 'Computationally relevant properties of natural languages and their grammars', *New Generation Computing* 3, 273–306.

Gazdar, G., G. Pullum, R. Carpenter, E. Klein, T. Hukari and R. Levine (1988), 'Category structures', *Computational Linguistics* 14, 1–19.

Gazdar, G., G. K. Pullum and I. Sag (1982), 'Auxiliaries and related phenomena in a restrictive theory of grammar', *Language* 58, 591–638.

Gazdar, G. and I. Sag (1981), 'Passive and reflexives in phrase structure grammar', in J. Groenendijk, T. Janssen and M. Stokhof (eds), *Formal Methods in the Study of Language. Proceedings of the Third Amsterdam Colloquium*, Mathematical Centre Tracts, Amsterdam.

Goldberg, J. (1985), 'Lexical operations and unbounded dependencies', *CLS* 21, 122–32.

Goldsmith, J. (1985), 'A principled exception to the Coordinate Structure Constraint', *CLS* 21, 133–43.

Green, G. (1985), 'The description of inversions in generalized phrase structure grammar', *BLS* 11, 117–45.

Green, G. and J. Morgan (1996), 'Auxiliary inversions and the notion "default specification"', to appear in *Journal of Linguistics*.

Grimshaw, J. (1974), 'Evidence for relativization by deletion in Chaucerian Middle English', *NELS* 5, 216–24.

Grimshaw, J. (1993), 'Minimal projection, heads and optimality', unpublished manuscript, Rutgers University.

Grinder, J. and S. Elgin (1973), *Guide to Transformational Grammar*, Holt, Rinehart and Winston, New York.

Grishman, R. (1986), *Computational Linguistics: An Introduction*, Cambridge University Press, Cambridge.

Grover, C. (1994), 'Rethinking Some Empty Categories: Missing Objects and Parasitic Gaps in HPSG', PhD dissertation, University of Essex.

Grover, C., T. Briscoe, J. Carroll and B. Boguraev (1988), *The Alvey Natural Language Tools Project Grammar: A Wide-Coverage Computational Grammar of English*, Lancaster Papers in Linguistics 23, University of Lancaster.

Gunji, T. (1987), *Japanese Phrase Structure Grammar*, D. Reidel, Dordrecht.

Haegeman, L. (1994), *Introduction to Government and Binding Theory* (2nd edn), Blackwell, Oxford.

Harman, G. (1963), 'Generative grammars without transformational rules: a defense of phrase structure', *Language* 39, 597–616.

Harris, Z. S. (1951), *Methods in Structural Linguistics*, University of Chicago Press, Chicago.

Harris, Z. S. (1962), *String Analysis of Natural Language*, Mouton, The Hague.

Heinz, W. and J. Matiasek (1994), 'Argument structure and case assignment in German', in J. Nerbonne, K. Netter and C. Pollard (eds), 199–236.

Heny, F. (1979), Review of Noam Chomsky, *Logical Structure of Linguistic Theory*, *Synthese* 40, 317–52.

Hinrichs, E. and T. Nakazawa (1989), 'Flipped out: AUX in German', *CLS* 25, 193–202.

Hinrichs, E. and T. Nakazawa (1994), 'Linearizing AUX in German verbal complexes', in J. Nerbonne, K. Netter and C. Pollard (eds), 11–37.

Hockett, C. F. (1954), 'Two models of grammatical description', *Word* 10, 210–31.

Hockett, C. F. (1961), 'Grammar for the hearer', in R. Jakobson (ed.), *Structure of Language and its Mathematical Aspects*, Proceedings of the 12th Symposium in Applied Linguistics, Providence.

Hoeksema, J. (1991), 'Complex predicates and liberation in Dutch and English', *Linguistics and Philosophy* 14, 661–710.

Horrocks, G. (1987), *Generative Grammar*, Longman, London.

Huang, C. T. J. (1993), 'Reconstruction and the structure of VP: some theoretical consequences', *Linguistic Inquiry* 24, 103–38.

Huck, G. J. and A. E. Ojeda (eds) (1987), *Syntax and Semantics 20: Discontinuous Constituency*, Academic Press, New York.

Huddleston, R. (1976), *An Introduction to English Transformational Syntax*, Longman, London.

Hudson, R. (1971), *English Complex Sentences: An Introduction to Systemic Grammar*, North-Holland, Amsterdam.

Hudson, R. (1976), *Arguments for a Non-Transformational Grammar*, University of Chicago Press, Chicago.

Hudson, R. (1984), *Word Grammar*, Basil Blackwell, Oxford.

Hudson, R. (1989), 'Gapping and grammatical relations', *Journal of Linguistics* 25, 57–94.

Hudson, R. (1990), *English Word Grammar*, Basil Blackwell, Oxford.

Hukari, T. (1989), 'The domain of reflexivization', *Linguistics* 27, 207–44.

Hukari, T. and R. D. Levine (1986), 'Generalized phrase structure grammar: a review article', *Linguistic Analysis* 16, 135–260.

Hukari, T. and R. D. Levine (1987), 'Parasitic gaps, SLASH termination and the c-command condition', *Natural Language and Linguistic Theory* 5, 197–222.

Hukari, T. and R. D. Levine (1988), 'Liberation and inversion in GPSG', *WCCFL* 7, Stanford Linguistics Association, Stanford.

Hukari, T. and R. D. Levine (1991a), 'On the disunity of unbounded dependency constructions', *Natural Language and Linguistic Theory* 9, 97–144.

Hukari, T. and R. D. Levine (1991b), Review of Pollard and Sag (1987), *Journal of Linguistics* 27, 262–7.

Hukari, T. and R. D. Levine (1995a), 'Adjunct extraction', *Journal of Linguistics* 31, 195–226.

Hukari, T. and R. D. Levine (1995b), 'On the status of adjunct-internal gaps', unpublished paper, University of Victoria and Ohio State University.

Huybregts, R. (1985), 'The weak inadequacy of context-free phrase structure grammar', in G. de Haan, M. Trommelen and W. Zonneveld (eds), *Van Periferie naar Kern*, Foris, Dordrecht, 81–99.

Jackendoff, R. S. (1975), 'Morphological and semantic regularities in the lexicon', *Language* 51, 639–71.

Jackendoff, R. S. (1977), *X-Syntax: A Study of Phrase Structure*, MIT Press, Cambridge, MA.

Jacobson, P. (1987a), 'Phrase structure, grammatical relations, and discontinuous constituents', in G. J. Huck and A. E. Ojeda (eds), 27–69.

Jacobson, P. (1987b), Review of Gazdar et al. (1985), *Linguistics and Philosophy* 10, 389–486.

Jacobson, P. (1990), 'Raising as function composition', *Linguistics and Philosophy* 13, 423–75.

Jacobson, P. and G. K. Pullum (eds) (1982), *The Nature of Syntactic Representation*, D. Reidel, Dordrecht.

Johnson, M. (1986), 'A GPSG account of VP structure in German', *Linguistics* 24, 871–82.

Joshi, A. K. (1987), 'Phrase structure grammar', in S. C. Shapiro (ed.), *Encyclopaedia of Artificial Intelligence*, Wiley, New York, 344–51.

Joshi, A. K., K. Vijay-Shanker and D. Weir (1991), 'The convergence of mildly context-sensitive grammar formalisms', in P. Sells, S. Shieber and T. Wasow (eds), 31–81.

Kaplan, R. and J. Bresnan (1982), 'Lexical-functional grammar: a formal system for grammatical representation', in J. Bresnan (ed.), 173–281.

Kartunnen, L. (1984), 'Features and values', *Proceedings of Coling*, 28–33.

Kasper, R. T. (1994), 'Adjuncts in mittelfeld', in J. Nerbonne, K. Netter and C. Pollard (eds), 39–69.

Kasper, R., B. Kiefer, K. Netter and K. Vijay-Shanker (1995), 'Compilation of HPSG to TAG', *Proceedings of ACL-95*.

Kasper, R. T. and W. C. Rounds (1990), 'The logic of unification in grammar', *Linguistics and Philosophy* 13, 35–59.

Kathol, A. (1993), 'Linearization and coordination in German', in A. Kathol and C. Pollard (eds), *Papers in Syntax*, OSU Working Papers in Linguistics 42, Ohio State University, 117–51.

Kathol, A. (1994), 'Passives without lexical rules', in J. Nerbonne, K. Netter and C. Pollard (eds), 237–72.

Kathol, A. (1995a), 'Verb-"movement" in German and topological fields', *CLS* 31.

Kathol, A. (1995b), 'Linearization-Based German Syntax', PhD thesis, Ohio State University.

Kathol, A. (forthcoming), 'On agreement in HPSG', to appear in R. D. Levine and G. Green (eds).

Kathol, A. and R. D. Levine (1993), 'Inversion as a linearization effect', *NELS* 23, 207–21.

Kathol, A. and C. Pollard (1995), 'On the left periphery of German subordinate clauses', *WCCFL* 14.

Katz, J. J. and J. A. Fodor (1963), 'The structure of a semantic theory', *Language* 39, 170–210.

Kayne, R. S. (1994), *The Antisymmetry of Syntax*, MIT Press, Cambridge, MA.

Kenstowicz, M. (1994), *Phonology in Generative Grammar*, Blackwell, Oxford.

Kilbury, J. (1986), 'Category co-occurrence restrictions and the elimination of metarules', *11th International Conference on Computational Linguistics: Proceedings of Coling '86*, Bonn, 50–5.

Klein, E. H. and I. A. Sag (1985), 'Type-driven translation', *Linguistics and Philosophy* 8, 163–201.

Kolliakou, D. (1995), 'Definites and Possessives in Modern Greek: An HPSG Syntax for Noun Phrases', PhD dissertation, University of Edinburgh.

Koopman, H. and D. Sportiche (1991), 'The position of subjects', *Lingua* 85, 211–58.

Kornai, A. and G. K. Pullum (1990), 'The X-bar theory of phrase structure', *Language* 66, 24–50.

Koster, J. (1978), *Locality Principles in Syntax*, Foris, Dordrecht.

Koster, J. (1986), *Domains and Dynasties: The Radical Autonomy of Syntax*, Foris, Dordrecht.

Koster, J. and R. May (1982), 'On the constituency of infinitives', *Language* 58, 116–43.

Krieger, H-U. and J. Nerbonne (1993), 'Feature-based inheritance networks for computational lexicons', in T. Briscoe, V. de Paiva and A. Copestake (eds), 90–136.

Kuno, S. (1972), 'Pronominalization, reflexivization and direct discourse', *Linguistic Inquiry* 3, 161–95.

Kuno, S. (1975), 'Three perspectives in the functional approach to syntax', in R. Grossman, L. J. San and T. Vance (eds), *Papers from the Parasession on Functionalism*, Chicago Linguistic Society, Chicago, 276–336.

Kuno, S. (1983), 'Reflexivization in English', *Communication and Cognition* 16.1/2, 65–80.

Kuno, S. (1987), *Functional Syntax*, University of Chicago Press, Chicago.

Kuno, S. and A. G. Oettinger (1962), 'Multiple-path syntactic analyzer', in *Information and Processing 1962*, North-Holland, Amsterdam.

Lakoff, G. (1986), 'Frame semantic control of the Coordinate Structure Constraint', *CLS Parasession on Pragmatics and Grammatical Theory*, Chicago, 152–67.

Lamb, S. (1962), *Outline of Stratificational Grammar*, Berkeley.

Larson, R. (1988a), 'On the double object construction', *Linguistic Inquiry* 19, 335–91.

Larson, R. (1988b), 'Scope and comparatives', *Linguistics and Philosophy* 11, 1–26.

Larson, R. (1988c), 'Implicit arguments and situation semantics', *Linguistics and Philosophy* 11, 169–201.

Lees, R. and E. Klima (1963), 'Rules for English pronominalization', *Language* 39, 17–28.

Lema, J. and M-L. Rivero (1989), 'Long head movement: ECP vs HMC', *NELS* 20, 333–47.

Lema, J. and M-L. Rivero (1991), 'Types of verbal movement in Old Spanish: modals, futures, and perfects', *Probus* 3, 237–78.

Levine, R. D. (1985), 'Right node (non-)raising', *Linguistic Inquiry* 16, 3–29.

Levine, R. D. (1989a), 'On focus inversion and the role of a SUBCAT list', *Linguistics* 27, 1013–55.

Levine, R. D. (1989b), 'Downgrading constructions in GPSG', *Natural Language and Linguistic Theory* 7, 123–35.

Levine, R. D. and G. Green (eds) (forthcoming), *Readings in Head-driven Phrase Structure Grammar*.

Ludlow, P. (1992), 'Formal rigor and linguistic theory', *Natural Language and Linguistic Theory* 10, 335–44.

Lyons, J. (1968), *Introduction to Theoretical Linguistics*, Cambridge University Press, Cambridge.

Maling, J. (1978), 'An asymmetry with respect to *wh*-islands', *Linguistic Inquiry* 9, 75–88.

Maling, J. and A. Zaenen (1982), 'A phrase structure account of Scandinavian extraction phenomena', in P. Jacobson and G. K. Pullum (eds).

Manaster-Ramer, A. and M. Kac (1990), 'The concept of phrase structure', *Linguistics and Philosophy* 13, 325–62.

Manzini, M. R. (1983), 'On control and control theory', *Linguistic Inquiry* 14, 421–46.

Marantz, A. (1995), 'The minimalist program', in G. Webelhuth (ed.), 348–82.

McCawley, J. (1968), 'Concerning the base component of a transformational grammar', *Foundations of Language* 4, 243–69.

McCawley, J. (1982), 'Parentheticals and discontinuous constituent structure', *Linguistic Inquiry* 13, 91–106.

McCloskey, J. (1979), *Transformational Syntax and Model-Theoretic Semantics*, D. Reidel, Dordrecht.

McCloskey, J. (1990), 'Resumptive pronouns, A-bar binding and levels of representation in Irish', in R. Hendrick (ed.), *Syntax and Semantics 23: The Syntax of the Modern Celtic Languages*, Academic Press, New York, 199–248.

McGee Wood, M. (1993), *Categorial Grammars*, Routledge, London.

McNally, L. (1993), 'Comitative coordination: a case study in group formation', *Natural Language and Linguistic Theory* 11, 347–79.

Miller, P. (1991), 'Scandinavian extraction phenomena revisited: strong and weak generative capacity', *Linguistics and Philosophy* 14, 101–13.

Miller, P. (1992), *Clitics and Constituents in Phrase Structure Grammar*, Garland, New York.

Miller, P. and I. A. Sag (1993), 'French clitic movement without clitics or movement', unpublished manuscript, U. de Lille 3 and Stanford University.

Monachesi, P. (1993), 'Object clitics and clitic climbing in Italian HPSG grammar', *Proceedings of the Sixth Conference of the European Chapter of the Association for Computational Linguistics*, Utrecht, 437–42.

Monachesi, P. (1994), 'Towards a typology of Italian clitics', *CLS* 30, 266–80.

Montague, R. (1974), *Formal Philosophy*, ed. and with an introduction by R. H. Thomason, Yale University Press, New Haven.

Moshier, M. A. and C. J. Pollard (1994), 'The domain of set-valued feature-structures', *Linguistics and Philosophy* 17, 607–31.

Muysken, P. C. and H. C. van Riemsdijk (eds) (1985), *Features and Projections*, Foris, Dordrecht.

Nerbonne, J. (1986a), '"Phantoms" and German fronting: Poltergeist constituents', *Linguistics* 24, 857–70.

Nerbonne, J. (1986b), 'A phrase-structure grammar for German passives', *Linguistics* 24, 907–38.

Nerbonne, J. (1994), 'Partial verb phrases and spurious ambiguities', in J. Nerbonne, K. Netter and C. Pollard (eds), 109–50.

Nerbonne, J., M. Iida and W. Ladusaw (1989), 'Running on empty: null heads in head-driven grammar', *WCCFL* 8, 276–88.

Nerbonne, J., K. Netter and C. Pollard (eds) (1994), *German Grammar in HPSG*, CSLI, Stanford.

Netter, K. (1992), 'On non-head non-movement', in G. Gorz (ed.), *Proceedings of KONVENS 92*, Springer, Berlin.

Netter, K. (1994), 'Towards a theory of functional heads: German nominal phrases', in J. Nerbonne, K. Netter and C. Pollard (eds), 297–340.

Newmeyer, F. J. (1986), *Linguistic Theory in America* (2nd edn), Academic Press, New York.

Oehrle, R. T. (1976), 'The Grammatical Status of the English Dative Alternation', PhD dissertation, MIT.

Oehrle, R. T., E. Bach and D. Wheeler (eds) (1988), *Categorial Grammars and Natural Language Structures*, D. Reidel, Dordrecht.

Ojeda, A. E. (1987), 'Discontinuity, multidominance, and unbounded dependency in generalized phrase structure grammar: some preliminaries', in G. J. Huck and A. E. Ojeda (eds), 257–82.

Ojeda, A. E. (1988), 'A linear precedence account of cross-serial dependencies', *Linguistics and Philosophy* 11, 457–92.

Ouhalla, J. (1991), 'Sentential negation, relativized minimality and the aspectual status of auxiliaries', *The Linguistic Review* 7, 183–231.

Partee, B. H. (ed.) (1976), *Montague Grammar*, Academic Press, New York.

Partee, B. H., R. Wall and A. ter Meulen (1990), *Mathematical Methods in Linguistics*, Kluwer, Amsterdam.

Pereira, F. C. N. (1981), 'Extraposition grammars', *Computational Linguistics* 7, 243–56.

Pereira, F. C. N. and S. Shieber (1987), *Prolog and Natural Language Analysis*, CSLI, Stanford.

Pereira, F. C. N. and D. Warren (1980), 'Definite clause grammars for language analysis: a survey of the formalism and a comparison with augmented transition networks', *Artificial Intelligence* 13, 231–78.

Perlmutter, D. (1970), 'Surface structure constraints in syntax', *Linguistic Inquiry* 1, 187–255.

Perrault, R. C. (1984), 'On the mathematical properties of linguistics theories', *Computational Linguistics* 10, 165–76.

Pike, K. L. (1954–60), *Language in Relation to a Unified Theory of the Structure of Human Behaviour*, Summer Institute of Linguistics, Glendale, CA (3 parts).

Pollard, C. (1984), 'Generalized Context-Free Grammars, Head Grammars, and Natural Language', PhD dissertation, Stanford University.

Pollard, C. (1985a), 'Lectures on HPSG', unpublished manuscript, Stanford University.

Pollard, C. (1985b), 'Phrase structure grammar without metarules', *Proceedings of the West Coast Conference on Formal Linguistics* 4, Stanford Linguistics Association, Stanford.

Pollard, C. (1988), 'Categorial grammar and phrase structure grammar: an excursion on the syntax–semantics frontier', in R. Oehrle, E. Bach and D. Wheeler (eds), 391–415.

Pollard, C. (1994), 'Towards a unified account of passive in German', in J. Nerbonne, K. Netter and C. Pollard (eds), 273–96.

Pollard, C. (forthcoming), 'On head non-movement', in W. Sijtsma and A. van Horck (eds).

Pollard, C. and I. Sag (1983), 'Reflexives and reciprocals in English: an alternative to the binding theory', in M. Barlow, D. Flickinger and M. Westcoat (eds), *Proceedings of the West Coast Conference on Formal Linguistics* 2, Stanford Linguistics Association, Stanford, 189–203.

Pollard, C. and I. Sag (1987), *Information-Based Syntax and Semantics*, vol. 1: *Fundamentals*, CSLI, Stanford.

Pollard, C. and I. Sag (1992), 'Anaphors in English and the scope of binding theory', *Linguistic Inquiry* 23, 261–303.

Pollard, C. and I. Sag (1994), *Head-driven Phrase Structure Grammar*, University of Chicago Press, Chicago.

Pollock, J.-Y. (1989), 'Verb movement, universal grammar, and the structure of IP', *Linguistic Inquiry* 20, 365–424.

Postal, P. M. (1964), *Constituent Structure: A Study of Contemporary Models of Syntactic Description*, Mouton, The Hague.

Postal, P. M. (1974), *On Raising*, MIT Press, Cambridge, MA.

Postal, P. M. (1986), *Studies of Passive Clauses*, State University of New York Press, Albany.

Postal, P. M. (1993), 'Right node raising and extraction', unpublished paper, IBM TJ Watson Research Centre, Yorktown Heights, NY.

Postal, P. M. and G. K. Pullum (1988), 'Expletive noun phrases in subcategorized positions', *Linguistic Inquiry* 19, 635–70.

Prince, A. and P. Smolensky (forthcoming), *Optimality Theory: Constraint Interaction in Generative Grammar*, MIT Press, Cambridge, MA.

Proudian, D. and D. Goddeau (1987), 'Constituent coordination in HPSG', CSLI Report 97, Stanford University.

Pullum, G. K. (1977), 'Word order universals and grammatical relations', in P. Cole and J. Sadock (eds), *Syntax and Semantics 8: Grammatical Relations*, Academic Press, New York.

Pullum, G. K. (1980), 'Syntactic relations and linguistics universals', *Transactions of the Philological Society* 1–39.

Pullum, G. K. (1982a), 'Syncategorematicity and English infinitival *to*', *Glossa* 16, 181–215.

Pullum, G. K. (1982b), 'Free word order and phrase structure rules', *NELS* 12, 209–20.

Pullum, G. K. (1985), 'Assuming some version of X-bar theory', *CLS* 21, 323–53.

Pullum, G. K. (1991), 'English nominal gerunds as noun phrases with verb phrase heads', *Linguistics* 29, 763–99.

Pullum, G. K. (1993), Review of Berwick, Abney and Tenny (eds) (1991), *Computational Linguistics* 19, 393–6.

Pullum, G. K. and G. Gazdar (1982), 'Natural languages and context-free languages', *Linguistics and Philosophy* 4, 471–504.

Pulman, S. (1987), 'Passives', *Proceedings of the 3rd Meeting of the European Chapter of the Association for Computational Linguistics*, Copenhagen, 306–13.

Pulman, S. (1988), Review of Barton, Berwick and Ristad (1987), *Journal of Linguistics* 24, 573–5.

Radford, A. (1988), *Transformational Grammar: A First Course*, Cambridge University Press, Cambridge.

Reape, M. (1994), 'Domain order and word order variation in German', in J. Nerbonne, K. Netter and C. Pollard (eds), 151–97.

Reape, M. (forthcoming), 'Getting things in order', in W. Sijtsma and A. van Horck (eds).

Rentier, G. (1994a), 'A lexicalist approach to Dutch cross-serial dependencies', *CLS* 30, 376–90.

Rentier, G. (1994b), 'Extraction in Dutch with lexical rules', ITK research report No. 53, Tilbury.

Riehemann, S. (1992), 'Word formation in lexical type hierarchies: a case study of *bar*-adjectives in German', MA thesis, University of Tubingen.

Rivero, M-L. (1991), 'Long head movement and negation: Serbo-Croatian vs Slovak and Czech', *The Linguistic Review* 8, 319–51.

Rivero, M-L. (1994), 'Clause structure and V-movement in the languages of the Balkans', *Natural Language and Linguistic Theory* 12, 63–120.

Rosenbaum, P. S. (1967), *The Grammar of English Predicate Complement Constructions*, MIT Press, Cambridge, MA.

Ross, J. R. (1967), 'Constraints on Variables in Syntax', PhD dissertation, MIT.

Ross, J. R. (1969), 'Auxiliaries as main verbs', in W. Todd (ed.), *Studies in Philosophical Linguistics 1*, Great Expectations Press, Evanston, IL.

Rounds, W. C. (1991), 'The relevance of computational complexity to natural language processing', in P. Sells, S. Shieber and T. Wasow (eds), 9–29.

Sag, I. A. (1987), 'Grammatical hierarchy and linear precedence', in G. J. Huck and A. E. Ojeda (eds), 303–40.

Sag, I. A. (forthcoming), 'English relative clauses', to appear in *Journal of Linguistics*.

Sag, I. A. and J. D. Fodor (1994), 'Extraction without traces', *WCCFL* 13, 365–84.

Sag, I., G. Gazdar, T. Wasow and S. Weisler (1985), 'Coordination and how to distinguish categories', *Natural Language and Linguistic Theory* 3, 117–71.

Sag, I. A. and D. Godard (1994), 'Extraction of *de*-phrases from the French NP', *NELS* 24, 519–41.

Sag, I. A., L. Kartunnen and J. Goldberg (1992), 'A lexical analysis of Icelandic case', in I. A. Sag and A. Szabolsci (eds), *Lexical Matters*, CSLI, Stanford, 301–18.

Sag, I. and C. Pollard (1991), 'An integrated theory of complement control', *Language* 67, 63–113.

Sager, N. (1981), *Natural Language Information Processing*, Addison-Wesley, Reading, MA.

Sampson, G. (1984), Review of P. Jacobson and G. K. Pullum (eds) (1982), *Lingua* 64, 371–92.

Schachter, P. and S. Mordechai (1983), 'A phrase structure account of "nonconstituent" coordination', *WCCFL* 2, 260–74.

Scobbie, J. (1991), 'Attribute-Value Phonology', PhD dissertation, University of Edinburgh.

Scobbie, J. (1993), 'Constraint violation and conflict from the perspective of declarative phonology', *Canadian Journal of Linguistics* 38.

Sells, P. (1984), 'Syntax and semantics of resumptive pronouns', PhD thesis, University of Massachusetts at Amherst.

Sells, P., S. Shieber and T. Wasow (eds) (1991), *Foundational Issues in Natural Language Processing*, MIT Press, Cambridge, MA.

Shieber, S. (1984), 'Direct-parsing of ID/LP grammars', *Linguistics and Philosophy* 7, 135–54.

Shieber, S. (1985), 'Evidence against the context-freeness of natural language', *Linguistics and Philosophy* 8, 333–43.

Shieber, S. (1986), 'A simple reconstruction of GPSG', *11th International Conference on Computational Linguistics: Proceedings of Coling 86*, Bonn, 211–15.

Shieber, S. (1987), *An Introduction to Unification-Based Approaches to Grammar*, CSLI, Stanford.

Sijtsma, W. and A. van Horck (eds) (forthcoming), *Discontinuous Constituency*, Mouton de Gruyter, Berlin.

Sobin, N. J. (1985), 'Case assignment in Ukrainian morphological passive constructions', *Linguistic Inquiry* 16, 649–62.

Spencer, A. (1991), *Morphological Theory: An Introduction to Word Structure in Generative Grammar*, Basil Blackwell, Oxford.

Stabler, E. P. (1993), *The Logical Approach to Syntax: Foundations, Specifications and Implementations of Theories of Government and Binding*, MIT Press, Cambridge, MA.

Steedman, M. (1991), 'Structure and intonation', *Language* 67, 260–96.

Stowell, T. (1981), 'Origins of Phrase Structure', PhD dissertation, MIT.

Stowell, T. (1982), 'A formal theory of configurational phenomena', *NELS* 12.

Tomita, M. (ed.) (1991), *Current Issues in Parsing Technologies*, Kluwer, Dordrecht.

Travis, L. (1989), 'Parameters of phrase structure', in M. Baltin and A. Kroch (eds), *Alternative Conceptions of Phrase Structure*, University of Chicago Press, Chicago.

Uszkoreit, H. (1984), *Word Order and Constituent Structure in German*, CSLI Lecture Notes No. 8, CSLI, Stanford.

Uszkoreit, H. (1986), 'Categorial unification grammars', *11th International Conference on Computational Linguistics: Proceedings of Coling 86*, Association for Computational Linguistics, Bonn, 187–94.

Vallduvi, E. and E. Engdahl (1995), 'Information packaging and grammar architecture', *NELS* 28, 519–33.

Verheijen, R. (1986), 'A phrase structure syntax for emphatic *self*-forms', *Linguistics* 24, 681–95.

Vikner, S. (1994), 'Finite verb movement in Scandinavian embedded clauses', in D. Lightfoot and N. Hornstein (eds), *Verb Movement*, Cambridge University Press, Cambridge.

Wacholder, N. (1995), 'Acquiring Syntactic Generalizations from Positive Evidence: An HPSG Model', PhD dissertation, The City University of New York.

Warner, A. R. (1988), 'Feature percolation, unary features, and the coordination of English NP's', *Natural Language and Linguistic Theory* 6, 39–54.

Warner, A. R. (1989), 'Multiple heads and minor categories in generalized phrase-structure grammar', *Linguistics* 27, 179–205.

Warner, A. R. (1993a), *English Auxiliaries: Structure and History*, Cambridge University Press, Cambridge.

Warner, A. R. (1993b), 'The Grammar of English Auxiliaries: An Account in HPSG', Research Paper YLLS/RP 1993–4, University of York.

Warner, A. R. (1995), 'Predicting the progressive passive: parametric change within a lexicalist framework', *Language* 71, 533–57.

Webelhuth, G. (ed.) (1995), *Government and Binding Theory and the Minimalist Program*, Blackwell, Oxford.

Wechsler, S. M. (1991), 'Argument Structure and Linking', PhD dissertation, Stanford University.

Wechsler, S. M. (forthcoming), *The Semantic Basis of Argument Structure: A Study of the Relation between Word Meaning and Syntax*, CSLI, Stanford.

Wells, R. S. (1947), 'Immediate constituents', *Language* 23, 81–117.

van Wijngaarden, A. (1969), Report on the algorithmic language ALGOL68, *Numerische Mathematik* 14, 404–10.

Yngve, V. (1958), 'A programming language for mechanical translation', *Mechanical Translation* 5, 25–41.

Zwicky, A. M. (1986a), 'Free word order in GPSG', in *Interfaces: Papers by Arnold M. Zwicky, Working Papers in Linguistics* 32, Ohio State University, Columbus, 125–32.

Zwicky, A. M. (1986b), 'Concatenation and liberation', *CLS* 22, 65–74.

Zwicky, A. M. (1987), 'Slashes in the passive', *Linguistics* 25, 639–69.

Zwicky, A. M. and J. A. Nevis (1986), 'Immediate precedence in GPSG', in *Interfaces: Papers by Arnold M. Zwicky, Working Papers in Linguistics* 32, Ohio State University, Columbus, 133–8.

Index

Note: page numbers in **bold** refer to detailed discussion of the topic.

Abeillé, A. 88
Abney, S. 6, 9
acquisition 55
Ades, A. 243
Adjunct Island Condition 155
adjuncts 15, 54, 56, 57, 71, 97,
    110–13, 135, 156, 161, 230, 232
AGR 33, 91–3, 100, 129–30, 160, 176,
    180
agreement 26, 29, 40, 92, 93, 100,
    102, 176, 228
agreement features 70, 102, 181
Aho, A. V. 21
Ajdukiewicz, K. 26, 242
Akmajian, A. 12, 15, 19
Alshawi, H. 3, 171
anaphora 6, 7, 139, **175–89**, 197
argument composition 89, 206, 227
Arnold, D. 113
attributes 24, 35–6, 54, 55, 69, 70, 72,
    73, 74, 78, 113, 181, 230, 231
attribute-value matrices (AVMs) 32, 35
auxiliaries 26, 34, 39, 40, 61, 89, 113,
    123, 141, 144, 153, 156, 206, 207,
    212, 213, 216, 218, 224, 227–8, 232

Bach, E. 12, 19, 242
Baker, C. L. 12, 15, 19, 122
BAR 32, 33, 110
Barton, G. 4, 6, 8, 18, 60, 241
Barwise, J. 68
Bear, J. 170
Bennett, P. 8, 9
Berwick, R. 4, 6, 8, 9, 18, 60, 241
Bird, S. 40

Blevins, J. P. 235
Bloch, B. 14, 16
Bloomfield, L. 16
Bolinger, D. 185
Borsley, R. D. 2, 8, 61, 62, 82, 87, 93,
    95, 109, 123, 133, 153, 210, 214,
    216–18, 230, 235
Bouchard, D. 187
Börjars, K. 122
Brame, M. 2, 128, 178
Bresnan, J. 2, 25, 39, 102, 146, 147
Breton 61, 218–19
Bulgarian 218
Bunt, H. 235

Calder, J. 37
Cann, R. 77
Carpenter, R. 4, 21, 40
Case 25, 37, 81, 84, 92–3, 100, 238–9
Categorial Grammar 7, 26, 33, 81, 85,
    86, 121, 150, **242–7**
Chamorro 171
Chichewa 201
Chomsky, N. 1, 5, 9, 11, 12, 13, 14,
    16, 18, 20, 24, 25, 26, 80, 106, 110,
    180, 238–9, 240–1
Classical PSG 3, 4, 5, **11–21**, 24, 27,
    29, 31, 44, 65, 80, 87
Clements, N. 40
clitics 215–16, 225–9
coercion 136–7
comparatives 172
complementizers 26, 87–8, 99, 102,
    109, 114–15, 137–9, 144, 159, 161,
    163, 171, 172

COMPS 82, 84–7, 94–9, 112, 134, 139, 150, 157, 180, 187, 199, 208, 214–16
computational linguistics 3
CONTENT 69, 70, 71, 73, 74, 77, 135, 137, 163–4, 181, 183, 188, 196
CONTENT Principle 72, 74
CONTEXT 69
context-free grammars (CFGs) 12, 17, 18, 20, 21
context-free languages (CFLs) 5, 17, 18, 21, 235
context-free Phrase Structure Grammar 3, 4, 16, 18, 19, 20
context-sensitive grammars (CSGs) 12, 17
context-sensitive languages (CSLs) 17, 21
context-sensitive Phrase Structure Grammar 3, 17, 20
control 7, 68, **126–44**, 179–80, 186, 187–9, 238
Control Agreement Principle (CAP) 60, 68, 91–2, 128–30, 153, 160, 180
CONTROL features 92, 129–30, 152–3, 160
Control Theory 135, 188
Cooper, R. 73
Cooper, R. P. 78, 123
Coordinate Structure Constraint 158
coordinate structures 14, **115–22**, 123
Coordination Principle 121, 158
Crain, S. 58
cross-serial dependencies 17, 223–4
Culicover, P. 161
Culy, C. 21
Czech 218

Daelemans, W. 40
Danish 221
Daughter Dependency Grammar 25
daughters 54
Davis, A. 78
Definite Clause Grammars (DCGs) 26
de Smedt, K. 40
determiners 87–8
directed acyclic graphs 32
discourse representation theory 7
Dowty, D. 77, 121, 232, 234, 235, 242
Dutch 171, 220, 222, 223–5
Dyla, S. 123

E-language 7
Elgin, S. 26
empty categories 15, 55, 61, 99, 122, 137–9, 144, 148–50, 163–6, 171, 187
Engdahl, E. 78, 248
Ernst, T. 122
European Portuguese 218
Exhaustive Constant Partial Ordering (ECPO) 48, 57, 62
extraposition 198–200

features 24, 25, 26, 29, 30, 31, 32, 33, 34
feature co-occurrence restrictions (FCRs) 33, 34, 51, 59, 176, 213
feature specification defaults (FSDs) 33, 34, 36, 51, 59
Flickinger, D. 40
Flynn, M. 246
Fodor, J. A. 25
Fodor, J. D. 3, 5, 34, 55, 58, 86, 122, 144, 148, 150, 161, 171, 209, 216
FOOT Feature Principle 50, 60, 151, 176, 244
FOOT features 34, 148, 151, 155, 158, 176
formal language theory 17
formalization 8, 240–1
free word order 55, **229–34**
Freidin, R. 2
French 89, 123, 225–9

Gazdar, G. x, 1, 2, 3, 4, 5, 8, 15, 17, 18, 21, 24, 26, 31, 32, 34, 35, 40, 48, 56, 59, 60, 66, 67, 77, 78, 85, 93, 100, 117, 119, 122, 128, 129, 131, 132, 140–1, 144, 147, 165, 166, 167, 169, 172, 175, 194, 232, 240
Generalized Phrase Structure Grammar (GPSG) x, 1, 2, 3, 4, 5, 6, 7, 15, 17, 18, 20, 24, 31–5, 38, 39, 40, 44, 46, 47, 48, 50, 53, 55, 56, 58, 60, 62, 65–8, 77, 80, 85, 86, 91, 102, 110, 113–14, 115, 117, 121, 123, 126, 128–33, 140, 144, 146, 147, 148, 150, 153, 154, 155, 158, 159, 160, 161, 168, 170, 175–80, 189, 190, 193–5, 199–200, 212–13, 240

German 57, 89–90, 171, 206–7, 212, 219, 220–3, 235
Godard, D. x, 88, 226
Goddeau, D. 123
Goldberg, J. 171
Goldsmith, J. 158
Government and Binding theory 1, 7, 239
Greek 122
Green, G. 37, 154, 235
Grimshaw, J. 61
Grinder, J. 26
Grishman, R. 40
Grover, C. 3, 172, 210
Gunji, T. 3, 90, 110

Haegeman, L. 110, 247
Harman, G. 16, 20, 24
Harris, Z. 11, 16
HEAD 35, 50, 51, 110–11, 115
Head-driven Phrase Structure Grammar (HPSG) x, 1, 2, 3, 5, 6, 7, 8, 17, 18, 19, 20, 21, 24, 31, 34, 35–8, 39, 40, 44, 46, 47, 50, 51, 53, 54, 55, 60, 61, 65, 68–72, 77, 78, 80, 85, 86, 102, 110, 114, 115, 121, 122, 123, 126, 133–40, 144, 146, 147, 148, 150, 153, 154, 159, 160, 161, 168, 180–9, 195–8, 199–200, 213–16, 240
Head Feature Convention (HFC) 50, 51, 53, 60, 81, 110, 119
Head Feature Principle (HFP) 50, 51, 53, 61, 83, 94, 108, 111, 115, 214
HEAD features 34, 35, 50–1, 110, 111, 119, 120, 155, 158, 218
Heinz, W. 114
Heny, F. 12, 15
Hinrichs, E. 89
Hockett, C. F. 14
Hoeksema, J. 235
Huddleston, R. 12
Hudson, R. x, 25, 87, 121
Hukari, T. 8, 34, 55, 93, 154, 156, 157, 161, 167, 171, 176–80, 183–4
Huybregts, R. 17

Icelandic 37, 161, 235
I-language 7
immediate dominance rules (ID rules) 31, 44–8, 49, 50, 51, 53–5, 57, 58, 59, 60, 61, 80, 81, 83, 84, 91, 93, 94, 108, 110, 111, 112, 114, 117, 118, 119, 149, 152, 153, 160, 193, 199, 210, 213, 216–17, 222, 224, 235
impersonal passives 200–1
inheritance 38
intensional logic 66
Irish 168
Island constraints 6, **154–62**, 169, 245

Jackendoff, R. S. 15, 39, 106
Jacobson, P. 58, 130, 139, 156, 218
Japanese Phrase Structure Grammar (JPSG) 3, 90–1, 110
Johnson, M. 86, 222
Joshi, A. 21, 248

Kac, M. 16, 18
Kaplan, R. 147
Kartunnen, L. 36
Kasper, R. 4, 40, 112, 232, 248
Kathol, A. x, 40, 78, 102, 171, 206–9, 232–4, 235
Katz, J. J. 25
Kayne, R. 241, 248
Kenstowicz, M. 40
Kilbury, J. 61, 194
Klein, E. x, 1, 40, 144
Klima, E. 175
Kolliakou, D. 122
Koopman, H. 140–1
Koster, J. 2, 4, 187, 239
Krieger, H.-U. 40
Kuno, S. 40, 185

Lakoff, G. 159
Lamb, S. 14
Larson, R. 121, 247–8
Lasnik, H. 5
learnability 34
Lees, R. 175
Lema, J. 218
Levine, R. D. xi, 3, 8, 34, 55, 154, 156, 157, 161, 167, 169, 171, 232–4
LEX 85
lexical rules 39, 136, 150, 161, 164, 192, 196, 197, 199, 201, 202, 209, 210, 215, 228, 232

Lexical Functional Grammar (LFG) 102, 127
lexicon 2, 38, 39
linear precedence rules (LP rules) **44–8**, 51, 53, 55, 56, 57, 58, 59, 217, 229, 246
list-valued features 36
Ludlow, P. 241

McCawley, J. 14, 15, 21, 169
McCloskey, J. 2, 168
McGee Wood, M. 248
McNally, L. 123
Maling, J. 154, 168
Manaster-Ramer, A. 16, 18
Manzini, M. R. 188–9, 190
Marantz, A. 247
Matiasek, J. 114
Mellish, C. 3, 17
metagrammars 59, 60
metarules 59, 62, 149, 150, 160, 161, 192, 193–5, 199, 200, 213, 235
Miller, P. x, 3, 21, 225–9
MOD 111
modals 140
model-theoretic semantics 65, 66, 243
Modern Phrase Structure Grammar x, 1, 2, 3, 4, 6, 7, 8, 9, 11, 16, 19, 20, 24, 26, 27, 29, 44, 51, 58, 65, 80, 89, 127, 128, 146, 154, 168, 212, 218, **237–47**
Monachesi, P. 229
Montague, R. 65–7
Montague grammar 25
Montague semantics 66, 248
Mordechai, S. 121
Morgan, J. 37, 54
Moshier, M. 4, 40

Nakazawa, T. 89
Nerbonne, J. 40, 86, 122, 201, 222
Netter, K. 86, 87, 122, 218, 219
Nevis, J. A. 58
Newmeyer, F. J. 9, 21
node admissability conditions 14, 15
Non-Local Feature Principle 50, 152, 244
NON-LOCAL features 148, 152

not 113, 122
Null-subject languages 99

o-binding 182
o-command 182
obliqueness 55, 56
Obliqueness Extraction Constraint 161–2
Oehrle, R. 2
Oettinger, A. G. 40
Ojeda, A. E. 3, 20, 58, 59, 118, 169, 217, 223–4, 230
Old Spanish 218
Ouhalla, J. 26

parasitic gaps 155
parsing 5, 18, 60, 248
Partee, B. H. 21, 25
partial VPs 222
Pereira, F. 3, 26, 171
Perlmutter, D. 226
Perrault, R. C. 21
Perry, J. 68
Peters, P. S. 77
phrase structure (PS) rules 2, 3, 12, 13, 14, 15, 19, 20, 21, 31, 44, 46, 47, 48, 59, 60
Pike, K. 14
Polish 123, 229
Pollard, C. x, 1, 4, 7, 37, 38, 40, 52, 54, 55, 56, 57, 60, 61, 68, 69, 71, 72, 73, 76, 77, 78, 82, 85, 88, 99, 100, 101, 106, 108, 110, 111, 112, 114, 120, 121, 122, 127, 135, 136, 137, 139, 143, 144, 153, 156, 157, 158, 161, 163, 165, 166, 167, 170, 171, 180–9, 190, 206–7, 216, 221, 222–3, 230–1, 235, 240
Postal, P. M. 12, 14, 18, 19, 127, 170, 204
pre-Chomskyan linguistics 1, 3
Prince, A. 61
Principles and Parameters framework (P&P) 1, 3, 4, 5, 6, 7, 8, 19, 20, 25, 26, 30, 44, 58, 61, 109, 113, 121, 123, 127–8, 140, 143, 153, 158, 163, 175, 180, 187, 198, 218, **237–42**
PROLOG 26

proto-sorts 207–8
Proudian, D. 123
Pullum, G. K. x, 1, 2, 5, 17, 21, 26, 32, 34, 35, 44, 53, 59, 110, 122, 127, 144, 235
Pulman, S. 210, 241

QSTORE 73, 74, 78
quantification 72–7
Quantifier Binding Condition 77
Quantifier Inheritance Principle 74

Radford, A. 110
raising 7, **126–44**, 193, 238
Raising Principle 134, 139–40, 164
Reape, M. 3, 231, 234, 235
Relational Grammar 19
relative clauses 2, 146–7, 163–6, 171
Rentier, G. 89–90, 171, 224–5
resumptive pronouns 168–9
rewrite rules 14, 15
Riehemann, S. 40
right node raising 169–70, 245
Ristad, S. 4, 6, 8, 18, 60, 241
Rivero, M.-L. 218
ROLES 208–9
Rosenbaum, P. S. 126
Ross, J. R. 140–1, 158
Rounds, W. 4, 18, 40
Russian 123

Sadler, L. 113
Sag, I. A. x, xi, 1, 2, 7, 32, 33, 37, 38, 40, 52, 54, 55, 56, 57, 60, 61, 68, 69, 71, 72, 73, 76, 77, 78, 82, 85, 88, 99, 100, 101, 106, 108, 110, 111, 112, 114, 120, 121, 122, 127, 134, 137, 139, 143, 144, 148, 150, 153, 156, 157, 158, 161, 163, 165, 166, 170, 171, 175, 180–9, 190, 216, 226–9, 230–1, 240
Sager, N. 25
Sampson, G. 3
Schachter, P. 121
Scobbie, J. 40, 61
SCOPE Principle 75
Sells, P. 158
semantic combinators 131, 193

semantic types 66–7, 129, 131–2, 194
semantics 2, 25, 37, 38, 54, **65–78**, 91–2, 108, 112, 114, 121, 133, 134, 171, 176, 185, 190, 193, 198, 199, 206, 209, 240, 243
Serbo-Croatian 218
set-valued features 36
Sharman, R. xi
Shieber, S. 3, 8, 17, 60, 61, 171
situation semantics 7, 68, 248
SLASH 33, 34, 37, 112, 147–54, 156, 157, 159, 160, 164, 167, 168, 169, 170, 218, 244
Slovak 218
Smolensky, P. 61
Sobin, N. J. 200
sorts 35, 38
SPEC 108, 115
SPEC Principle 109, 115
Spencer, A. 201
Sportiche, D. 140–1
SPR 107
Stabler, E. 9
Steedman, M. 242, 243, 248
Stephens, J. 218
Stowell, T. 44, 60
structure-sharing 36
SUBCAT 37, 70, 71, 81, 82, 83, 90, 91, 94–9, 106, 134, 180–7
Subcategorization Principle 83, 94
SUBJ 82, 84, 85, 86, 87, 94–9, 107, 133, 134, 135, 139–40, 157, 176, 180, 186, 188, 208, 214–16
Subject Condition 155, 157
subsumption 30
Swedish 122, 158
Swiss German 17
syntactic categories 2, 4, 19, 20, **24–40**, 45–8, 67, 69, 70, 80, 81, 82, 86, 88, 93, 95, 119–20, 133, 147, 148, 149, 150, 151, 152, 158, 159, 160, 170, 176, 195–8, 199–203, 206–9, 214–16, 224–5, 227–8, 232, 238, 239, 242, 244, 246
Syrian Arabic 235

tags 36
Tenny, C. 6, 9

ter Meulen, A. 21
there-insertion 202–3
Tomita, M. 9
'tough' constructions 166–8
Trace Principle 150, 161
Transformational Grammar (TG) 1, 6, 7, 12, 15, 16, 19, 20, 146, 149, 166, 221
transformations 2
Travis, L. 58
Tree Adjoining Grammar 248

Ukrainian 200
Ullman, J. D. 21
unbounded dependencies 2, 7, 26, 33, 67, 112, **146–74**, 187, 216, 235, 239, 244–5, 246–7
unification 6, 52, 53, 61
Uszkoreit, H. 33, 57, 221

Valence Principle 84, 95, 108, 111, 115, 153, 214, 240
Vallduvi, E. 78, 248
van Wijngaarden, A. 62
variables 30
verb-second 220–2
Verheijen, R. 190

Vijay-Shanker, K. 21
Vikner, S. 221
Visser's generalization 132, 189

Wacholder, N. 40
Wall, R. 21, 77
Warner, A. R. 33, 34, 40, 102, 120, 122, 123, 140–1, 144, 216
Warren, D. 26
Wasow, T. 40
weak generative capacity 17, 18, 20
Wechsler, S. 71, 208–9
Weinberg, A. 18
Weir, D. 21
Wells, R. 14
Welsh 29, 40, 210, 212, 214–16, 235
wh-phrases 78
wh-questions 2, 109, 146–8

X-bar theory 80

Yiddish 235
Yngve, V. 24

Zaenen, A. 154, 168
Zwicky, A. 58, 203–6, 210, 216–17, 230, 235